# Contrails

A
Boeing
Salesman
Reminisces

*To Don*
*With all best wishes*
*E. Be*
*Cyp  2/5/97*

# Contrails

## A
## Boeing
## Salesman
## Reminisces

*by*
*Eugene E.*
*Bauer*

*TABA Publishing, Inc.*
*Enumclaw, Washington*

Published by TABA Publishing, Inc.
24103 SE 384th Street
Enumclaw, Washington 98022

ISBN 1-879242-07-9

Library of Congress Catalog Card No. 96-90165

Illus. – The Boeing Family of Airplanes, December 31, 1979. Courtesy of The
Boeing Company Historical Archives

Book and cover design by Bridget Culligan Design, Seattle, Washington, from
photos by Eugene E. Bauer

Printed in the United States of America at Gilliland Printing, Inc., Arkansas
City, Kansas

*"Upon those that step into the same rivers,*
*different and different waters flow. . . .*
*It scatters and . . . gathers . . . it comes together*
*and flows away . . . approaches and departs.*
*"All things are in process and nothing stays still. . . . "*

HERACLITUS

*"We must take the current when it serves,*
*or lose our ventures."*

WILLIAM SHAKESPEARE

To my many dedicated Boeing compatriots
who stepped into those rivers with me,
I salute you.

# ACKNOWLEDGMENTS

The author is indebted to DR. PAUL SPITZER, retired Boeing company historian, for a comprehensive review of the manuscript.

Special thanks are extended to TOM LUBBESMEYER, archivist for the Boeing Company, who enthusiastically searched out historical information.

Special thanks are also extended to ROBERTO CITTADINI, VAN-REX GALLARD, JEFF YOUNG, and KEITH BERGSTROM of the Boeing international sales staff, and analyst SANDY PETERSON, for providing current (1996) fleet makeup of my old customer airlines.

# PREFACE

Incorporated as Pacific Aero Products on July 15, 1916, by restless visionary William E. (Bill) Boeing—who left Yale at the end of his junior year in engineering to come west—the company evolved to become The Boeing Company. Passing his legacy of dedication to excellence to eight subsequent presidents, six of whom were engineers, Bill Boeing molded the largest and most respected aircraft manufacturing enterprise in the world.

Engineers were represented in the management structure of every department, including the factory. On average, degreed engineers, represented about 12 percent of the company's total labor force.

Indeed, for decades, even the sales staff reported to the engineering department. The company sales strategy was simple—just build the best product—a strategy that lived on into the dawn of the jet age in the '50s.

"As long as Boeing builds the best airplanes, it will be sufficient. The world will recognize the superior product and buy it."[1]

Those words, spoken by William M. (Bill) Allen, fifth president and first with a law background, continued to embrace this philosophy. At the time, the battle was raging between the Boeing 707 and the Douglas DC-8, and the director of sales suggested that Boeing hire local representatives in Europe and South America. When the decision was passed up to Bill Allen, he was adamant that Boeing not do it.

Embodying the straight-laced ethics of Bill Boeing, Allen would not make payments to middlemen, nor would he accept gifts from customers. Even though he led Boeing as its president from 1945 to 1968, and as Chairman until 1972, he continued to refer to himself as an employee, subject to the same company rule which forbad the acceptance of gifts from anyone doing business with Boeing.

However, in the late '50s, two Englishmen, including one former official of British Overseas Airways (BOAC), now British Airways, were hired to help sell airplanes to BOAC. Despite the reluctance of Bill Allen and those close to him, it was apparent that such practices were becoming necessary.

Then, in the late '60s, the company was brought to its knees when a commercial market slump coincided with the end of the moon landing program, and the beginning of a recession in the U.S. economy. Over the period of 1969–71, employment at Boeing was savaged—reduced from 142,400 to 56,300.

Seattle and the Puget Sound region became an economic disaster area. Someone erected a huge billboard sign adjacent to Interstate Highway 5, with the grim admonition: "Will the last person leaving Seattle, turn out the lights"—not bothering to say please.

However small, a silver lining appeared on the dark clouds, and the year of 1970 became the harbinger of the role that overseas sales were destined to play in the fortunes of the Boeing Company. That year, $716 million of foreign sales were booked, while not a single airplane was sold in the United States market. In fact, domestic sales showed less than zero net due to the cancellation of existing orders.[2]

Those foreign sales were made predominately to old customers from the early days of the Boeing 707 and 727—well established airlines—while the remaining foreign markets were primarily in the developing countries of Latin America, Africa, and Asia.

Selling in those countries presented a whole new set of problems not faced before. Most of the airlines were government owned, and most were poor, tending to purchase used equipment. Competition had drastically stiffened, and the great "jumbo war" of the late '60s among the Boeing 747, the Douglas DC-10, and the Lockheed L-1011, was still in full swing. The Boeing 737 was high on the list of candidates for the many small airlines in those countries, but it faced an awesome uphill battle. The Douglas DC-9, which came out two years before the 737, had already captured the entire U.S. market with the exception of United Airlines, as well as most of Western Europe. In fact, 236 DC-9s were flying when the first 737 rolled out of the factory.

Rumors of payoffs and bribes were rampant, and seemed to be the normal way of doing business in many countries. Referred to as *cumshaw, boobol, baksheesh, hongbao, chongtok, mordida,* and many other names, the practice was viewed among the indigenous population as simply "dealings among friends."

This new dimension of selling put added stress on Boeing, a company that had refused to consider any but honest business negotiations throughout its history.

Nevertheless, change was the order of the day. In 1969, sales and marketing had been elevated to vice presidential status, when Clarence F. (Clancy) Wilde, an aeronautical engineer who had left Northwest Airlines as its superintendent of maintenance, was appointed to the new post. Then in 1972, in what proved to be one of the most significant decisions in the history of the company, Boeing targeted overseas commercial airplane sales as its top priority. In a major reorganization, the Commercial Group became the Commercial Airplane Company, with its own president, super salesman Ernest H. (Tex) Boullioun, reporting to corporate headquarters.

Significantly, Boeing squarely faced the problems of in-country representation. Consultants were retained in most overseas accounts, and commissions paid on a contingency basis. Those commissions were legitimate sales costs, and if there was no sale, there was no commission.

Boeing's own salesmen had diverse backgrounds. Most were engineers. Many had business education as well. Some were ex-U.S. government employees; State Department, Commerce, Defense, as well as retired military—however, a preponderance were Boeing career people. The international sales force included some foreign born American citizens—still comfortable in their native tongues—who were assigned to the regions of the world of their origin.

Salesmen were given the title of regional directors, and were responsible for covering six to ten airlines. These regional directors, via their area directors, were authorized to commit the company on price, delivery, and maintenance terms.

Tenure was tentative. Clancy Wilde was ruthless in getting the right people in the right slots. Thus, a regional salesman might be gone after one year, or might carry on for ten or more.

The decade of the '70s would prove to be the crucible in which was forged a new dominance of Boeing products in the world's airlines, leading to the massive backlogs of the late '80s and early '90s, peaking at nearly $93 billion in 1991.

This book is a personal account of the day-by-day experiences of one of those frontline salesmen in Latin America, over a period of five years during that watershed decade.

1. Private communication.
2. T. Wilson, *U.S. House of Representatives Testimony on Foreign Trade*, 14 May 1973.

# PROLOGUE

In 1966, after twenty-five years in the Boeing engineering department, I decided to launch a new career within the company, initiating a double duty trek toward an MBA. My plan was to intersect the impending supersonic airplane era—an active program at the time—at an early phase of its production, and to sell airplanes overseas.

Working full time as head of one of the technical staffs, I stretched my day at Boeing to accommodate a marathon five-year program at the University of Washington. In March 1971, the United States Congress canceled the SST, and graduating the following December with an MBA in international business, I found myself swimming on a strange new, uncharted ocean.

However, good fortune smiled on me and I was assigned the international desk in the newly formed Office of Corporate Business Development (OCBD), in Boeing headquarters.

After the major downsizing of the 1969–71 aircraft sales depression, Boeing had adopted a "lean and mean" philosophy, with product diversification as the new watchword.

The OCBD had been set up to formulate a ten-year business plan as well as to screen the flood of new ideas coming from the divisions. Our staff, consisting of eleven MBAs—most also with engineering degrees—reported to vice president Henry K. (Bud) Hebeler, who in turn reported directly to the Chairman of the Board, Thornton A. "T" Wilson.

After two years of searching the world for opportunities to market our new, non-airplane products, Brazil—among others—came into focus as a potential customer for fast rail, and hydrofoil boats.

The Spanish that I had learned in night classes during my MBA program would be useless in Brazil, so I began to study Portuguese.

In September 1973, Hebeler sent me on a fact finding trip to Brazil, a country which at the time was undergoing an "economic miracle." I expanded the trip to include a short vacation which allowed me to travel widely in the country, testing my newly minted language ability.

At the time, a Boeing 727-200 airplane was being displayed and demonstrated at Brazil's First International Air Show in José dos Campos, near São Paulo. There I met Clancy Wilde, and was impressed with the scope and intensity of the Boeing sales campaign. Perhaps here was an opportunity for me to get involved in a still more exciting adventure.

# Contents

# 1

As my Varig Airlines 707 approached Rio de Janeiro in early September 1973, I was overcome with a sudden surge of anxiety.

Had I made the right move when I stepped out of the boat in 1971—
from my comfortable position in engineering—to face a strange, foreign world?

This was my first trip out of the United States—since soldiering in
WWII—to a new country, embracing an unfamiliar culture.

At Boeing, management expectations were always for success, and
the spotlight was sharply focused on this mission.

Pride prevailed.

Resolutely, I stepped out of the plane, almost oblivious to the blast
of tropical air, carrying my briefcase in one hand and my suit bag over
my shoulder, as I descended the loading ramp to the hot tarmac.

I was unprepared for the primitive facilities at Galeão, Rio's international airport. Baggage was handled manually. Not even a moving belt
was in evidence. While waiting, I headed for the restroom. To my dis-
may, there was no paper in the doorless stalls. I learned that toilet paper
was in short supply and was stolen by the local poor. Indeed, even airline

employees made off with the paper. From that day on, I carried a partial roll in my briefcase.

I had made meticulously detailed plans by mail and phone from Seattle, and my appointments had been confirmed by our consultant in Brazil.

Immersing myself into the Brazilian scene, I checked out the hydrofoil boat which commuted between Rio and the bedroom community of Niteroi across the bay; rode the aerial tram to the top of Sugarloaf Hill; and peered into the excavations in the center of the city where a new subway system was beginning. My goal was to get Boeing involved in replacing the small Italian hydrofoils with the much larger ones that Boeing was offering, and to provide subway rail cars. I quickly found that Rio's pleasant facade of sun, beaches, and beautiful women masked a tight government bureaucracy that stifled progress. After a week of frustrating meetings, with our consultant trying to steer me, realism began to set in. It became clear that concrete results would be hard won—and well into the future.

The following week I headed north—on vacation—and on my own. I went to old Brazil; to the sertão, the parched and poverty-stricken northeast, to Recife and Bahia. I flew on Cruzeiro, second largest of the four Brazilian airlines. Cruzeiro also operated Boeing planes—727s—purchased secondhand. Like many other South American airlines, they had been unable to afford new equipment. The word cruzeiro quickly entered my vocabulary—it was the same as the Brazilian currency.

My halting Portuguese sounded like a cracked record, but I was learning. Impervious to strange glances and blank stares, I had decided to swim on this new ocean—and planned for success.

I explored the central city of Recife—divided by rivers—an ideal situation for rapid transit in the city of two million, served by ancient buses. But the poverty of the region gave me a clear signal that such a project could never be afforded.

The poverty in Bahia was no better. Inhabited predominantly by blacks, the city had been the center of slave trade from Africa in the days before emancipation.

Nevertheless, I felt the potential energy of the people everywhere. The Trans-Amazon highway was nearly complete, irrigation projects were being constructed in the São Francisco River basin, and new industrial parks were being created.

Leaving Bahia, I flew to the new concrete, steel, and glass city of Brasilia. An extravaganza of functional, modern buildings, carved out of the jungle 600 miles from the coast, the city was created in 1955 by President Kubitschek to force the development of the vast interior of the country.

From Brasilia, it was on to José dos Campos, the International Air Show, and Boeing business. Considering that it was Brazil's first attempt, they hosted a grand show.

The high gross weight, advanced Boeing 727-200 demonstration airplane was a winner. Hours-long lines formed—oblivious to the 100 degree heat—for a chance to walk through for a brief glimpse of the interior.

The white tarmac, reflecting the dazzling sun, assailed the eye, while the damp heat numbed the mind.

Overhead, the minions of modern airpower roared and snorted. The huge, moth-like British bomber, Vulcan, plowed ponderously through the hot skies. The British Harrier stood still in the air, motionless over the runway, even performing a retrograde maneuver—then suddenly zoomed skyward on twin streams of gray smoke.

The European Airbus consortium's new commercial A300 twinjet—on a world demonstration tour—came in for a landing, hinting at a future confrontation. At Boeing, we had not yet recognized the seriousness of the Airbus program.

The U.S. Air Force was strongly in evidence. Its mammoth cargo plane, the C-5 Galaxy, squatted lazily on the apron, its gaping mouth open in a yawn big enough to swallow the largest tank—or a thousand troops. Far up in the sunbathed sky, the Blue Angels pranced and weaved in fantastic loops and spins.

It was in the Boeing booth near the 727 demonstration airplane that I first met Clancy Wilde. I decided to toss my hat into the foreign sales ring.

I had grown to like the OCBD and the exciting work under Hebeler and Wilson. I felt the old longing for rootedness settling in—but only for a moment.

"I'd like to try my hand at selling commercial airplanes," I announced, shortly after returning from Brazil.

"Why don't you call Clancy and discuss it?" Hebeler replied. "I'll recommend you."

A few weeks later, in December, I said goodbye to OCBD and joined the Latin American sales force as a regional director.

As sales directors, the world outside the U.S. was our domain. No corner of the globe escaped our attention. No country was too small, no government too recalcitrant, no revolution too intimidating, no climate too harsh, and no schedule too severe.

We were few in number, not more than thirty actively assigned to the front lines as regional directors, but our loyalty was intense. Our customers came to view us as not simply Boeing employees—*we were Boeing*.

With personnel like Clancy three deep in most departments, a company rock-solid in technology, with an integrity to match, a product that was family-wide and globally tested, supported by a customer service organization covering six continents, it was easy to see why Boeing airplanes were so successful—barely short of inevitable.

The difficulty lay in convincing customers in developing countries to take the long view. The entrenched philosophy to "buy cheap and plan short" would be hard to change. Perhaps of even greater significance was the common practice of accepting—even demanding—clandestine payoffs.

I had set my sights on selling airplanes in Brazil, an account to which Boeing had a regional director already assigned. Nevertheless, the country is larger than the contiguous United States, and seemed to be on the threshold of significant expansion in air travel. With VASP, second largest carrier, already talking of purchasing at least twenty 737s, the logic of two directors to cover Brazil seemed compelling.

There was a natural reluctance for the existing regional director to see his turf cut in half. Thus, several months elapsed while the adjustments were being made in personnel.

During this period, Boeing had targeted AeroPeru, the newly formed, government-owned and-operated flag carrier in Peru.

AeroPeru was formed in October 1973, to fill the gap left by the failure of two private companies, LANSA and APSA, as well as a government owned forerunner, SATCO. At one time APSA had operated DC-8 and Convair 990 aircraft to Miami and Europe. The new airline—not much more than a name—inherited a total fleet consisting of three old DC-8s, leased from Douglas, and one used Boeing 727-100, purchased from Eastern Airlines.

The second carrier in Peru, Faucett Airlines—a private company with no authority for international flights—was a direct competitor of AeroPeru on domestic routes. The airline had purchased a new 727-100 from Boeing in 1968. The remainder of its fleet consisted of British BAC-111s, DC-6s, DC-4s, and even one old DC-3. They were achieving phenomenal performance from their 727—boasting a load factor of 85% (industry average is in the 60% range)—and were hopeful of replacing their two BAC-111s with larger and more efficient 737s.

With Faucett already in the Boeing camp, sales to AeroPeru were elevated to "campaign" status, a designation which triggered all supporting organizations to extend the highest priority to the airline.

A costly series of demonstration flights was made in Peru with the 737-200, pitting it against the Fokker F-28. It was a major mismatch, with the 737 showing vastly superior performance from the short, high-elevation airfields of the country's domestic network. Boeing was elated. The superior product had prevailed.

Boeing's consultant in Peru, a lawyer with extensive ties to government officials, notified our sales director.

"The sale is in the bag," he crowed. "The *Ministro* will sign the contract next week."

Two days later, AeroPeru stunned Boeing, announcing the purchase of three Fokker F-28 twinjets from the Netherlands.

The purchase of the Fokkers triggered a chain reaction in the Boeing sales department. The regional director was transferred out of sales—a brutal reality of the intensely competitive climate in the front lines.

Later, it was learned that the decision had been "cast in concrete," even before the 737 airplane arrived in Peru, as a result of passing *mordida* (Spanish for *"the bite"*) of $1.5 million on the $12 million order.

The outcome of this campaign in 1974, provided bitter proof of the hidden forces that were increasingly shaping airline purchase decisions in many parts of the world. In Latin America at the time, the practice of accepting bribes was almost universal, and the Europeans had no inhibitions concerning this practice.

John Broback, area director for Africa, Spain, and Latin America, called me in.

"Gene, I'm giving you the Peru accounts. Now that they have the F-28s for domestic operations, we need to target their regional routes. I want you to call General Soto right away and arrange to meet with him in Lima next week with a firm proposal to sell 727-200 airplanes to AeroPeru. We should be able to show them much better returns than the DC-8s on their South American routes, maybe even to Miami."

Broback paused. "And very important," he added sternly, "we just fired our consultant there. You'll have to start over. Whoever you find, he better be good!"

I stared at the huge map of South America on the wall behind his desk. I knew nothing about Peru—and had never heard of General Soto.

# 2

My first flight south in the summer of 1974, on Avianca Airlines, was a milk run, stopping three times on the way to Lima, Peru. After leaving Los Angeles two hours late, we landed in Mexico City in the middle of the night. I recall waking to see a mass of Mexicans pouring into the plane.

It was beginning to get light when I first caught sight of Bogota, Colombia, home of Avianca, where we made a brief stop. Located in a lush mountain valley over 8,000 feet above sea level, its climate is perpetual spring, striking a delicate balance between the humid heat of the coast only 200 miles distant, and the cold and snow a scant 5,000 feet up the mountain.

Our next stop was Quito, Ecuador, the legendary second capital of the ancient Inca Empire, another jewel locked in the mountains, even higher than Bogota.

The plane remained in Quito for only a few minutes. Then I was off to Lima, where some of the most interesting, demanding, and frustrating events of my sales career awaited.

The extravagance of nature in forming the Andes Mountains is awesome. So immense is their scale that a view from the air is the only way to appreciate their magnitude. From the sea they appear as an unbroken chain, stretching from the Straits of Magellan on the south, all the way north to Panama. For the ground-based visitor, it is only after reaching the tablelands that the separate peaks are discernible.

Leaving Quito, the air route follows along "volcano alley" on the spine of Ecuador. The volcanoes stand as lonely white sentinels, marking the way. On the left, fifteen minutes out of Quito, the world's highest active volcano, 19,347-foot Cotopaxi, was in full view.

In the distance stood mighty Chimborazo, known as "king of the Andes." One after another, the volcanoes came marching by: Illiniza, Tungurahua, Altar, and finally Sanguay, the legendary site of buried Inca treasure.

Three *cordilleras* of the Andes in the north merge into two as they stretch southward. In the *Cordillera Negro*, nearest the ocean, rain is so rare that cactus is barely able to survive.

Paralleling it on the east is the Cordillera Blanco. Its snow-covered slopes and massive snow cornices are mute testimony to the unceasing precipitation that it receives. The continental jungle creates a continuous pattern of clouds, which are driven toward the coast by the prevailing easterly winds. Torrential rains rush down the mountainsides the year around, forming hundreds of cascading rivers, which join to create the mighty Amazon at Iquitos.

Such was the terrain where modern jet airplanes were flying their daily patterns.

Peru is a large part of that land of extremes, extending more than 1,400 miles along the west coast of South America, its third largest country. The high mountain valleys and trapped tablelands stand out as well-watered jewels of emerald green, or as barren dust bowls, captives of the capricious whims of nature.

A narrow strip of land, from thirty to 100 miles wide, borders the ocean—land which in its natural state would be waterless desert. Where a few rivers break through the mountain chain to the sea, there are green oases. Lima, the capital and largest city, is situated at the mouth of the Rimac River, the principal waterway reaching the Pacific.

Peru contains some of the most rugged terrain of the Andes, precipitous bastions of rent and splintered granite, impassable for the most part, where surging torrents roar endlessly through the *quebradas*, the hideous gashes which appeared from the air to have no bottoms.

However, the geographic location of Lima, at sea level and mid-continent, gives it the potential of a major international air hub, one of the most opportune locations on the entire continent.

My sales strategy was twofold: first, to provide data revealing this immense regional and international potential; and second, to develop an optimized fleet plan to match. Peru, a nation both ancient and modern, struggling to join the western technological society and yet wedded to antiquity, is a strange mixture of western and pre-Columbian cultures.

Knowing the history and culture of a people was one of the central axioms of my sales philosophy. To be successful, I knew that I must learn to "walk in their shoes."

Cuzco, Peru's oldest city and third largest, represented an important element in my sales strategy. At an altitude of 11,204 feet, Cuzco would require airplanes with extremely high performance—an ideal match for Boeing equipment. Cuzco was also the gateway to Macchu Picchu, ancient capital of the Incas, and one of the premier tourist attractions in the world.

Situated at the very top of a spire of jungle-covered granite, with nearly sheer walls, Macchu Picchu was as close to being an impregnable fortress as the imagination could conjure.

Peru's first recorded civilization centered around Cuzco, adding to its lure and mystery. Its exact origin is lost in the shadows of history, compounded by myth and legend.

During the flight, I was reading Prescott's classic history of the Inca civilization, and Pizarro's conquest in 1532. Prescott cautions that the tradition of the Incas is not the only account that has been current among the Peruvians. Another legend speaks of strange bearded men who advanced from the shores of Lake Titacaca and established domain over the natives. Whatever the origin, evidence of civilization dates back more than 4,000 years, and the existence of the Incas for nearly 400 of those years is well documented. Exactly how they got there, who they really were, and what sorts of civilization filled the centuries before them remains a mystery.

Though the Incas were only one of the many civilizations to inhabit Peru and the neighboring mountains, their story is the most awesomely romantic. Their deeds are universally admired and their passing universally mourned.

It was another forty years after Pizarro, before Peru was settled under total Spanish rule as one of its viceroyalties. Independence was proclaimed in 1821, and after the Monroe Doctrine was declared in the United States in 1823, the Spanish hold on the Western Hemisphere was abandoned. Peru developed a constitutional government in 1828, with a president and a senate. However, the land was owned by twenty-one families, legacy of the huge land grants made by the King of Spain. With that heritage of history, it was easy to understand the intensity of the intertwining network of "friends."

There had been an occasional revolution, military coup, and war with its neighbors—Ecuador to the north, and Chile to the south. Nevertheless, constitutional government hesitatingly prevailed—until 1968. In that year, General Velasco led a military coup which resulted in a harsh leftist dictatorship. Foreign business interests were purged from the country, and most of their property expropriated.

The fishing fleets, perhaps the most important industry in Peru, were taken over by the government—as well as the mines and factories. Government corporations were created to manage each sector of the society.

Newspapers, radio, and television stations were seized, and all unfavorable dialogue silenced. Velasco even initiated a campaign to replace Spanish with *Quechua*, the ancient Inca language. A torrent of decrees poured forth from the government presses, directing every facet of Peruvian life. Naturally, initiative faded, and Peru became an economic graveyard.

That was the Peru that greeted me on that sunlit August day in 1974, when I landed in Lima.  Filled with trepidation, I invented my own optimism.

# 3

Approaching Lima, two features predominated.

First, the city seemed captured by the coastal desert—a green oasis in its midst. The Rimac, largest of the few rivers that penetrate the cordillera, is the irrigation source for the surrounding farmlands, as well as the water supply for the city of one million inhabitants. As the river, by then pitifully small, leaves the city, it serves as an open sewer to the ocean.

Second, I was startled to see the hundreds—perhaps even thousands—of fishing boats in the harbor. These were the anchovy fleets, used to harvest the enormous annual crop provided by *Él Nino*, the great, mysterious current that courses its way northward from the Antarctic. Anchovies, processed for fertilizer, represented a significant fraction of Peru's exports.

As we landed at the Jorge Chavez airport, coming straight in from the north, I expected to find similar conditions as at Galeão in Brazil. To my surprise, I was greeted by a modern facility.

The airport—brand new and still in the final stages of construction—boasted a 10,000 foot runway. The airport portals were guarded by soldiers whose frozen countenances betrayed no emotion. Their rifles had bayonets fixed, and burp guns hung loosely at their belts. Silent, hostile stares were returned for attempts to be friendly. I was fearful—and completely respectful—having heard about South American jails.

Passing immigration was simple—no visa was required—only my American passport. After collecting my baggage from the gleaming new stainless steel moving belt, I felt a surge of confidence. However, clearing customs proved to be difficult, occupying nearly an hour.

As a standard promotion practice, I was bringing a plastic desk model of the 727-200 for presentation to the president of AeroPeru. Customs officials—brusque and rude—demanded exorbitant duties, which I resisted. It was clear that they hoped I would abandon the model—so they could have it for themselves. Finally, I asked to talk to the *jefe*.

The chief was more polite, but nevertheless demonstrated the proud and pompous attitude which I found to be commonplace in Peru. The matter was resolved when I feigned a loss of patience, raising my voice and waving my arms.

"*Este modelo está una regalo especial para Él Ministro da Aeronautica!*" I declared, playing my ace.

The chief hesitated, and then a broad smile crossed his brown, leathery face. Perhaps he could gain a little favor in the *Ministerio*.

"*Está bien,*" he said, reaching for his seal to stamp my document.

I opened my briefcase and brought out a small airplane tie tac, which I handed to him.

"*Gracias, bueno, bueno.*"

He smiled again and extended his hand.

I was learning. On subsequent trips, I armed myself with about a dozen of those little tie tacs. Boeing stocked them in every airplane model. They were like gold everywhere that Boeing salesmen traveled. Was this bribery?

My fluency in Spanish was nearly complete. Nevertheless, I found the subjunctive tense to be the most important—and the most difficult.

My next introduction to realism was my encounter with Lima's taxicabs. Relics of the pre-World War II era, most were 1942 models. Poorly maintained, they appeared to be fugitives from a junk yard. Faced with the constant hazard of breakdowns, I began planning my arrivals at the airport two hours in advance of flight departures.

The route from the airport—through the slum district—seemed endless. Perhaps it was only because of the overwhelming poverty. On all sides were block after block of the barest of living accommodations; clusters of galvanized sheet and cardboard shacks interspersed in a sea of small, unfinished, brick buildings. The river banks were heavily populated with women washing clothes in the polluted water, and everywhere clotheslines were laden with brightly colored apparel.

I began to wonder if there really was a city. Soon however, the streets were filled with cars, trucks, and buses, honking and pushing. Scores of three-wheeled vehicles wove in and out among the traffic, with loading trays mounted over the two front wheels. Ragged, lean-muscled boys and wrinkled old women pedaled them along under overburdening loads. Rusty and creaky, they were carryovers from a technology of bygone days.

The streets became more narrow and congested, but abruptly widened at *Avenida Pierola*, the main thoroughfare. Here, the sidewalks were blanketed with squatting vendors—their wares spread on multi-colored carpets before them. Normally, from midday until late in the evening in downtown Lima, the street was a cacophony of sound from the hawking vendors. Soldiers patrolled the main intersections.

Downtown, there were no traffic lights. Instead, from an elevated box located in the center of each intersection, a uniformed policeman directed the flow of traffic with hand signals and whistles.

We turned on Union, oldest street in the city, finally reaching *Avenida de República*, the first modern, divided boulevard I had encountered. Along its sweeping curves, the new Lima loomed in the distance. That was the direction of Miraflores and San Isidro, the suburbs where the middle and upper class lived—elegant districts with large, extravagantly landscaped homes. Iron or stone fences, well manicured lawns, flowering trees, fragrant hibiscus, and graceful palms clothed the mansions with an aura of comfort and security. The line of demarcation between

the two Limas was at the square near the Sheraton Hotel—a line separating two worlds.

Facing *Avenida de República*, the Sheraton was an impressive, modern, twenty-one-story structure, decidedly out of place among the old,
ornate, Spanish-style buildings. To the casual eye, it was a well-appointed
hotel, equal of many in the United States. But there was a dramatic
difference. Behind the facade, managers grappled with nearly unsolv-
able problems to keep it running. The employees were of a different
culture, responding to a different drumbeat. There, as everywhere in
Latin America, the cleavage between technology and antiquity meets the
businessman with stunning force.

The natives—always referring to us as Americans, while in fact, they
are Americans as well—could never comprehend our furious urgency.
They really didn't believe it was necessary. This traditional condition,
more than any single factor, became the greatest frustration in dealing
with Latin Americans.

There was always mañana. As salesmen, we were squeezed between
the demanding expectations of our own technology-oriented company,
and the people-oriented organizations which were our customers.

It was early Wednesday afternoon when I checked in to the Sheraton,
and my first priority was to contact the airline. When General Soto tele-
phoned Boeing, requesting a firm cost proposal for the acquisition of a
new 727-200 airplane, he stated pointedly that he was in a hurry. My
appointment was for the next morning, so it was of some urgency that I
make my presence known without delay.

Our initial contact, indeed the required prelude to any visit with
airline personnel, was with the president—a fact of Latin American protocol.

The president ran everything, personally presiding over the minut-
est details. Often it would take days to arrange a meeting, and then
cancellations at the last minute were the expected norm. Advance planning scarcely helped. Airline presidents seldom considered previous
commitments to be binding. Thus, salesmen were constantly in the posi-

tion of beggars of a few minutes of "rug time."

After nearly a half hour of continuous dialing, I finally broke through the thicket of busy signals. A pleasant feminine voice greeted me.

*"Hola, como está,"* I announced.

*"Muy bien, quien habla?"*

*"Aqui está senor Bauer, da Boeing—usted habla Engles?"*

*"Si*—who would you like to speak to?"

Elation seized me—my lucky day—the secretary spoke excellent English, and had recognized my accent.

*Easy,* I mused.

I was pleased to discover that many Latins knew English—and preferred to speak it—happy for the practice.

Before I could utter another word, she announced, "The General just left for the *Ministerio.*"

That response proved to be standard reply number one.

"Well, you remember that I called from the United States last week and the General said a meeting on Thursday would be fine."

"The General is very busy."

That proved to be standard response number two.

Giving my room number, I agreed to call *en punto* at 9:00 a.m. the next morning, knowing full well that no one was ever on time. I vowed to get better acquainted with the secretaries. Since all contacts had to be initiated through the president's office, they were the barrier—or the conduit to reach the boss.

It didn't seem proper to invite airline secretaries to lunch, but on subsequent trips, I faithfully brought a supply of tiny boxes of chocolates—four pieces in each—one box for each of the secretaries I would be calling on. My percentage of successful meetings with airline executives improved dramatically. I was learning about *mordida* on a modest scale.

Next, I rang Faucett Airlines, requesting a meeting with General Revoredo. After the AeroPeru experience, I was startled at the warm reception. The new 727-100 they had purchased from Boeing in 1968 was a money-maker. With its quick, powerful takeoff capability, the airplane had proven to be outstanding for the high mountain airfields and short runways in Peru.

Faucett was nearing the final payment on the airplane and was pleased with the cordial association with the people of Boeing.

Elsa, the General's secretary, did not even bother to ask him.

"Why don't you come down to the office between 8:30 and 9:00 in the morning?" she suggested.

I gulped, immediately in trouble. Having already promised to call General Soto at nine, I would be in his competitor's office, with no opportunity. There was no retreat. Impulsively, I agreed.

"Fine, fine, that will be very nice. Thank you very much, and the best to the General," I replied.

Elsa had sounded pleasant. The relationship with Faucett was obviously well joined. My task would be to develop the same rapport with AeroPeru.

Later that afternoon, I called Mrs. Giesela Plenge, Boeing's public relations consultant in the country. She had gone to the mountains for a vacation.

The next morning I decided to phone AeroPeru at 8:30—on the chance that Lila was already there—and before leaving for Faucett.

"The General has not come in yet," Lila announced. This became standard reply number three, and was good for an entire morning.

"Why don't you call about 9:30?"

My heart sank. Another nail in my coffin, I thought. I felt a growing antagonism toward Soto, and hadn't even met him. Perhaps the real reason for my feelings was the knowledge that he had been a consultant for McDonnell Douglas just before he was chosen as president of AeroPeru, and I viewed him as 100 percent sold on Douglas airplanes. I believed he was simply using Boeing as a stalking horse.

"Okay," I replied pleasantly, remembering my allegiance to the customer at all costs.

Grabbing my briefcase, which was packed and ready by the door, I rushed madly for the elevator and a taxi. Traffic jams were already forming, and Faucett headquarters was located adjacent to the airport—on the other side of the city.

It was already fifteen minutes to the hour. My first appointment, and I was going to be late! I cursed General Soto under my breath.

I arrived at fifteen minutes after nine, profuse with apologies. Elsa took no notice, cordially offering me *cafe*, and announcing my arrival to General Revoredo. A few minutes later I was ushered into the General's office.

Meticulously groomed, in a trim, powder blue suit and tie, Revoredo greeted me warmly. He immediately began talking about the 727, putting me at ease. My confidence returned.

"Our plane will be paid off next April!" he exclaimed proudly. Faucett had not missed a single payment.

Revoredo stepped out from behind his desk and we embraced, as was the custom among friends in Latin America. He motioned me to a chair.

Faucett, third oldest airline on the entire continent of South America, had been consistently operating at a profit. Under ordinary circumstances, the airline would have been taken over along with the rest of the private industry. The company was spared in deference to its managing director and CEO, General Armando Revoredo Iglesias, a Peruvian air hero.

The Peruvians were partial to their heroes, particularly airmen, and Peru had its share.

Notable in the annals of air history was Jorge Chavez, the first aviator in the world to fly over the Alps from France to Italy. An unlikely event—that someone from a little-known country thousands of miles away should steal that glory away from the Frenchmen.

Born in the Peruvian embassy in Paris, the young Chavez became a fearless aviator. In September 1910, he broke the world's altitude record, flying up to 2,680 meters. A few days later, he made the successful crossing of the Alps. During the landing maneuver, he encountered strong winds and lost control of his fragile Bleriot airplane. Witnesses reported that at 200 meters of altitude, the wings broke off and fell like leaves to the ground. Chavez was grievously wounded and died on the 27th of

September, 1910, at the age of twenty-five. The Peruvians had named the new airport in his honor.

Peru produced many daring airmen, but none reached the world recognition that Chavez enjoyed until Commandante Revoredo flew non-stop in a single engine Stinson in 1937, from Lima on a direct compass course route to Buenos Aires, over the highest portions of the Andes. It was he who showed the world that the airplane was the instrument of transportation that could join the landlocked regions of South America together.

Revoredo was an uncommon man. After two careers, first as a successful surgeon, and then as a test pilot for the Peruvian Air Force, he joined Faucett Airlines in 1953 as its Director of Operations. He was fifty-six at the time, and he attacked the problems of commercial aviation with the vigor of a man thirty years his junior. The company was facing crucial decisions on new equipment.

Few could match Revoredo's abilities to evaluate a new airplane. In the '60s, he successfully convinced the board of directors that the right course for Faucett was to purchase the 727 trijet, even though its price was more than the entire worth of the company. With the delivery of that airplane in 1968, Revoredo had led Faucett into the jet age.

My goal was to replace their two BAC 111 twinjets with the larger and more efficient 737s.

Revoredo was seventy-seven years old when I first met him. No one would have guessed. He ran the airline with a disciplined hand, paying personal attention to the smallest detail. A pleasant man, with hawk-like features, his piercing blue eyes were kind and understanding behind thick, gold-rimmed glasses. His hair had thinned considerably and the gray had completely obliterated the red of his youth. He was short and slight of build, almost fragile, but his athletic body still gave testimony to a man in a hurry.

"Clancy and Tex send their kindest regards," I announced, sitting down. "They asked me to congratulate you personally on the great job Faucett is doing."

"Thank you very much, Mr. Bauer, I had a pleasant meeting with them in New York last spring," he confided.

When I showed him the performance data for the advanced 737-200 model, his face lit up and his eyes danced.

"Mr. Bauer, I really like that airplane," he said. "But Faucett can't afford new machines right now—only used. We're looking at another 727-100 from World Airways."

"General Revoredo, I can make an excellent case for a new 737. It will earn far more money for the airline than a used 727-100."

"I'd like to see the figures, but we still need to find the money to buy it. That's the big problem. We can buy a used 727 for about $3 million. What does the new 737-200 cost?"

"Around $6 million, depending on engines and options."

"Well, you see, there it is. We could buy two used 727-100s."

"That's an easy overview, but it doesn't take into account the higher maintenance costs for the older airplanes, the higher operating costs for three engines, or the remaining life of the old airplanes. Those 727s already have about 30,000 hours on the airframe. That's equivalent to ten years of operation."

Revoredo smiled—and sighed—at about the same time.

"You're probably right, Mr. Bauer, but we couldn't finance a $6 million dollar deal. The government won't back us up."

A pained expression clouded his face.

"Anyway, we should be able to get 60,000 hours out of those Boeing planes," he added slyly. "The one AeroPeru bought from Eastern had more than 30,000 hours, and it's flying beautifully."

"I can't argue with that. Boeing won't be surprised if they last 80,000 hours—but that doesn't change the facts of maintenance and operating costs continuing to escalate with age. Nevertheless, you've made your point. I'll ask Boeing to conduct an economic analysis comparing the two machines over the next ten years of operation, and we'll discuss it on my next trip."

"That's fine."

Recalling the remark the general had made about government backing, I realized that would be the biggest problem. Boeing's standard policy for sales in foreign countries was to require a government guarantee on the loans—and the new dictatorship wouldn't be doing Faucett any favors. They were just waiting for Father Time to take care of the old general.

I said my goodbyes, glancing hurriedly at my watch—already ten o'clock—and sprinted to the airport to call AeroPeru. In the 90-degree heat, loosening my tie and carrying my suit jacket, I arrived sweating profusely.

I ran to the nearest public phone, suddenly realizing I had no local coins. I believe it was at that moment that I developed one of the two most important axioms that I continued to use throughout the rest of my sales career. *Don't panic. There's plenty of time to panic later!*

No one was willing to give change for Peruvian currency. They had more faith in the brass coins. However, as soon as I offered an American dollar bill, change became available immediately.

I rushed to the phones. Two of the three were out of order, and the third was occupied. I decided not to wait. Hailing a taxi, I headed back to the hotel.

"*Prisa! prisa!* I urged the driver, constantly glancing at my watch.

It was nearly eleven o'clock when I reached Soto's secretary. The general had gone to the *Ministerio*. I was told to call after lunch, around two-thirty. *Siesta* time was inviolate.

Considering events so far, my surprise was complete when I called back in the afternoon. The meeting was scheduled for 4:00 p.m.!

I walked the seven blocks to AeroPeru headquarters on *Cailloma* Street, near the center of the city. At precisely four o'clock, I was invited into the president's office—extravagantly furnished in every detail—in sharp contrast to that of General Revoredo.

General Soto had retired from the Peruvian Air Force two years before, becoming a consultant for McDonnell Douglas, and dropping that account after being appointed to the presidency of the airline.

The 727-100 that AeroPeru had purchased from Eastern in May was competing with Faucett on the longer domestic routes.

The three new, recently purchased F-28 twinjets were being employed on the short routes. For the regional and international service, AeroPeru utilized their three old DC-8s.

Soto, pleasant but official, was a handsome man, short and muscular, with a dark complexion, neatly combed wavy hair graying at the temples. He impulsively drew on his cigarette, blew a cloud of smoke, squinted his eyes, and talked in quick, short bursts—in perfect English.

As requested, I had brought a proposal to sell one new 727-200, the stretched version of the original 727, with a capacity increase of forty seats in an all-tourist configuration. I reviewed the important parameters.

The plane had significantly longer range than its predecessor, ideal for the continental route additions that they were considering. By adding auxiliary fuel tanks in the cargo holds, the plane could also reach nonstop all the way from Lima to Miami, roughly 2,300 miles.

Soto listened politely.

"AeroPeru will need two airplanes," he abruptly announced, watching me closely for effect.

"We want a proposal immediately—with price and delivery dates," he added.

"Boeing can put a proposal together over the weekend, and telex it to Lima on Sunday afternoon," I said.

"How about me bringing it over first thing Monday morning?" I added.

This sudden, unexpected response caught Soto off guard. He got up, walked a few paces, and returned to his chair.

"Monday and Tuesday are impossible. Bring it over on Wednesday, and we can talk about it." He blew another cloud of smoke. Then, in an apparent second thought, "Does Boeing have a consultant here?"

"Not at the moment, but I'm looking for a suitable candidate who can work with the airline."

Soto did not respond to the bait, and I made my departure.

My meeting on Monday morning with Giesela Plenge reinforced my feeling of no confidence in the government. She was furious with the way they were mistreating the press. Everything was censored. Giesela verified that *mordida* was the standard way of doing business. She reminded me of the competition between the 737 and the F-28, and how the complexion of the sale changed overnight when the money was passed "under the table."

"Boeing needs to develop friends here," Giesela said pointedly, her dark eyes flashing. "And Soto is Dooooglas," she added in her heavily accented English.

"That's part of my mission, to find a good consultant," I revealed. "I'll need all the help I can get."

Finding a consultant was difficult, requiring care and discretion. After discussion with the management in Seattle, it was decided to invite Lt. General Benjamin "Ben" LeBailly, recently retired from the United States Air Force, along on the next trip to help in the search. Ben was already a part-time consultant for Boeing, working on a retaining fee. Prior to his retirement, he had been chairman of the Inter-American Defense Board, and was personally acquainted with the Air Force generals, both active and retired, in most of the countries of Latin America.

Early the following Wednesday, I called AeroPeru for an appointment. General Soto had gone to Miami. Tiring of the runaround tactics—without phoning in advance—I went directly to his office. Lila was taken by surprise.

"The general didn't get back from Miami," she informed me. "But he'll be here later this afternoon. Why don't you call back tomorrow morning?"

"Okay," I replied, forcing myself to be cheerful.

I used the remainder of the day to finish other important visits, following up on Revoredo's invitation to meet his maintenance and operations managers, Jorge Corpancho and Francisco Arteaga. It was our policy to become immersed in airline operations to better understand their needs. Both men proved to be fast friends of Boeing—the result of flying and working with the 727.

I also met with the vice president of maintenance and engineering for AeroPeru, Hernando Vasquez, who had only recently become an outspoken supporter of Boeing equipment. The 727 they had purchased from Eastern less than a year before was doing an outstanding job on the

Lima-Cuzco, Lima-Arequipa, and Lima-Iquitos routes—the main money-makers for both airlines.

Hernando was casual and open, his round face and pleasant countenance a perfect complement for his short, heavyset body. I immediately felt as if I had known him forever. Hernando complained bitterly about the maintenance-prone F-28s, hoping aloud that AeroPeru would not make the mistake of buying any more of them. He mentioned the strong pressure that Fokker was making, promising a later version of the F-28, the - 400.

I was pleased to find someone in the organization who appeared to be open minded, but I was beginning to wonder if anything made any difference except the level of payoffs.

Later in the day, I checked on the promised Friday meeting with Soto.

"You have an appointment with the general at 4:00 p.m. tomorrow afternoon," Lila reported cordially.

I hardly knew what to expect the next day—perhaps still another postponement. Arriving early, as was my custom, I nevertheless was prepared for a long wait. But Soto was on time. Twice in a row!

He was less formal, addressing me by my first name, unusual for the short relationship. He listened to the terms of the new proposal—asking only cursory questions and nervously blowing clouds of smoke—and thanked me.

When I inquired what he thought about the proposal, Soto relaxed and became talkative.

"Well," he said, "the government has decided to look at wide-bodies instead. They'll form a commission to study all the possibilities."

"When will that be done?"

"Right away. The schedule is to get the Commission named within the next thirty days. We need airplanes by the middle of July 1976. Our DC-8 lease expires then. We plan to start flying to Los Angeles and New York. We'd like to see a technical presentation on the 747SP as soon as possible."

Soto's apparent candor did not lessen my suspicions that he was simply using Boeing as a yardstick to promote his personal interest in McDonnell Douglas equipment.

# 4

The best conceived strategies often had to be changed overnight at the whim of the customer, and in the developing countries, this proved to be the rule rather than the exception. Salesmen developed a repetitive cycle—prepare, travel, present, and review—and then start all over again. To make a sale during the first contact was rare. Indeed, many sales campaigns spanned two or more years, often resulting in no sale at all. Salesmen were on the road about 60 percent of the time. It wasn't long before I began to feel like the man who came to dinner. Still, the lure of capturing a new customer made it all worthwhile.

The 747SP airplane for which General Soto had requested a proposal was a derivative of the original 747. However, it was a rare occurrence in commercial airline history—the body was shrunk rather than stretched, *actually shortened 46 feet and 7 inches from the original.*

This design decision was the result of several evolutionary developments. In the late '60s, a market emerged for a machine with passenger loads somewhere between the DC-8/707 airplanes and the jumbos, capable of connecting distant city pairs.

McDonnell Douglas decided to stretch the DC-8 to serve those "long thin routes," offering the DC-8-62. Boeing chose not to stretch the 707, and that market was captured by McDonnell Douglas.

Then in 1972, luck and timing ratcheted to Boeing's advantage, when McDonnell Douglas shut down the DC-8 line altogether—concentrating on the DC-10.

In 1973, Boeing decided to challenge this growing market with an airplane larger than the '62s, but smaller than the jumbos, with a spectacular increase in range—on the order of 7,000 miles—far exceeding any airplane in the commercial field. This new machine was designated the 747SP—for Special Performance.

The SP retained the wing, engines, and lift devices of its parent; thus also providing higher cruising altitude, superior takeoff and landing characteristics, and improved fuel economy.

Typical capacity was 44 first class and 261 economy, 81 passengers more than the DC-8-62.

With these attributes, the SP should have sold itself. On the contrary, a totally unexpected disadvantage appeared. With first flight almost a year in the future, it was being viewed as a "paper airplane"—something that might never come to be—and I was back at square one.

The first step was to bring specialists to Lima to study AeroPeru's route system, and to make a growth forecast based on local, regional, and world economics. A favorable projection of traffic growth was all important, and it was crucial to obtain customer concurrence—thus validating earnings expectations.

After three weeks of preparation in Seattle, we returned to Lima in mid-September. Ben LeBailly came along, and while our staff people were working with their counterparts in the airline—to create a five-year traffic forecast—Ben and I initiated our search for a consultant.

Ben was a happy, extroverted man with boundless energy and untempered enthusiasm, always smiling and joking. A veteran pilot, he made contacts easily, even arranging a meeting with the *Ministro* himself.

We interviewed dozens of candidates. Whenever things went badly, Ben would put on his full-face smile and declare, *"La vida está un fandango!"* Then we would both laugh, slap hands, and charge ahead. Selling airplanes in Peru was indeed a dance!

The conventional wisdom for hiring a consultant in Latin America was to zero in on retired air force generals. They knew the workings of both the airlines and the government.

Probably of greatest significance, retired generals had held positions of importance in the government, and their opinions were highly valued. Although we decried dishonesty, it was not our business to pry into their private lives. The key was legitimacy. For myself, I sought, first and foremost, a man with honesty and integrity—since if he lacked it, he might secretly sell sensitive concession information to our competitors.

We quickly narrowed the field to three—all generals, retired from the Peruvian Air Force.

I was particularly impressed with General Chamote, a man who had been retired less than a year and had worked under the current *Ministro*— whom he regarded as a personal friend.

In a country where special favors were considered entirely appropriate among friends, I was elated to have discovered General Chamote. An added bonus was his open candor and apparent honesty—in the image of the archetype of a Boeing career man. He had four children, two still in high school. With mandatory retirement from the military established at age fifty-five, retirees found themselves in need of supplementary funds. Thus, I felt certain that Chamote would be highly motivated.

John Broback concurred with my recommendation, and we signed a one-year contract. I sent letters to Soto and Revoredo the next day, notifying them that General Chamote had been chosen as our consultant in Peru.

Salesmen kept in close contact with home base, dispatching daily telexes. However, in the knowledge that the messages were often monitored, we resorted to telephone conversations for sensitive information, using code words in many instances.

Consultants worked as independent contractors in all respects, with no authority to obligate Boeing in any manner whatsoever. The consultant was also required to assume all expenses and pay all costs in relation to carrying out his duties, receiving no compensation until the airplane was sold. Nevertheless, the incentive was huge. Commissions ranged from 0.5 percent to 2.5 percent, and perhaps in a rare instance would be increased to three. The contract with Chamote called for a commission of 2.5 percent. The 747SP airplane was selling for about $44 million at the time—a potential bonanza of $1,100,000 for the consultant.

Many consultants worked through two or more years of one-year contracts, spending much of their time, and potentially considerable of their own money, betting on a favorable outcome of a sales campaign, only to find an empty pot at the end of the rainbow. No commissions were offered for the sale of used airplanes, which made up the total fleets of many small operators.

Reports of multimillion-dollar commissions earned by a few legitimate consultants around the world were highly publicized. Nothing was ever said about the dozens of others who never made a penny, and in some cases lost their life's savings on one wrong perception.

With the consultant selection completed, Ben departed for Seattle, but I received new instructions.


"Gene, I want you to go down to Cochabamba, and deliver a proposal to LAB Boliviana," John Broback directed.

"Am I being assigned the Bolivia account?" I inquired.

"Not right now, but since you're in the area, I want you to pick this one up—and stop in at Quito on the way back to see what's going on in Ecuador. You should introduce yourself to the airlines and scout around to see if we need a consultant there. Better yet, why don't you keep Quito on your regular visit list. It's on the way to Lima, and we can kill two birds with the same stone."

"What about my Brazil assignment?"

"Don't worry about that, it's in the works."

I knew that Bob Steiner, the salesman for Brazil, was resisting the division of his territory, but had faith in John's promise.

"O.K., see you in Seattle," I said.

Salesmen had to be prepared to be dispatched to anywhere in the world by a late night phone call. Seattle was three time zones earlier than Peru and four earlier than Rio.

Hastily rearranging my flight schedule, I flew to Cochabamba with the proposal that had been telexed to Lima. Peter Stross, the regular salesman for Boliviana, would be following up on his next trip, so I limited my visit to a short meeting with the president.

After a quick stop in Lima, I was on to Ecuador.


Arriving in Quito, I was greeted by a crystal blue sky with unfiltered sunlight of magnificent brightness, the clear, sharp mountain peaks delineated as if painted on the horizon. It was a tranquil scene at the age-old city—timeless—welcoming man in his many costumes: from the Incas who came on their slave-borne thrones, followed by the *conquistadores* with the rattling of muskets and the fierce chop of swords, the Peruvian army bent on empire, and finally the expectation of hordes of camera-carrying, jet-borne *turistas*.

Those who claim for Ecuador that it is the healthiest climate in the world are the sun worshippers who have come to the country, straining to get ever closer to that golden orb. Indeed, if measured from the earth's center, 20,700-foot-high Chimborazo would be the highest point on the earth—exceeding mighty Everest.

Lying astride the equator, Ecuador does not depend on latitude for climatic variations. Instead, temperature and rainfall vary almost entirely with altitude. Myth and rumor has it that hidden valleys high in the mountains harbor scores of natives over 100 years of age. Quito, the capital and second largest city, lies in one of the most beautiful of those valleys at an elevation of over 9,000 feet, only fifteen miles from the equator. Similar to Bogota, temperature variations are scarcely noticeable throughout the year. For this reason it has been called the "Land of Eternal Spring."

The largest city, Guayaquil, in the coastal region, is spared the blistering heat of its equatorial location by *Él Nino*, the moderating Humboldt Current, flowing offshore.

Entry into Ecuador required only a passport, and I found the people to be pleasant and friendly. I decided to concentrate initially on Ecuatoriana de Aviación SA, known throughout the world as simply Ecuatoriana.

Originally established in 1957, the airline struggled with outmoded equipment, primarily old Caravelles, Viscounts, and Avros, finally building a small route network to the neighboring countries of Peru, Colombia, and Panama. By August 1972, they were on the verge of bankruptcy, not uncommon for many of the airlines of Latin America. To maintain solvency, the government acquired 51 percent of the stock. Success was elusive, and two years later, the government assumed complete control.

Three used Electras were purchased, and the Quito-Guayaquil-Miami route was won, giving Ecuador its first toehold in the United States market. Unfortunately, the airline still lacked the rigor necessary to maintain the airplanes properly, resulting in a crash of one of the Electras, and in September 1974, the Federal Aviation Authority (FAA) of the United States denied flights to the U.S. That order grounded the planes—portending doom to Ecuatoriana. My arrival in Quito, on September 30th—without advance notice—was a surprise to the airline management, but I had no difficulty in arranging a meeting with Colonel Fernandez, the president. Perhaps he had read something into the timing.

Headquarters for the airline was downtown, a pleasant walk from the Colon Hotel on that serene, sunlit Monday morning. Located in modest surroundings on the second floor of what appeared to be a small apartment complex, Ecuatoriana's headquarters could easily have escaped notice, except for the small sign on the top of the building.

After a short wait, I was ushered into the Colonel's office.

*"Hola! Como está?"* he greeted, extending his hand.

*"Bien, bien, e usted?"* I responded.

"Not so fine today, Mr. Bauer—you may speak English. I've made many visits to the States—in fact, I took some jet training in Texas." He smiled.

"Thank you, Colonel Fernandez, I appreciate you taking time from your schedule to receive me. As you know, my interest is in helping Ecuatoriana obtain modern equipment."

Fernandez motioned me to a chair, sat down at his desk, and began toying with a paperweight of an Electra model.

"I'm sure you know of the grounding last week? Does Boeing have some influence with the FAA?"

"Not in the least! We, of course, interface with them constantly, but they're a government agency, and Boeing is a private company."

We discussed the fleet problems, and I briefed Fernandez on availability and costs of various models of Boeing planes. He was most interested in the Model 720B, and I promised to telex him a list of the present owners, since Boeing no longer produced it.

The meeting ended on a cordial note; however, my report to management regarding sales potential was not optimistic.

Since no one from Boeing had been in Ecuador previous to my visit, I took the opportunity to meet with the commercial attaché in the U.S. Embassy, a procedure which we always followed when entering a country for the first time.

My primary interest was to assess the political and business climate, and to hear their views on the need for consultants for conducting business in Ecuador.

"Here, everything is handled by a process of payoffs. In my experience, it's just as bad—maybe worse than in Peru," Mr. Blackie advised.

# 5

Throughout its history, Boeing demonstrated an amazing propensity for attracting dedicated people, and whatever I may have lacked in other attributes, I made up in dedication. On a scale of one to ten, I expect my rating would be eleven. With my sales assignment still less than a year old and my new role as prime mover in the company's efforts for sales in both Peru and Ecuador, the new responsibility weighed heavily on my shoulders.

Divorced in 1972, I had been as guilty as anyone in putting my job ahead of my family—a trait shared by many Boeing engineers and managers. Single for nearly three years, I had begun dating Beth—also divorced—a journalist with many common interests. Recognizing that married men would be better received as salesmen in Latin America, and facing a "pressure cooker" schedule, we decided to get married between sales trips. Beth was excited about the challenge of my new job, and eager to support me as the wife of a "traveling salesman." We were married in a simple ceremony on November 3rd, resolving to concentrate on the happy attributes of continual reunions, rather than on the stress of separations. A few days later, I was off to Peru, taking a team of six specialists.

The three-hour presentation to General Soto and his vice presidents the following morning covered the entire spectrum; from the five-year traffic forecast, through the 747SP technical data—and performance on the AeroPeru routes—to the financial analysis at the end.

My strategy for offering the SP model was to add a new dimension to AeroPeru's capability, while at the same time closing the door on the competing airplanes.

Normally, a traveler to Cuzco, gateway to Macchu Picchu, was required to change planes in Lima, stay overnight, and transfer to the domestic system. The DC-10 and L-1011 lacked the performance for direct flights, whereas the SP could fly nonstop to Cuzco from New York, Miami, or Los Angeles, reducing the total trip time for a visit to Macchu Picchu from five days to three. For the hardy—who would not mind flying at night—the round trip would be possible over a single weekend! The difficulty was in convincing the conservative Peruvians to think in such bold concepts.

Now, in spite of the encouraging traffic forecast, General Soto—who had asked for the SP in the beginning—showed concern about the size of the airplane, expressing doubts that it could attract enough passengers. However, he was sufficiently interested to invite the team to remain in Lima, repeating the presentation to the newly formed Commission. I was beginning to feel we were making progress.

Wednesday morning, the day of the presentation, was hectic. We had been invited to the headquarters of the Peruvian Air Force, located on the edge of town.

The heavy brass showed an intense interest in this spectacular new flying machine, and there were few interruptions. But we were caught by surprise in the question period which followed.

General Soto stood up, paused for attention, stared directly at me and shouted, "Why did the 747 crash in Nairobi?"

Leaving the hotel early, no one on the team had read the morning paper, not even the headlines, and none of us had listened to the news on the radio.

"I'm sorry, General Soto, but I'm not aware of any 747 crash in Nairobi."

Soto waved a newspaper, unfolded it and pointed to the large headlines.

Those were the times that tried salesmen's souls. I was inwardly furious with Soto for grandstanding in front of the Air Force brass, but dared not show the slightest irritation.

*Zapped by Murphy's Law!* I thought. Calmly, I replied.

"The 747 has been flying with dozens of airlines—all over the world—for over five years without a crash. The plane has surpassed all previous safety records in commercial airline history."

This was a well-known, and well-publicized, fact. Soto harrumphed but did not reply.

"We can't answer your question right now, as the cause will not be immediately known; however, Boeing has the utmost confidence in the airplane."

There was nothing more to say. But the psychological impact had been made. Soto had exploited a perfect opportunity to discredit the 747.

With the technical presentations completed the day before Thanksgiving, the team departed. I remained in Lima to assess further reaction and competitor response.

Accident/crash propaganda began appearing in the Lima newspapers. I could only assume it was being planted.

From Nairobi, it was soon learned that the Lufthansa crew had failed to deploy the leading edge slats, causing the airplane to crash on takeoff. The plane had never become airborne. All but fifty-nine passengers survived. There had been two previous 747 hull losses, both the result of bombs while the planes were on the ground, neither resulting in fatalities.

Meeting with Giesela, we counterattacked with a vigorous publicity campaign in the Lima newspapers.

I had a standing invitation from General Revoredo to fly to Cuzco and visit Macchu Picchu. The trip seemed to be integral both to my familiarization with Faucett's 727 operations and my strategy for the 747SP sale. I called the general, accepting his invitation, and arranged to fly to Cuzco on Thanksgiving Day, occupying the observer's seat behind the pilot. It was our standard policy to decline a seat in the passenger cabin of our client's airplanes, unless we paid the full fare.

A visit to Cuzco, the ancient capital of the Incas, was a sufficient reward in itself; however, the added bonus trip to Macchu Picchu defies description.

The Cuzco airport is situated in a natural bowl in the mountains at an elevation of 11,204 feet, at the time exceeded in the world only by the 13,000-foot-elevation airport in La Paz[1], Bolivia. We flew in through a heavy cover of clouds.

Looking directly over the pilot's right shoulder at the blanked-out windshield was an unnerving experience, and I developed a bad case of sweaty palms. Visibility was zero until we reached the final approach—when suddenly we broke through the clouds into brilliant sunshine. It is common for the clouds to hang on the mountain peaks, completely surrounding the city.

Arriving in the early afternoon, I rented a taxi to visit the old Inca fortress of *Sacsayhuaman* on the hills above Cuzco. Here, giant stones from the crumbling fort still stand—one upon the other—so tightly fitted that a knife blade cannot be inserted in the joints. How these stones, some weighing several tons, were put in place remains a mystery.

The idea entered my mind about bringing Beth along on some future visit. I spent the night in a rustic hotel in Cuzco, and at 6:30 a.m. headed for the railroad station. Promptly at seven o'clock the daily train departed for Macchu Picchu. The locomotive labored back and forth, with six switchbacks along the mountain face, finally lifting itself up and out of the bowl.

This was the beginning of the trip, and its highest point. We now began weaving down a mountain valley in tortuous turns toward Macchu Picchu—the seventy-five-mile journey requiring three and a half hours. The train stopped at *Puente Ruinas*—literally, "the point of ruins," at about the 8,000-foot level. We had arrived at the base of a sharp mountain spire which thrusts up 1,200 feet above the surging Urubamba River.

From there, buses negotiate the fourteen hairpin turns of a gravel road which disappears in a boiling cloud of dust, as the drivers play "chicken" in negotiating the turns. It is a white-knuckle ride—even for the bravest.

My thoughts harked back to the American professor from Yale, Hiram Bingham—who in 1911 discovered the Inca fortress that had been hidden for four centuries. Hacking his way up the sheer side of the jungle-covered mountain, accompanied by an Indian guide, he was suddenly in the midst of an intricately designed stone city, perched on its very pinnacle. It appeared that the top of the mountain had been cut off—providing a relatively flat plateau.

"It fairly took my breath away," he wrote. "Surprise followed surprise. I could scarcely believe my senses."

Arriving at the top shortly after midday, we were allowed only four hours to tour the ruins and return to the train. A seventeen-room hotel was located at the top of the serpentine road, where lodging could be arranged—weeks in advance—with extreme difficulty and questionable assurance.

I visualized a modern tourist hotel near the base, perhaps a few miles away so as not to upset the pristine natural beauty of the site.

The campaign for the sale of the 747SP was firming up in my mind. The centerpiece would be the Cuzco/Macchu Picchu connection to New York, Miami, and Los Angeles.

With the help of Chamote, I began the long process of cementing personal relationships with the management of AeroPeru. I also hoped that he could be successful in acquiring copies of our competitors' proposals. Keeping aware of other offers was an intense and deadly serious activity. How he accomplished it was his own business. I was aware that our own proposals were in the hands of our competitors—in particular, McDonnell Douglas—within twenty-four hours after our presentations. General Soto would see to that.

Occasionally, I was invited into the homes of the executives. Those were my favorite times, since it gave me the opportunity to meet the families. I always brought flowers for the *Señora* and trinkets for the children. Those were personal gifts—not charged to the Boeing sales account. *La mordida?* Bribes? Gifts to friends? I wondered how many flowers equalled a bribe.

I did charge the Johnny Walker Black Label which I always brought for the airline officials. Peruvians love scotch whisky, and it was exorbitantly expensive—$40 a fifth in Lima, whereas I purchased it at the duty-free stores for less than one-fourth of that price.

Personally, it never occurred to me at the time that such gifts might be viewed as bribes, but later, when news of the large illegal payments by Lockheed were revealed, I began to wonder where the line would be drawn.

Other than the interfaces with airline executives, my social life on the road was essentially nonexistent. In Lima, however, I was fortunate to make the acquaintance of Camillo Bozzolo—manager of *Banco Continental*—who had been associated with the purchase of Faucett's first Model 727 in 1968.

Camillo, and his wife Isabel, invited me to their home for dinner on my second visit to Lima. On subsequent trips, as my schedule permitted, I had the pleasure of visiting with them and their two small sons. Those experiences were the closest thing to home for me, and we still exchange cards at Christmas.


The sixty days allocated for the Commission's decision passed rapidly. General Galindo, Commission president, felt he needed more time for the evaluation. AeroPeru was already entering a period of instability. Meanwhile, General Soto was coming under increasing criticism from the government. The first full year of operations under his leadership had been a dismal failure. He had devoted most of his resources to creating an elegantly furnished central headquarters in downtown Lima.

The F-28s were spending an inordinate amount of time in maintenance on the ground, and the old DC-8s were not competing well with U.S. based Braniff airplanes. The only part of the fleet that was still operating at a profit was the 727.

Rumors were strong that Soto would be replaced the following August, the biennial date for the selection of a new *Ministro da Aeronautica.* Perhaps no one could have done better in so short a time, but General Velasco needed a scapegoat for every government corporation with a failing record, and Soto was being postured as the "it" man of AeroPeru.

Unrest and violence erupted in the streets, each time put down by increasing force, portents of worse to come.

After a quick trip home for Christmas, bringing a favorite Inca poncho for Beth, I returned to Lima the next day, to be on hand at perhaps a crucial moment.

Nothing happened, and I spent my first New Year's Day outside of the United States since World War II, alone in my hotel room, marking time.

On the 2nd of January, 1975, General Galindo announced an extension to the middle of February. I returned to Seattle for a month, my longest stay for the next four years. On the way, I visited Air Panama and Copa, two Panamanian airlines, both considering the purchase of Boeing airplanes.

At the February meeting, with all the combatants back on the scene, General Galindo moved the decision date still further into the future.

There was a brief flurry of excitement when the Concorde arrived at Jorge Chavez airport and opened its doors to invited guests. It was a publicity stunt—the Concorde was the last thing Peru needed—or could afford.

General Revoredo was honored when he was given the opportunity to fly copilot from Lima to Bogota, tracing the route he had pioneered nonstop in a single-engine Stinson, forty years before. His historic, 1,675 mile flight took nearly fifteen hours. The Concorde required less than two.

Revoredo was not impressed. The romance was all in the past. "The flight was very smooth," he remarked, "but it is very crowded inside."

When I returned home on the last day of February, the Commission was still postponing the decision and making new predictions, each one followed by no action. After the blush of optimism from my first meeting with General Soto, there now seemed to be no end to the process. It was like a contrail, initially so bright in the sky, and then fading, diverging, and disappearing in the clouds.

John called me in immediately upon my return. "Gene, I want you to get ready to leave for Brazil next week," he said. "You'll have responsibility for the Cruzeiro and Transbrasil accounts."

I could barely hide the elation.

Bob Steiner had been replaced by Adolfo "Dolf" Rischbeiter, a native Brasileiro engineer, who had emigrated to the United States to work for Boeing. He was assigned to the Varig and Vasp accounts.

"Good," I replied. "But aren't we in the middle of a wide-body campaign in Peru?"

"Those people will never buy anything! You can cover Peru, but Brazil will be your primary responsibility. It's up to you to figure out how to do it."

The following Tuesday, March 4th, 1975, I was on an airplane on my way back to Brazil.

1. In May 1995, La Paz was relegated to second place in altitude, when a China Southwest Boeing 757 inaugurated commercial service to Bangda, Tibet, at an elevation of 14,219 feet.

# 6

It was a cold, dreary morning with a solid roof of slate-gray clouds over Seattle when I embarked on my next venture to Brazil, where Boeing was doubling its sales force.

I traveled on Boeing wings, Seattle to New York on a Northwest 747, and on to Rio on a Varig 707. Flying on customers' airplanes afforded the opportunity to talk to the flight crews. I was invited to sit in the observer's seat by simply presenting my card to the stewardess.

Flight crews always had strong opinions about airplanes—and often about management's plans. Many were willing to talk.

My fact-finding mission to Brazil the year before had provided an authentic perspective of its geography, history, and business climate—but above all, the potential of its four airlines to purchase new equipment.

Brazil is a massive subcontinent—the fifth largest country in the world. Its latitudes stretch from the temperate zone of 40 degrees south in Rio Grande do Sul, to beyond the equator in the north, where the State of Rioraima extends past the southern border of Guyana.

In width, it spans four time zones, lying astride the continent, and encompassing all but the Andes spine on the west, the coastal regions on the north, and the pampas on the south.

A colony of Portugal, and originally a slave country, Brazil declared its independence in 1822, forming a republic in 1891. A succession of presidents failed to solve Brazil's diverse problems, and in 1964, a benign military government took charge. Their task was to establish order and progress in a country where many of the people were illiterate, and nearly half of the farm acreage was owned by 1 percent of the land owners.

Foreign banks eagerly loaned hundreds of millions of dollars, and a bewildering array of programs—from social to scientific—streamed forth from the government offices.

"From today forward," they announced upon taking office, "there will be no place in Brazil for *Jeca Tatu*." He was the legendary tramp who wandered about the vast country with his worldly possessions on the end of a stick over his shoulder, his clothing in tatters, and a self-rolled cigarette hanging from the corner of his mouth.

"*Jeca Tatu morrei,*" appeared on billboards and in advertisements all over the country. It appeared that *Jeca Tatu* was indeed dead.

In the parched northeast, where the sertão buried its would-be conquerors in an annual cadence of searing droughts, water was promised. To traverse the unspannable northern Amazon jungles, a transcontinental highway was promised. In the basin of the mighty Parana River, the largest hydroelectric power generating plant in the world was promised.

Brazil had the resources to accomplish all of those things. What had been lacking was a marshalling of the national will and a stability of government that would attract foreign capital.

Boeing had also caught the fever. All except John Broback, a veteran in Latin American sales. He was a doubter, but he viewed my extensive studies of Brazil while in OCBD as a valuable bellwether of the modern turn of events.

"Gene, give me the straight scoop. Is this another false start, or does it signal a real turnaround?" he inquired one day.

"It's real," I said, "you can bet your bottom dollar."

We charged ahead with unrequited enthusiasm.

Varig is the second oldest airline in South America, surpassed only by Avianca in Colombia. Founded in 1927 with the technical assistance of the German Condor syndicate, it grew to 15,000 employees by 1978, becoming Brazil's largest. Varig operated an extensive network, including the U.S., Europe, Asia, and Africa, and was the sole carrier with international routes.

Led by ramrod Erik de Carvalho, simply "Dr. Erik" to his close associates, Varig's ever-present shadow appeared whenever political maneuvering threatened to upset the status quo of Brazil's airlines.

Varig was an early customer of Boeing, purchasing two 707-420s in 1960. Most of the eleven follow-on airplanes were the convertible model—capable of being configured in all-passenger, all-freight, or a combination. In 1973, Varig purchased ten 737s.

The second largest carrier, Vasp—always breathing on Varig's neck for domestic business—was busily expanding its fleet of 737 airplanes, which by the end of 1978 stood at twenty-four, largest of all non-U.S. airlines.

Cruzeiro, third largest, had just purchased six 737s, complementing its existing 727 fleet. My first mission was to meet with Dr. Leopoldino Cardoso de Amorim, airline president, to determine if their impending route expansion would justify additional planes.

Transbrasil, my second account, and smallest of the four airlines, led by Dr. Omar Fontana, a gregarious pilot with a degree in law, was only beginning to make its mark. Transbrasil had just purchased a used 727-100, which was intended to form the nucleus of a modern fleet.

The government succeeded too well, creating a success story heralded around the world. By the early '70s, GNP was growing by a real factor exceeding 10 percent annually. Inflation appeared to be defeated by the crawling peg, a series of mini-devaluations of the cruzeiro, while allowing fixed assets and personal savings to increase in value with the rising cost of living.

The economic turnaround became known as the "Brazilian miracle." Capital investment flowed into the country in a growing stream. Skilled labor became increasingly scarce, and demand exploded. New millions of Brazilians entered the economic mainstream, their thirst for western goods swelling imports to a dangerous level.

By the mid-'70s, the balance of payments had tilted to the negative side. The government was forced to impose import controls and put strong brakes on capital expansion, with the result that the economy slowed to less than half its previous growth rates. Subsequent events, primarily the fallout from massive debt and a general slowing of the world economy, plunged Brazil into an inflationary spiral.

The airlines were one of the first to feel the pinch on imports of foreign equipment. However, I remained confident of the opportunities to demonstrate increased efficiency by replacing old aircraft with new machines.

When I arrived, the government was demanding improved efficiencies, as all four airlines were competing on the same domestic routes. Rumors were rampant that Cruzeiro and Transbrasil—both privately owned airlines—would merge, a result desired by the government.

A power struggle developed, with Varig determined to orchestrate the outcome. Further, Amorim and Fontana vied for the executive position in the proposed merger, with Amorim appearing to have the inside track.

However, the maverick was Transbrasil—and Dr. Fontana. Brilliant and stubborn, he had no mind to follow lockstep into a merger as second in command. In fact, he visualized Transbrasil as the emerging domestic giant in Brazil.

Boeing viewed the recent purchase of the 737-200 airplanes by three of the four airlines as a harbinger of a market explosion. The airline network was spreading out over the country and reaching its far corners. Considering its size, Brazil would need hundreds of airplanes. The airline executives' infighting was viewed as a temporary aberration.

My unenviable task became that of working the Brazil accounts without loosing control in Peru—at the opposite side of the continent. Commercial flights were sparse. Cruzeiro and Varig were the only two airlines flying to Lima, and they were usually overbooked. Reservations had to be made weeks in advance. Predicting the whims of Soto, Amorim, and Fontana compounded the difficulty.

Brazil was at the crossroads in its airline history. The most favorable outcome appeared to be the merger of Cruzeiro and Transbrasil, hopefully resulting in profitability for the remaining three companies.

Thus, we decided to promote the process. A meeting between Tex Boullioun, president of the Boeing Commercial Company, and both Amorim and Fontana seemed to be a place to begin. Amorim made it a reality by extending a formal invitation. We were delighted when he also invited Fontana. The Boullioun visit was scheduled for the first week in April, less than a month away, and I was beginning to get a comfortable feeling about the future.

Arriving on Wednesday, March 5th, I spent the next two days setting up the social agenda for the Boulliouns. Dolf had come along to begin his regular contacts with Varig and Vasp. I leaned on his native experience to be certain that protocol was meticulously followed.

On Saturday, March 8th, I left again for Lima to prepare for a Boeing team presentation to the wide-body commission on the following Tuesday.

The Commission had speeded up their decision timetable. The new deadline for recommendations to the *Ministro* was April 1st, only three weeks away, and two days after the Boulliouns were to arrive in Rio. April Fool's Day! *Was it an omen?*

At the Tuesday presentation, Soto was abrasive.

"Does Boeing expect us to believe their performance figures for the 747SP? These are only numbers on paper."

We remained calm, referring again to the payload/range chart, which was firmly validated by 747 operations around the world.

"But we know Cuzco," Soto insisted. "Our people don't believe the airplane can take off from there with a full load."

"The SP can not only take off, it can fly nonstop to New York with a full payload," we replied. "On the other hand, the trijets—the L-1011 and the DC-10—can only reach Caracas. They require a technical stop in Lima for refueling, which will add at least three hours to the trip time."

Soto maintained his smug demeanor. There appeared to be no way to convince AeroPeru, short of making a full flight demonstration from Cuzco.

Naturally, the Lockheed and McDonnell Douglas strategies were to push for a stop in Lima. The extra performance of the SP would be wasted. Indeed, the fourth engine would be an albatross! The battle was clearly joined.

Soto, obviously pushing for the DC-10, had still more ammunition.

"How can we be certain the SP will be committed to production, after the first airplane flies?"

"There is no question about production. We already have firm orders from three airlines, including Pan Am," I replied.

"What about spare parts?"

"The 747SP has a 90 percent commonality with the original -100 model. The preponderance of spare parts are already available."

"How can you claim lower maintenance costs? On what basis? The plane has not even flown," Soto continued.

Again, we produced detailed data on maintenance costs, based on over five years of service with the worldwide fleets of the -100.

Soto's barrage had a single goal—to raise doubts in the minds of the Commission members. If they selected the DC-10, he stood to get a nice slice of the commission. I had reliable information that both McDonnell Douglas and Lockheed were offering commissions of 5 percent.

My task would be to sell the lower seat-mile cost of the SP, which had twenty-nine more seats than the competitors—and to convince AeroPeru and the Commission that they could fill the seats. The Peruvians remained skeptical, in spite of the favorable traffic forecast.

Before leaving again for Rio, I called General Galindo.

"The general is not available," was the reply. Checking with Chamote, I found that Galindo would not be meeting with any salesmen prior to the decision.

"The Commission is split," he advised, "but I think they are leaning toward the SP."

I fretted.

"Don't be in a hurry," he said, smiling. *"Whenever you're in a hurry, you must take plenty of time."* I adopted this advice as the second important axiom of my sales career.

Leaving Peru to the care of Chamote, I left again on Sunday for Rio. The Amorim banquet arrangements for the Boulliouns were all in place for Wednesday, April 3rd. Dolf had taken the opportunity to invite Dr. Erik of Varig for a banquet the previous Monday. That left Tuesday open. I called Col. Gabriel, Transbrasil's public relations manager, inviting Fontana and Vice President Alvarenga to a separate banquet, to show Boeing's high regard for the airline management. I was delighted with Gabriel's reply. *"Muitos obrigadas, Señor Bauer!"*

Everything was comfortably in order.

I called Chamote every day, to keep his feet to the fire. He seemed too complacent. Either Boeing was actually gaining the inside track or Chamote was seeing the handwriting on the wall.

"I think we can win it," he said, "but the biggest thing now is the difference in maintenance costs. And there's still the worry about filling the seats."

The competition was narrowing down to Boeing versus McDonnell Douglas. It was apparent that Boeing needed a little extra push to go over the top. I called Seattle, finally convincing them that we must add still another concession. We decided to offer a cost/revenue-sharing plan. Under the plan, Boeing would cover the differential in direct operating costs for the first full year of operations. In return, Boeing would share in the revenue obtained from the increment of passengers on all loads greater than the 276 seats of the DC-10.

Biting the bullet, I decided to rush back to Lima one more time, delivering our latest concession to the Commission in person.

Alas! There was only one flight to Lima—a Cruzeiro flight on Sunday, March 19th. It was fully booked! With the grand banquet in Rio eleven days away, getting to Lima might mean I would be stranded there. I decided to go for broke!

I called Dr. Amorim. Impossible to connect. I grabbed a taxi and rushed over to his office, begging for a minute of his time.

Amorim was calm, unworried. "Don't worry, Señor Bauer, you have to know us Brasileiros. We have a bad habit of booking on several flights way in advance—so to be sure to get on one of them. I can arrange for a seat."

I was profusely thankful. "Dr. Amorim, you saved my life!" I exclaimed, giving him the Brazilian abrazo.


Reaching Lima, I told Chamote about our cost/revenue proposal, and asked him to deliver it to Galindo. Chamote expressed tremendous confidence. "Good, good," he said, "this should do it."

In the U.S., the Civil Aeronautics Board had just released a report showing passengers preferred 747 airplanes for long trips. I directed Chamote to pass this new information also. My confidence was going up. I secretly thought of the elation in Seattle, when I would call to tell them we had won the battle.

The Commission was impressed. In a worst case scenario, the offer would have cost Boeing over a million dollars. However, offers and counter-offers move through the airline grapevine with computer speed. Both competitors responded by increasing their own concession packages.

Chamote then offered to apply a major part of his own commission fee to the Boeing offer of goods and services. I was a little skeptical—believing that the *Ministro* was expecting a share.

The Commission continued to drag their feet, and I was beginning to think about a new strategy—support the idea of postponement! Delay would allow the traffic pressure to continue to build, while giving the SP breathing room to gain flying time and airline experience with our three firm international customers. A few solid arguments for such a course of action, planted in the right minds, would be sufficient to derail the program for a year or more.

The April decision deadline was pressing, and I felt compelled to be close to the action. I remained in Lima as long as I dared, and attempted to book a flight to Rio on Varig on Sunday, March 30th, the same day that the Boulliouns were scheduled to arrive.

Varig was booked solid. Maybe now was the time to panic. I called Dolf in Rio.

"Dolf, I need a miracle," I announced. "You have to get me on Varig flight RG 831 for Sunday."

"I'll do what I can," Dolf assured me.

"And by the way, I can't be there for the welcoming arrival of Tex. Please give my regrets."

Dolf called the next morning. "Sorry, Gene, the plane really is fully booked. Varig would have to bump somebody."

I tried to speak, but nothing came out.

"But don't panic—I got you on the observer's seat."

"You bastard!" I replied, kidding. "You scared the hell out of me."

"Have a good flight," he laughed.

I was overjoyed for the opportunity to sit in the cramped little seat behind the pilot for the 2,100 mile flight.

The easy strategy would have been to remain in Brazil, relaxing on the beaches. But that scenario was unacceptable to me. During those five weeks of March and early April, I made six trips over the Andes between Rio and Lima.

# 7

The Boullions arrived in Rio on Sunday, as planned. Dolf met them at the airport and escorted them to the Sheraton, a new hotel nestled below the cliffs of *Dois Irmãos* on the beach of Leblon.

The grand dinner party being hosted by Dr. Amorim in the Boullioun's honor was the main event, scheduled for Wednesday. Early on Monday morning, Dr. Amorim called me, requesting an urgent meeting. I hurried to the Cruzeiro offices in downtown Rio, wondering what the urgency was about.

Dr. Amorim was cordial, but nervous. "Mr. Bauer, I have a difficult problem," he said, looking at me expectantly.

"I must ask Boeing a favor."

I nodded, hiding my feeling of panic.

"The government people have asked me to come to Brasilia on Wednesday," Amorim continued. "I'm afraid it's about the merger. It's crucial that I be there!"

"I understand," I replied, almost biting my tongue.

"Well, you see what it does to our social schedule. I'm really terribly sorry! It looks as if I'll have to ask you for the kindness to change the dinner appointment with the Boulliouns to this evening."

My mind raced, blanked out, raced again. The entire delicately balanced schedule was going up in smoke. It was Monday morning and the dinner with Dr. Erik, so carefully arranged by Dolf, would have to be switched to Wednesday! I dared not suggest that Amorim consider changing his business meeting in Brasilia, in any case most probably a command performance.

Perhaps Dr. Amorim's motive was to upset the Varig meeting. Nevertheless, since he had made the original invitation for the Boulliouns to visit Brazil, it was proper to acquiesce.

I was petrified. My brain buzzed—how could we change Varig at the last minute? The implications for infuriating Dr. Erik were huge. I took the coward's way out.

"Mr. Boullioun is looking forward to the dinner meeting, and I'm certain he wouldn't want you to shift your business plans. Let's go ahead with the change to this evening."

Amorim heaved an audible sigh of relief. "I really appreciate that," he said, smiling and extending his hand. "We'll see you tonight at eight o'clock."

*What the hell have I done?* I thought, as I went down the elevator. *Now we have both meetings scheduled for tonight!*

The events that followed can only be rationalized in the humor of the situation, but from a business point of view it was nearly a disaster.

The Tuesday appointment with Fontana and Alvarenga had been a natural, considering the main dinner party was to follow on Wednesday. However, with the principal dinner affair already over, it would look devious to Dr. Amorim if a separate meeting were held with Transbrasil the following day, particularly since Amorim had invited both Fontana and Alvarenga and their wives.

With precious little time to unwind the schedule, I called Dolf with the bad news. There was a silence of unbelief.

"Gene, you bastard, this is no time for jokes! Do you realize that this could be my ass with Varig? Actually both our asses."

"What in hell could I do? We brought Tex all the way down here at Amorim's invitation. You'll just have to ask Dr. Erik to be understanding."

Dolf calmed down. "Let's see what I can do. I'll run over to Varig right now and try to make peace with Dr. Erik."

I prayed. *Lord, please get me out of this one!*

The next two hours seemed like days, but around eleven, Dolf called back.

He was in good spirits. "I saved our butts," he announced. "I've rescheduled our Varig meeting to Wednesday evening."

"Thank God!" I said.

Tex took the sudden change in signals in stride—probably more expected than not.

Canceling the Tuesday night dinner with Transbrasil proved to be more difficult. The Brazilian telephone system came close to defeating me. It was worse than Peru, so bad that many executives followed the practice of hiring young boys to carry handwritten notes between offices. There was a three-year waiting period for phone installations.

Dr. Fontana was impossible to reach. He was in Brasilia. My only hope was Alvarenga, who was in São Paulo. My worries mounted when the first two hours of calling produced nothing but busy signals. The local custom of going home for lunch and a *soneca* saved the day.

I began a steady barrage of end-to-end calls to Dr. Alvarenga's home. The strategy worked.

"I'm sorry to bother you at lunch, Dr. Alvarenga," I began, "but there is a matter of some importance that I need to discuss."

"Oh, that's no problem, Mr. Bauer."

"It's about the dinner arrangements. I assume you are aware of the change in Dr. Amorim's plans."

"Oh, yes, Dr. Fontana called me from Brasilia this morning. He'll be back in time. I think Monday is better than Wednesday anyway."

"Well, there is one thing. I was thinking since we will all be together tonight, it would be easier for you and Dr. Fontana if you didn't have to make a trip to Rio two days in a row."

After a short silence, he replied.

"Yes, it would be more convenient for us, but it's really no great effort. I'll leave that up to you."

It was a tender situation. I feared making a social blunder, finally deciding that Dr. Alvarenga would rather avoid the extra trip but was being politely flexible. The Brazilians used the word "convenient" quite often and it usually indicated a preferred situation. That was the clue.

"Let's leave the Tuesday engagement out then, and we look forward to seeing you and your wife tonight."

"Thank you very much for calling. I'll pass the word to Dr. Fontana."

I breathed a sigh of relief, having avoided a potentially alienating event in the amiable new relationships leading to the merger of Cruzeiro and Transbrasil.

Tex Boullioun and his charming wife were gracious guests. With his wit and her presence, they overwhelmingly contributed to the success of the Monday evening extravaganza. The food and wine were served in grand style, typical for Brazilian aristocracy.

The interaction between Drs. Amorim and Fontana was rewardingly genial—at least nothing penetrated the facade. Toasts were exchanged, all manner of pleasantries were expounded, and warmth and cordiality spread over the room like a snug blanket.

In the spontaneity of the moment, after the appropriate period of arm twisting and cajoling, during which time he lamented how "poor a student of the instrument" he indeed was, Dr. Fontana went to the piano and attacked it with the fury of a lion in a pen of lambs. His style and command of musical theme astounded the audience, and his broad smile attested to the sheer joy he felt. Clearly, he was an artist with an unusual ability to put his soul into the music.

Seated beside Dr. Alvarenga, Transbrasil's director of Operations, I learned that Dr. Fontana was not only nationally recognized as a musician, but also as a composer of serious music.

That day, Monday, March 31, 1975, was a day to be remembered. I was left with a comfortable feeling about progress in Brazil. The horizon was bright. The country obviously presented a more equitable sales environment than Peru, indeed much better than most of the other

Latin American countries. I found it unnecessary to retain a consultant, not only eliminating commission payments but avoiding the bribery issue altogether. True, there was bribery in Brazil—known as *jeitinho*, however, it was not in evidence in our business.

I was completely unprepared for the cruel joke that fate dealt me on the morrow—*April Fools Day!*

With the dinner party a smashing success, I looked forward to a short respite from the pressurized schedule. We had Tuesday off. The multiple trips to Lima had worn me down. It would be Wednesday before the Varig dinner, and I did not have to attend as that was Dolf's territory. I was free to prepare for the next turn of the wheel in Lima.

The last few weeks had also been hectic for the Boulliouns. Jean, viewing her first trip to Rio as both business and pleasure, looked forward to an escape from the "prim and proper" circuit. The Boulliouns planned a quiet Tuesday evening in their suite. They ordered dinner to be served in their quarters at nine o'clock, but as a social gesture, and for the opportunity to review progress in a relaxed atmosphere, they invited the rest of us to an early evening cocktail.

Dolf, John Broback, and I were seated around the broad, luxuriously appointed living room in their suite, enjoying the magnificent night view of the bay and the city, when the phone rang in the kitchen. John Broback answered. It was 7:30.

After a few words, John looked into the room and motioned for me to join him in the kitchen. He had hung up the phone. He turned to me with a horrified stare.

"It's Dr. Fontana! He's downstairs in the lobby! He has Dr. Alvarenga with him, and they have been trying to call my room. What the hell's going on?"

My brain turned cartwheels. *Impossible!* I thought. *They can't be here!*

The bits of data flowing through my mind at that moment would have jammed a Cray computer. Figuratively speaking, my first impulse was to jump out the window.

"I don't understand!" was all I could muster. Then I added quickly,

"We agreed yesterday to cancel the Tuesday night dinner, since we were already together last night."

"I told them to come up," Broback said with a baleful expression. A cool operator, he usually knew how to handle tight situations.

We returned to the room where the others were waiting.

"It was Dr. Fontana," John said matter-of-factly.

"What did he want?" Dolf blurted.

"He's downstairs. He and Dr. Alvarenga are coming up."

Tex did not realize what was happening, but Dolf, wise in the ways of the Brazilians, was galvanized into action.

He headed for the door.

"I have to leave," he stammered. "It's your account, Gene." He gave me a pitying glance and rushed out, heading for the stairs.

Tough situations like this were commonplace in the lives of Boeing salesmen. I was learning fast.

With Broback's experience and Tex's tolerance, we were able to make the best of a potentially damaging episode—but not without a few more harrowing moments.

John and I went to the kitchen and quickly mapped out a plan. After the introductions, I would excuse myself and go downstairs to belatedly set up a banquet. Then, one by one we would slip out and change from our casual attire.

Once again, I was saved by the local customs. I scheduled the dinner for 10:30, perfectly normal in Brazil. If one arrives at a restaurant before 9:00 or 9:30 he will probably be the only customer there.

Our plans almost went awry when the bellboy rang at nine o'clock—right on time with the Boulliouns' dinner.

I rushed to the door, slipped out, and quickly closed it behind me.

"*No quermos,*" I announced calmly, pointing to the food trays. "*Volta para la cocinha.*"

The bellboy was incredulous. We had ordered the dinners and here they were, exquisitely prepared—and we wanted them returned to the kitchen!

He handed me the bill. I took out my pen and signed it.

*"Siga, siga,"* I urged, anxious for him to take the food and leave.

I reached into my pocket and handed him a ten dollar bill. *"Presa! presa!"* I exclaimed.

He took the bill, still unbelieving. As he pushed the food-laden cart down the hall to the elevator, he glanced back over his shoulder. I could read his thoughts—what in hell is the matter with these crazy Americans?

The dinner meeting went off without a hitch. Dr. Fontana monopolized the conversation in projecting the image of Transbrasil as the rising star in Brazil, and revealed his plans for fleet expansion.

I never found out what caused the mix-up—not daring to ask the Brazilians on subsequent visits.

On Thursday morning, April 3rd, I flew back to Lima.

# 8

I n Lima, the April 1st decision deadline for the wide-body selection had passed, and a new element abruptly entered the competition.

Eastern Airlines, in a fleet modernization program, offered to sell some of their Lockheed L-1011s at bargain prices. The airplanes were the original model, designed for U.S. domestic routes.

To serve New York and Los Angeles, those short range planes would require a stop at Miami or Mexico City, even when taking off from sea level at Lima.

Suddenly, Lockheed jumped into the middle of the negotiations, encouraging AeroPeru to accept Eastern's proposal and offering to trade the "interim" airplanes for the longer range -250s in the future. Thus, AeroPeru was thrust into the position of considering still another "paper" airplane.

McDonnell Douglas was quick to react, slashing $3 million off the price of each DC-10.

Boeing's offer on the 747SP was already at the zero profit point, and we "drew our line in the sand." Thus, McDonnell Douglas and Lockheed had gained the inside track, willing to accept a loss to crack the market.

Chamote remained optimistic, advising that the Commission favored the SP, four votes to three.

Our competitors hatched an elaborate new smoke screen on minor details of performance, economics, Mach numbers, route distances, and indirect operating costs.

Bewildered by the blizzard of conflicting claims, General Galindo called for still another postponement, as the business climate in Peru was drifting back toward the old philosophy to "buy cheap and plan short."

Nevertheless, Boeing refused to throw in the towel. The SP was still the best machine for Peru's proposed international routes. I requested the technical team to return to Lima. Airplane performance holds no secrets for capable analysts, and Boeing was quick to develop range/payload charts for the newly announced Lockheed L-1011-250. General Galindo was pleased to receive our data, and the mill continued to grind.

The safety issue persisted in the Lima newspapers. Coincidentally, the movie *Airport* was showing at the Lima theaters that week. The movie was extravagant in its praise of the 747 and its ability to withstand unusual punishment. *A stroke of good fortune!* I thought.

But it worked out exactly the opposite! Soon thereafter, when I was visiting the AeroPeru offices, one of the secretaries approached me scornfully, demanding, "Why did Boeing make the *Airport* movie?"

Surprised, I responded, "Boeing had nothing to do with it."

"But it's a Boeing airplane."

"Of course. But American Airlines bought the airplane from Boeing, and the movie studio leased it from them. That's their business, not Boeing's."

She was unfazed by the facts.

"I still think it was exaggerated," she shot back. "No airplane could do that. I think Boeing is dirty to make claims which are so far from the truth," she huffed.

I threw up my hands in exasperation. *Chocolates had their limitations.*

Of all the times when I needed our local publicity agent the most, she was sick in the hospital! *Murphy's Law is still as reliable as the law of gravity,* I thought.

Good news came the next day. I arranged an appointment with General Galindo.

*"Buenos dias, mi General,"* I greeted, having developed an easy familiarity over the many months.

*"Buenos dias,* Mr. Boeing," Galindo replied, smiling.

He seemed relaxed, belying the work hidden in the huge stacks of documents and correspondence on his desk and two surrounding tables.

"I have some very important news," I announced.

Galindo jerked his head up.

"Yes?"

"Aerolineas Argentinas has notified Boeing that they will purchase a 747-100. It will be the first for any South American airline."

*"Pues no,* that makes our work more interesting," he said. "But we will have to wait and see," he added. "I know those people."

When I departed I felt a new optimism, in spite of Galindo's doubts. *The Peruvians will bust a gut to keep the Argentinians from outdoing them,* I mused.

With Giesela in the hospital, I played news reporter, contacting Aerolineas Argentinas to arrange for stories and photos in the major Lima newspapers. It felt good to get some irrefutable facts to the public.

Honesty and integrity were being stretched all along the line. McDonnell Douglas delivered a document to the Commission which reportedly compared the DC-10 with the 747SP. Chamote obtained a copy. It was replete with deliberate inaccuracies.

I decided it was time to get down to bare knuckles. Securing a copy of a new book—just out—*The Rise and Fall of the DC-10,* by John Godson[1], I delivered it personally to General Galindo. The dust jacket had a drawing of a DC-10 with the fuselage shaped like a coffin.

The main thrust of the book was the loose ethics of McDonnell Douglas. Godson highlighted the crash of the Turkish Airline DC-10 in a Paris woods on March 3, 1974. At the time, it was the worst commercial airline crash in history. He also reported that the faulty cargo door which caused the crash had been certified by McDonnell Douglas to have been modified in their plant. However, the door, picked up at the crash scene, had not been modified.

Galindo requested Boeing to extend its offer—which expired on April 1st—to the end of May, with no delay in the delivery date. Time was bunching up. In order to deliver as promised, initial parts would have to go into the production line before the end of April. Boeing decided to take the risk since initial parts in the line were common to all the SP airplanes.

Having spent five continuous weeks in Peru and Brazil, I returned to Seattle to regroup. My first order of business was to develop a strategy for the Cruzeiro/Transbrasil fleet consolidation.

Following an extended slump, Cruzeiro was beginning to achieve improved traffic growth. Dr. Amorim hoped to be first to introduce jets on the *Ponte Aerea*, the shuttle between Rio and São Paulo known as the "air bridge." Varig had a hammerlock on the route with their Lockheed Electra turboprop fleet, with flights on the hour—around the clock.

Dr. Amorim wanted to introduce 737 airplanes on the *Ponte Aerea*, competing with the Electras. With the superior performance and added comfort of the 737s, that would be an unequal contest.

The government had the final authority, and had not yet decided to allow jets to operate out of the Santos Dumont airport—in the heart of Rio. The runway was only 4,300 feet long, located on a small spit which extended into the bay, nearly surrounded by water. A further hazard was Pão de Açúcar, the famous tourist attraction known as Sugarloaf. Jutting up 1,200 feet, directly in the flight path, the Electras needed a 5-degree turn on takeoff to miss it. The 737 could easily clear Pão de Açúcar without a turn.

While government planners were studying the problems, Dr. Erik was lobbying intensely to get the right decision for Varig.

Cruzeiro would need two more 737 airplanes in the event of a favorable decision for jet operations, and the sale would be in the bag.

Aware that the 737s had demonstrated a capability to take off from runways less than 4,000 feet long, Dr. Erik began to fear the outcome. He played his last ace.

In order to foreclose the faintest possibility of competition on the *Ponte Aerea*, he offered to purchase Cruzeiro—lock, stock, and barrel.

Varig had plenty of cash, and the offer went to the Cruzeiro stockholders for a vote.

I was home only for a week, enjoying the short reunion with Beth and planting my early spring garden. Returning to Rio in mid-April, by way of Lima, I was on the Rio-Lima merry-go-round again until the middle of June. When I came back to Seattle, I began to hear rumors that the Brazilian government had approved the Varig purchase of Cruzeiro, and that the stockholders, eager for cash, had quickly acceded.

I headed back to Rio to discuss the buyout with Dr. Amorim. Brazilians had none of the pomposity and facades of the Peruvians, and Dr. Amorim agreed to meet with me the next morning.

"Well, Mr. Bauer, the rumors are true," Dr. Amorim sighed. Then he laughed. "It's time I got out of this business. I'm already past the usual retirement age."

He paused for a moment, adding, "I've been fighting airplanes all my life."

"I'll be sorry to see Cruzeiro disappear," I said. "It's been a pleasure to work with your people."

"Cruzeiro will still be around. Varig is taking over, but the integration will allow Cruzeiro to fly certain routes where we have good name identification—and duplication will be eliminated." A serious expression flickered across his round, flushed face.

"What about Cruzeiro insignia on the planes, and promotion?"

"Oh, the colors will stay the same, and promotion will be integrated." He smiled again.

"I suppose it will be nice to retire."

"The only thing I'm retiring from is the airline. I'll continue as president of several other firms—but I may do a little fishing."

His eyes lighted up as he glanced out the window. I knew the fishing was good in Brazil but had not had the time to try it out. I hesitated.

"I must take this occasion to say goodbye," I said. "Varig is served by my compatriot, Dolf Rischbeiter."

Amorim crinkled his brow, his bald head shining under the bright lights.

"Oh, I see. But I hope you will keep coming to Brazil."

"Yes, Brazil is a favorite country for me, and I've found many Brasileiro friends here. I'll still be supporting Transbrasil."

It was time to go. "I must say goodbye to the rest of your staff. *Muito bom acaso!"*

*"Igual por você."*

Amorim came around the desk and we exchanged the traditional Brazilian abrazo.

I made the other visits to my new-found friends of only two months. Mario Cesar, presidential assistant, was expecting to be laid off. His replacement from Varig would take over soon. Mario would be seeking a new job—not easy—as he was middle-aged and in mid-career. Uncertainty had become the order of the day.

I would also be saying goodbye to Rio. It was my seventh trip, and on June 7, 1975, I left Rio for the last time, to return to Lima. Future visits to Brazil would be directly to São Paulo to support Transbrasil.


In Peru, the time had come to implement a strategy of postponement. Boeing could no longer meet the requested delivery date of December 1976, and our pricing policy was to make increases on an annual basis—each January. With Lockheed and McDonnell Douglas employing an incremental pricing adjustment policy by the month, January was the least competitive month for Boeing to deliver an airplane. I urged Chamote to begin trumpeting the merits of taking more time for study.

The Peruvian economy proved to be the best ally for my new strategy, sinking to new lows every month. The Commission finally rejected all the wide-body offers—recommending the renewal of the DC-8 lease agreement for another two years. That decision put me back at square one for the AeroPeru account. A full year of our intensive efforts was down the tube.

Clouding the future still further in Peru, it was announced that the *Ministro de Aeronautica* would change in August. That meant certain corporate death for General Soto.

Faucett Airlines was slowly improving their position, working within their own financial capability and without the guarantee of the government on outside loans. They were able to complete the final payment for the Boeing 727 in April, and had applied for an Ex-Im Bank loan guarantee for the purchase of a second 727, a used airplane from Braniff Airlines.

With Giesela's help, I kicked off a publicity campaign in the Lima newspapers for the rollout and first flight of the 747SP, and headed for home.

The sales organization was making tentative plans for a round-the-world demonstration flight with the SP. I was jubilant. *It would be my opportunity to trump the doubters about operating out of Cuzco.*

By the end of July, I was ready for the road again, heading back to Lima, then on to Brazil.

At Aeroperu, activity was beginning to quicken. General Soto had been targeted to be sacked in September, a new president was being sought, and the wide-body program was starting a second round. General Galindo was reported to be interested in pursuing the Cuzco potential, and the new *Ministro* was actively studying it.

It was an opportune time to be in Lima with my ear to the ground. Giesela was always full of fresh rumors, the U.S. embassy was sometimes helpful, and my visits with second-tier managers in the airline generally turned up new information.

Thus I lingered over the August 9th weekend to be on hand for new government announcements expected the following week.

Wary of robbers, I usually stuck to the safe areas, but noting that a native fair was scheduled for the weekend—over the *cordillera* at Huancayo—the tourist in me took over. I envisioned a rare opportunity to acquire some real Inca artifacts.

Bona fide tourists took the safe way—a special sightseeing bus. Feeling comfortable in the language, I decided to "go native," taking the train.

No matter that I had no old clothing, no beat-up suitcase or backpack like the others. *It will be an exciting weekend,* I thought as I hurried through the deserted city early that Saturday morning. Indeed it was!

The train station was located in the center of the city, immediately behind the palace, and as I turned the corner bringing it into view, I had a sinking feeling—a tremendous crowd was milling around in front of the great iron gates. The women were dressed in slacks and worn blouses, the men in baggy pants, a few with the traditional woolen ponchos draped loosely over their shoulders. *No place for a gringo,* I thought.

From dilapidated walk-up flats, old and dingy in the sooty railroad environment, more travelers trickled out, all hurrying to the station to assure a seat by the window. Some were obviously Americans and Europeans, youth with faded jeans, open shirts, and backpacks.

I was acutely conscious of my neatly pressed trousers and bright sport coat. Instinctively, I touched each pocket where I had carefully stowed the individual valuables: passport, native money, billfold with credit cards.

*There was no reason to be alarmed,* I told myself. There were a number of policemen, *pistolas* on their hips in leather holsters, standing in the waiting areas near the gates. The impending opportunity for a fine view, riding through the magnificent Andes mountains, pushed all other thoughts to the back of my mind.

My movie camera hung from my left shoulder and the locked attache case in my right hand held the necessities for a weekend in a strange place. Gripping the ticket tightly in my left fist, and congratulating myself for the foresight of purchasing it several days before, I advanced confidently toward the gate.

The attendant, cowering behind the massive iron gate, which he held open only a small crack—barely sufficient for one person at a time to squeeze through—was shouting, *"Solo billetes por lo mano!"* I raised my left hand high to display the ticket. Then, as if from some hidden signal, the crowd began to surge toward the gates.

The pressure and shouting increased to a crescendo—a regular melee. I was swept forward to the small passageway. Something struck my forearm, as if to dislodge my briefcase.

Then, as suddenly as it had begun, it was over. I was propelled like a bundle of straw through the portal.

*What a relief!* But even as I contemplated my success in getting to the front quickly, I grabbed for the camera and checked my pockets. The camera was intact, but my back pocket was flat!

"The bastards stole my billfold," I screamed.

A cold sweat broke out on my neck and forehead, as the list of valuables paraded through my mind: bank, gasoline, travel, phone—all the credit cards. Driver's license, social security card, photographs—even a fishing license. Finally, almost an afterthought, the money. Very little. All in U.S. currency, and less than thirty dollars.

Whatever must be done, must be done quickly. *At this very moment the robbers were probably running away as fast as possible.* At least ten seconds had elapsed.

I bolted back to the gate, now firmly locked, the crowd still shouting and pounding on the outside. The plot dawned. I was the victim of a planned operation. The gate attendant—who had now disappeared, was apparently a part of it.

I began to scream, *"Ladrones! Policia! Ladrones!"*

The police were nowhere in sight!

Recognizing the impossibility of getting any assistance, I resigned myself to the situation. There was no opportunity to report the theft until Monday, so I decided to finish the trip.

Fortunately, I had stowed my local currency in the front pocket of my trousers, and I was able to complete my original mission—poorer and wiser.

Being robbed in a foreign country was a new experience for me.
Early on Monday morning, I called home to cancel my credit cards, and
proceeded to the U.S. embassy to seek advice. I was told to report to the
local police station and obtain an official paper, recording the robbery.

The events that followed were hilarious—even though deadly
serious.

At the station, the police were aloof and disinterested, turning posi-
tively hostile after I told my story.

*"Senor Bauer, será necesario para visitar outra distrito,"* the officer shouted
grandly, claiming to lack jurisdiction, brushing me aside.

*"Donde está?"*

*"Cerca la estación de tren."*

My first appointment was not until noon—lunch with Chamote—
and except for a short meeting with Galindo and a visit with the chief of
planning at AeroPeru headquarters in early afternoon, I was free to go.

I located the police station near the palace with ease, and felt a sudden surge of optimism as I glanced at my watch.

Two hours later, my optimism had evaporated. The first requirement
was to write out a detailed description of the *denuncia,* or accusation.
Then after being shuffled from one official desk to another, I was told to
return at one o'clock.

Hastily rearranging my schedule, I arrived back at the station *en punto.*
The officer at the desk claimed total ignorance of the morning event.
He was adamant—I would have to fill out the paper all over again. Com-
plying, I was told to come back at five in the afternoon.

I arrived at fifteen before five.

*"Captain Vallero no está,"* I was told. *"El vuelto a la casa."*

I threw up my hands to demonstrate my irritation. Pointing to my
watch, I demanded, *"Que pasa? Tenga un compromiso a las cinco horas!"*

*"No se, vuelva mañana."*

*"Que hora?*

He looked at the clock. *"A las un."*

The light was beginning to dawn. No one wanted to admit the

robbery in writing, and they planned to wear me down with delays until I gave up. My determination stiffened.

Time was running out. I had a confirmed ticket to São Paulo on Thursday morning, and firm appointments with Transbrasil.

The trips across town were wearying and time consuming. Returning at one o'clock on Tuesday, I was told that Captain Vallero had changed his schedule and would be back at five.

I arrived at four, surprising Vallero.

Deciding attack was better than defense, I launched into a tirade over the delay, and how it was threatening my schedule, invoking names of high-level people in the government.

He became apologetic, saying in cases involving foreigners, it was necessary for the chief of the division to sign and officially stamp the paper.

*"Él jefe no está,"* he lamented, putting on a sad face.

*"Cuando el regresa,"* I inquired.

*"No se."*

I saw red. Impulsively, I decided I would stick with the captain until he took action. Picking up my chair, I moved it to the back of his desk, and sat down beside him.

*"Yo voy esperar!"* I exclaimed. I had decided to stick with Captain Vallero like glue, following him everywhere, even to the bathroom.

He gave me a sideways glance, saying nothing. Then he went about his paperwork.

Twenty minutes passed. I merely sat.

After about another half hour, his glances became more frequent and a worried expression crossed his face.

Abruptly, he pushed his chair back, got up and strode briskly into the back room. I tried to follow, but he slammed the door.

I waited. Soon, I heard angry voices, and curses.

After about ten minutes, Captain Vallero came out. He had a big smile on his face as he showed me a document. It appeared to be official. One entire page was covered with stamped seals, four in all, including one belonging to the chief of the division.

*"Queiro una copia, por favor,"* I requested.

*"Este is para usted,"* he replied, handing it to me.

I had won the battle. *"Muchas gracias,"* I said, departing.

Obviously, they had completed the paper much earlier, but were reluctant to deliver it. The last line stated: *"Obra como constancia para efectos de los documentos."*

I knew the documents would never be recovered, but I needed the official record. Indeed, the case was closed the minute I walked out the door.

1. John Godson, *The Rise and Fall of the DC-10* (New York: David McKay Company, Inc. 1975).

# 9

On Thursday, I was back in Brazil, aiming to sell 737 airplanes to Dr. Fontana. His headquarters was located in an old hangar at the Congonhas Airport in downtown São Paulo—little changed from the days when the airline had a single DC-3, hauling meat. A couple of bare-bones offices were situated on a small mezzanine area above the hangar floor.

Fontana was not concerned about his modest office facilities, instead focusing on his fleet of airplanes. Always brash and optimistic, he was concentrating on expansion—and moving Transbrasil to Brasilia—the power center where everything of importance was decided.

Driving his employees relentlessly, he pushed himself even harder. Working sixteen-hour days, he took his regular turns as a pilot, flying the standard eighty hours a month. His first love was the sky, and he left most of the administrative work to Dr. Alvarenga.

Fontana conceived his symphonies while flying. Music came naturally to his mind, and he wrote it down later. *Jonathan Livingston Seagull* was his favorite story, from which he constantly quoted.

The wings of the plane became his own, and in the air he was free, the world of flight circumscribing his entire being.

He maintained two residences—one in São Paulo and one in Rio—not unusual for Brazilian businessmen who found it difficult to wean themselves from the beaches and nightclubs of Rio.

He seldom took time for sales people—secure in his own convictions—but the next day he invited me to visit his home high in the hills of Rio. John Broback, who was in Rio at the time, joined us.

With his giant-sized ego, Fontana took charge, playing his music and telling yarns of his flying exploits, all the while quoting poetry and philosophy. I made a note of his favorite saying—which he repeated often—storing it in my memory for future use. Although he always quoted it in Portuguese, he would follow in English for emphasis—and to demonstrate his command of the language.

*"Pensar, Saber, Lutar, Vencer — Por Deus."* "To think, to know, to fight, to win—for God."

"Transbrasil can't afford to buy new airplanes," he announced. "So you might just as well forget your sales pitch."

"We know better than to try to sell you anything," John retorted. "We just demonstrate our product, and it sells itself."

*"Muito bom,* now we understand each other," Fontana said, returning to the piano. He played and played—far into the night. Then he stopped abruptly, waving his broad meaty hands.

"It's time for food!" he exclaimed. It was nearly midnight, not unusual for dinner in Brazil. He rang a little bell and the servants brought out a veritable banquet. Fontana was enjoying himself to the fullest.

"Let me tell you my plans for expanding the fleet," he announced, pouring the wine.

"You're probably laughing. As you know, we just have the one jet, a used 727-100—the rest of the fleet is BAC-111s and some old Dart Heralds. But just watch us. We can't afford to buy new equipment—especially with all the bargains on the market. We plan to build a fleet of 727-100C convertibles—less than $3 million apiece—compared to your price of $6 million for a new 737."

Fontana paused, reared back, and let that sink in.

"We'd still like to make the case for new equipment, Omar, but you're the doctor. You decide," John replied.

"*Muito bom*, but listen to this. We're going to train our crews to change from passenger to cargo configuration and back every twenty-four hours. We'll fly cargo at night. Then, early in the morning, we'll convert to passengers and pick up on the heavily booked morning flights."

"It's definitely possible," John said, "but you'll need to make the turn-around in less than two hours."

"Your biggest problem will be finding time for maintenance, particularly unscheduled maintenance," I added. "And that's where the new machines have a great advantage."

Omar smiled again. "You'll see!" he exclaimed, raising his glass.

"To Transbrasil—*Un gran sucesso*," we chimed in unison.

"As you know, Boeing doesn't handle used airplanes, but we know where they are, and you can count on us to help locate potential sellers," Broback promised.

At the time, total sales of the 727 series had reached a new record in commercial jet aviation history, and with many U.S. airlines upgrading their fleets with newer models, used Boeing planes were proving to be the strongest competitors for new Boeing planes. It was difficult to make a case based on price alone, so we emphasized the passenger appeal and operating cost advantages of new planes.


Ecuatoriana was starting to show new potential. Following the grounding, the government had purged the airline management, transferred the Electras to TAME, the principal domestic airline, and leased an old, out-of-production 720B from Pan Am. They contracted major maintenance to an approved facility outside the country, and the FAA promptly lifted the flight restrictions, allowing resumption of the Quito-Miami flights. Load factors zoomed, with many flights completely booked.

"Gene, with Cruzeiro out of your hair, I want you to bore in on Ecuatoriana," John announced. "Ecuador has lots of mountains, and maybe the SP is a good prospect for their next buy."

"Good idea, they'll need the SP for nonstop service to the main U.S. markets, because of the 9,000-foot elevation of Quito."

Ecuador had captured my imagination ever since that first Avianca "milk run" flight the year before. Having done considerable climbing in the Pacific Northwest of the United States, I had visions of conquering some of those mountains. Hopefully, I would discover someone in the airline with the climbing fever. If so, I could achieve that rare combination of business and recreation, while getting closer to their hearts.

But climbing would have to wait. There was urgent business at hand.

Quito had easily become my favorite city in South America, with its brilliant sunlight and fresh mountain environment, even though the altitude sometimes caused a small headache the first day.

Adhering to the axiom of flying on my customers' planes whenever possible, I had booked my flight on Ecuatoriana from Miami. Entry was smooth, and the airport was only a few miles from the Colon Hotel.

I walked over to Ecuatoriana headquarters to meet with their new president, Colonel Banderas. There was a fresh crispness in the office atmosphere, and the secretary quickly ushered me in. A little apprehensive about this first meeting, I was pleasantly put at ease when Banderas welcomed me in impeccable English. The colonel was an impressive figure in his brass-buttoned blue uniform, a tall handsome man in his late thirties.

"Good morning, Mr. Bauer," he greeted, extending his hand. "How was your flight?"

"I came in on your 720B. Everything was fine, the flight was outstanding—and nearly fully booked."

Banderas smiled, happy with the knowledge that I had selected Ecuatoriana over a U.S. carrier.

"Please have a seat," he said, motioning to the couch.

We sat down, facing each other across a little hand-carved table. "We really love that Boeing plane, and the airline made its first profit in July," Banderas beamed proudly.

"We're negotiating with Pan Am to buy two more airplanes," he added quickly, lighting a cigarette.

"Good, good, Pan Am has always done an excellent job in maintenance. You couldn't do better anywhere."

I paused. "But with your fast growth, it won't be long before you'll need a wide-body, and Boeing has just the ticket," I volunteered.

Banderas' interest quickened, and I explained the 747SP program and the performance that we could achieve.

"The probability that we will do a demo around the world is very high," I said, when we completed our discussion.

"You can count on us, Mr. Bauer. We would definitely like to see what the airplane can do. Just let us know your schedule as soon as possible."

Banderas got up and walked across the office. Turning, he announced, "We have already applied for entry to New York, and expect to be ready for Los Angeles next spring."

"Fantastic! We know you can do it. I'd like to meet your operations people so we can see where you need help on your Boeings."

"Good. You should meet Colonel Lara. His office is out at the airport. I'll call and tell him you're coming over."

Thanking Colonel Banderas for his hospitality, I took a taxi to the airport and went directly to Colonel Lara's office.

Lara was extremely pleasant, exuberant over his "new 720B" which they were keeping in the air nearly eleven hours a day—considerably higher than the industry average.

"I need a little help from Boeing," Lara volunteered. "Our operations and flight manuals are not up-to-date. I wonder if you could arrange to get us some new ones."

Ordinarily, Boeing didn't furnish manuals to operators who purchased second-hand machines. The manuals were supposed to go with the airplanes. It was very complicated to recreate new manuals for old airplanes.

"You know, Colonel, there is some difficulty in obtaining manuals. They are customized to specific configurations, and when Pan Am purchased the 720Bs, they received all the manuals. Now, every time they make a single-airplane deal, they don't have enough copies to give away."

"That's just the problem. They tell us they need to keep them for the rest of their fleet, so we have some poor copies that aren't being kept up-to-date."

"Colonel Lara, stop worrying," I volunteered. "I'm taking an action item to get new manuals for Ecuatoriana."

Lara's face lit up. "But we really don't have a budget," he lamented. I waved my hand. "There'll be no cost."

Thus began a very cordial working relationship with Ecuatoriana.

Returning to Seattle, I found that Boeing had firmed up its plans to fly the 747SP around the world, demonstrating its exceptional performance to potential customers and inviting their pilots to fly the plane. Sales directors were requested to identify interested airlines in their regions. I added Ecuatoriana to my list, and Boeing management included both Peru and Ecuador in the flight program.

A sense of urgency was assigned to the venture, and a four-week flight itinerary was developed, to begin the first week of November. The spotlight quickly focused on eighteen cities scattered around the world. Two of them—Cuzco and Quito—were in my territory. I had to move fast.

That same month, the international sales department underwent a major reorganization at Boeing. Latin America and Africa were becoming too heavy a burden for John Broback, and he gave up all of Latin America except Brazil and Mexico, while retaining Africa.

Spain and the remainder of Latin America were assigned to Alfredo Dodds, who was promoted to area director. That action put me in the awkward position of having one foot on the east and the other on the west side of the continent, reporting to two different directors. With the Brazilian airlines down to three, those accounts were consolidated under Dolf Rischbieter, and I left John's domain, reporting to Alfredo.

Further, the company decided to give me some additional accounts, and assigned Trinidad and Tobago, Guyana, and Surinam.

Dodds had been deputy area director under Broback, responsible for Spain and part of Latin America. A native of Argentina, where he graduated in engineering and served in their air force, he emigrated to the U.S., joining Boeing in 1958.

Alfredo had made his mark as a rising star in sales when he completed a $225 million deal with Spain's Iberian Airlines, for twenty-seven Boeing 727s in 1971.

I personally regretted the management change, as I related strongly to John's strict ethics. On the other hand, Alfredo, reared in the atmosphere of "dealings among friends," had an aggressive tendency to "push the envelope." We had already clashed over consultant philosophy in Peru and Ecuador.

I departed from Seattle on September 20, 1975, with a heavy heart. The reorganization was weighing on me—but more importantly, it was the birthday of my only daughter, Cheryl. It seemed as though I was always somewhere else on important family days, but customer demands had priority. Adding to my depression was the realization that I was on the way to Brazil for the last time. I made brief visits to Copa, Air Panama, Ecuatoriana, and AeroPeru, and finally to Transbrasil in São Paulo.

Dr. Fontana and I had become good friends—discovering a strong common interest in poetry—and I wanted to give him a special parting gift. Purchasing a Brazilian flag on a previous trip, I had given it to Cheryl to use for a color match, and asked her to make a needlepoint of Fontana's favorite quotation.

The Brazilian flag is blue, green, yellow, and white. She made the needlepoint with a yellow background, and arranged the words in a column. *Pensar, Saber, Lutar, and Vencer,* were alternately green and blue, and it was completed in white with *Por Deus.* The result was beautiful in her fine handiwork. I made a frame of limed oak.

When I arrived in São Paulo, Dr. Fontana was out of town. I would not be in Brazil again, so I extended my stay and requested an appointment. He was extremely busy, having been gone for more than a week, and was only taking urgent appointments.

*"Por favor, dice Dr. Fontana, este reunion está muito importante,"* I informed his secretary. I felt a twinge of guilt, but there was no other way to make it happen.

Dr. Fontana was apparently unable to believe there could be such a thing as an urgent requirement for a meeting with a salesman—from Boeing or otherwise. I believe he accepted the appointment out of pure curiosity.

"I'm sorry to break into your busy day," I said. "I'll only take a few minutes of your time."

Fontana was calm and attentive.

"I came to say goodbye. I'm being reassigned."

I handed him the framed needlepoint. "It's a gift from my daughter."

If we had been negotiating a sales contract, I believe Fontana would have signed it on the spot. Brazilians are noted for being driven by emotion.

He took the frame in both hands and held it at arm's length, admiring the beautiful colors of his country's flag—spelling out his favorite phrase.

He was silent for a long moment. Then he turned to me and stretched out his huge hand. His face was wreathed in a great full-face smile, and I even imagined a little tear in the corner of his eye.

*"Muchisimo obrigado!"* he exclaimed, hugging me with the Brazilian abrazo.

*"Muito bom acaso por você e Transbrasil!"* I replied. Hesitating for a brief moment, I picked up my briefcase and walked out the door.

Thinking back, I wondered if the SEC would classify my gift as *jeitinho.*

I felt a loss at leaving Brazil, but welcomed the opportunities in my new territories. It had been difficult to deal with both Portuguese and Spanish from one week to the next.

With a heavy accent in both languages, my friends in Brazil jokingly called me a *"Castellano gringo,"* and on the west side, they called me a *"Brasileiro gringo."*

I would always respond, *"Yo estoy un gringo todo del mundo!"*

There was no urgency to visit my new accounts in the Caribbean, and I turned my full energies to the impending world flight of the 747SP. At last we would be able to dispel the doubts about operations out of Cuzco. Nevertheless, I wanted to make certain there were no flight restrictions hidden in the fine print, and I telexed the technical staff at Boeing to review their analysis one more time. After all, taking off at 11,000 feet with a full load—even from an adequate runway—and flying all the way to New York staggered the imagination!

The reply came back: *The 747SP can do everything you promised.*

I prepared a letter to General Berckemeyer, the new president of AeroPeru, and formerly responsible for civil aeronautics in the transportation ministry. The message read in part—

*"The Boeing Company is pleased to announce an around-the-world\* demonstration flight with the 747SP, our newest member of the family of commercial airplanes. We would be pleased to fly the airplane from Cuzco to prove its superior performance from high elevation airfields. . . ."*

---

\* Not around the world in a literal sense; however, the airplane logged 72,152 miles, equivalent to nearly three times around the globe.

# 10

P an American, the globe-hopping pioneer, was first to purchase the 747SP. Deliveries were scheduled to begin in early 1976, and the SP that flew around the world was actually the first Pan Am airplane. After the tour, it would return to Boeing to trade its red, white, and blue coating for the blue and white of Pan Am.

In eighteen cities scattered over the globe, Boeing salesmen were hammering together the agenda for the demo.

Having completed the preliminary steps by telex and telephone from Seattle, I headed south to finalize the details and await the arrival. I visualized an easy time in Lima, as the Peruvians seemed anxious to prove us wrong on the Cuzco operation, and Ecuatoriana appeared to be a certainty.

My November 11th arrival in Quito was the same day that the 747SP was taking off from Seattle, bound for New York, in its preparation for the initial fourteen-hour flight to Tokyo.

The ambitious demonstration schedule included three dramatic giant leaps: New York to Tokyo, Sidney to Santiago, and Mexico City to Belgrade.

The Sidney-Santiago flight—6,120 nautical miles over the vast South Pacific Ocean—was the longest. In its ambitious schedule, the plane would leapfrog continents and oceans to prove its prowess in shrinking the globe.

As a country, Ecuador had considerable catching up to do to achieve its industrial ambitions. The government was in turmoil. The constitutional republic under Velasco Ibarra, which began after the elections of 1968, rapidly turned into a dictatorship only two years later, and itself was overthrown in a coup by the Army, under General Guillermo Rodriguez.

Over the centuries, Ecuador had been torn with both internal strife and incursions from without. Historically, both Peru and Colombia had designs on the rich little mountain country.

Internally, animosities persisted between the *serranos* (highlanders) and the *costenos* (lowlanders), which carried into the modern politics of the country. This polarizing rivalry, bordering on fanaticism, and centered in Quito in the mountains and Guayaquil on the coast, had a powerful influence on the direction that growth in industry and commerce would take, particularly the expansion of commercial airline routes. In fact, the choice between Quito and Guayaquil as the international gateway became the centerpiece of the wide-body competition in Ecuador. Technically, it was a replay of the Cuzco-Lima airplane performance battle.

The government under Rodriguez that greeted me on that November day in 1975 was already on shaky ground, and new rumors of plots to overthrow him were rampant.

At the time, in spite of the turmoil in the government, Ecuador was enjoying one of the healthiest economies in all of South America. The country was no longer a "banana republic," even though bananas were still the principal agricultural crop. The new heavy contributor was oil. The recently constructed pipeline from the jungle fields to the sea had a capacity of 280,000 barrels a day. Ecuador was a member of the

Organization of Petroleum Exporting Countries (OPEC), and a major fraction of its oil was exported.

The time was fast approaching for Ecuatoriana to begin serious planning for the acquisition of a wide-body airplane.

Three European airlines—KLM, Iberia, and Lufthansa, already flying through Quito and Guayaquil—would soon offer service with DC-10s, and Air France was lobbying to begin 747 service. For Ecuatoriana to gain a fair share of the expected traffic, it would be necessary for Colonel Banderas to take the first step toward a major equipment decision within the next twelve months.

There was no time to lose, and central to perceived success was the retention of a consultant who had influence with the airline and its multilayered government bureaucracy. I was mindful of the caution that the U.S. commercial attaché had given me on an earlier visit, but was leaning toward the advice of Colonel Banderas. When I approached him about the subject, he had been adamant. "We're married to Boeing, and the airline will choose the equipment." I kept thinking about his words, but after the experience in Peru, I decided to enlist Ben to help me in lining up a consultant as soon as the demo was completed. *If we were to err, let it be on the safe side.*

The runway at Quito was a narrow asphalt strip, originally built to serve DC-6 airplanes, recently lengthened to accommodate jet operations. Lying north and south, its approaches were guarded by mountains. Pilots had to trace their way between and around the peaks as they approached the landing field. There were no lights, forcing the airport to close before dark. At the equator, there is no twilight, and minutes after the sun dips below the horizon, total darkness descends. It was common for flights destined to Quito to be diverted to Guayaquil.

Ecuatoriana was bullish. Colonel Banderas had brought a new energy to the company, drawing the tight little force of 600 closely around him.

Projections were being made fifteen years into the future, including service to Madrid and other points in Europe as soon as traffic matured.

The director of civil aviation, Colonel Suarez, also had extensive plans for new, modern airports for both Quito and Guayaquil.

I felt a good deal of comfort when I arrived at the terminal at Mariscal Sucre International Airport in Quito to find that Colonel Banderas had sent Ecuatoriana's director of Ground Operations, Alfonso Fiallos, to meet me.

Alfonso stayed with me the next two days, while we arranged the details of the 747SP visit.

We planned to fill the 305 seats of the airplane, and because of the stratified society in Latin countries, it was necessary to establish a pecking order. General Rodriguez himself was invited, although we knew that the probability of acceptance was near zero. Next in the pecking order was Senor Alcalde Duran, mayor of Quito, followed by the United States ambassador to Ecuador, the Honorable Robert Brewster—and  so on.

We could not have done it without Edison Teran, director of publicity for Ecuatoriana. His knowledge of the correct people to invite, and in what order, proved to be a godsend. I put Edison on my "most favored" list for the future, and we developed a lasting kinship that endured throughout my sales campaign in Ecuador.

Almost as difficult as the selection of guests was the seat assignments. Latins abhor forming orderly lines, and I feared a rush to the best seats unless it was done by the numbers. With the help of Alfonso, I enlisted the airline hostesses, and we issued boarding passes as in any regular flight.

On Friday, November 14th, I sent a telex to Seattle reporting that all was in readiness, and the plane would have no trouble coming to Quito— the city was prepared to welcome it with a *grande abrazo*.

Triumphant, I flew to Lima to complete the other half of my double demonstration duties.

# 11

The official schedule for the world tour was already "cast in concrete," and highly publicized. The airplane was in the sky, winging its way over the Pacific, at the very moment that I was flying in to Lima.

At each stop, Boeing planned to make demonstration flights, technical presentations, or both, depending on the local conditions, as defined by the salesmen. For the Quito visit, since the high-elevation performance would be amply proven by simply landing and taking off on the narrow asphalt runway, no additional flights would be made. The plane would serve as a theater on the ground.

In Peru we planned a more complex scenario. After fully loading with government officials, representatives of the press, and airline personnel at Lima, we would fly to Cuzco, carrying a fuel load equivalent to an actual arrival from New York. At Cuzco, we would add fuel to simulate a takeoff bound for New York, fly around for a couple of hours to burn it off, and return to Lima. Meanwhile, on board, the technical presentations would be made, and a press conference would be offered.

*I could hardly wait to see the Peruvians' eyes pop!*

My enthusiasm and confidence suffered a small setback, however, when I emerged from customs at the airport and saw no one from AeroPeru there to meet me—only Chamote. I quickly dismissed this slight in protocol, since I had been coming regularly for about a year and knew my own way around. Besides, I had found the Peruvians to be more reserved than the Ecuadoreans. Nevertheless, a new, nagging feeling was beginning to focus as I thought again about the official response to our original Boeing request to land in Peru—telexed by our flight operations as a required formality. Scarcely three weeks before, when I departed from Lima, enthusiasm was high for the demonstration.

The protocol for requesting permission to enter most countries was simply a form letter. Boeing flight operations had sent all the requests by telex over a month in advance.

For Peru, the message was addressed to the *Ministerio de Transportes*, which had jurisdiction over all civil airplane operations in the country. The telex was brief:

"The Boeing Company, Seattle, Washington, requests approval to operate 747SP airplane N40135 into Lima on Monday, 24 November 1975. The airplane is participating in an extensive demonstration tour of South America, Asia, Europe, and Africa. The 747SP is basically a 747 airplane with the fuselage reduced by 47 feet. It is powered by four Pratt and Whitney engines. Details follow:

1. Flight crew: J. Waddell, Pilot in Command.

T. Edmonds, Pilot . . . .

The remainder of the message covered the certification of the airplane, numbers of passengers and crew expected to be on board, arrival and departure schedules, and ended with a request:

Please forward approval by cable to the undersigned.

Mr. N. E. Jepsky, Flight Operations"

From Lima, there had been only silence. There was no recourse except to make a followup request and wait. The second telex was even shorter:

"Reference cable requests approval for 747SP airplane N40135 to operate one hour local demonstration at 1100 hours, 25 November 1975.

Boeing requests approval to conduct this demo into Cuzco if weather permits. Activities at Cuzco will include landing, taxi to turn around, and takeoff performance.

Please forward approval via cable to the undersigned."

Before I left Seattle, I had reviewed all the messages, and was surprised by the coldly polite reply which came on October 31st.

"We thank you for your communication of October 28, about the demonstration flight and landing at the international airport in Lima and Cuzco with the 747SP equipment stop but negative for reasons of technical operations stop."

However, upon thinking it over, I was less concerned. In the first place, I felt the message had not received the attention of General Galindo in the *Ministerio de Aeronautica,* whom I presumed would have the final word, in spite of the protocol that the request be made to the civil authorities. Further, noting the reasons were "technical," I felt that they could be easily overcome with support from Boeing.

On November 3rd, I had directed Boeing flight operations to send still a third message:

"Your reply to Boeing cables B-7911-637 and 721 requesting approval to operate the 747SP airplane into Lima on November 24 states there are technical difficulties. Please furnish information to clarify reasons for disapproving. Boeing can revise schedule if there are conflicts, and offers to furnish specialists to work with government authorities to resolve technical questions. Please reply via telex."

When three days passed without a reply, I decided it was time for more direct action. I phoned General Victor Velazques, chief of staff for the Peruvian Air Force, second in command in the *Ministerio de Aeronautica.* Velazques had most recently been the Peruvian military attaché in Washington, D.C., and had taken his flight training in the United States. He understood the problems in moving large aircraft like the 747SP into and out of airports. Telephone calls from the U.S. usually commanded immediate attention. General Velazques was extremely cordial and promised to look into the matter.

In anticipation of many technical questions on my return to Peru, when I departed from Seattle on November 11th, I requested Mr. Herb Skeels, a Boeing runway engineering specialist, to proceed to Lima, where I would meet him after completing my business in Quito.

I then called Chamote, requesting him to meet Skeels at the airport and to introduce him to the authorities to begin quickly to resolve their technical concerns.

My fears were abruptly reinforced when I met Chamote at the airport on November 16th.

His smile and outstretched hand belied a hidden concern.

"*Buenos dias,* Chamote," I shouted, eagerly shaking his hand. "I expect you have already solved our little problem."

Chamote shook his head. "I can't seem to get through to them," he lamented. "There's a struggle between the *Ministros.*"

"There must be a way. Let's find it!" I exclaimed.

It was already late in the afternoon on Friday.

"I want you to get the critical people together right here at the airport first thing Monday morning for a meeting," I demanded. "They can show us first-hand what the technical problems are. If necessary we'll go on to Cuzco in the afternoon! There's not much time—the SP is already in Japan!"

Chamote frowned. "Gene, I don't think it's so easy. They're not telling us everything."

"*No problema,* now is the time for us to do a small miracle," I said, pounding him on the shoulder.

The next day I breathed a little easier when Chamote called to announce the meeting was arranged for the control room at the airport at nine o'clock on Monday morning.

On Monday, the Peruvians arrived—*en punto*—a good sign of the importance they ascribed to the meeting. Herb Skeels spoke no Spanish, and for myself, I needed to be careful not to create any misunderstanding when using my shaky subjunctive tense, so I stuck strictly to

English. Chamote translated.

"Gentlemen, as you know, Boeing has offered the 747SP airplane as the machine to suit the needs of AeroPeru on its international network in the not-too-distant future. The airplane is unique in its ability to perform out of high-elevation airfields. Our technical specialists have determined that it can take off from Cuzco with a full load of 305 passengers and baggage, and fly them nonstop to New York City."

While Chamote translated, I watched the intent faces and noticed a quickening interest and obvious surprise—and perhaps unbelief—as they exchanged glances.

"Therefore, we propose that the airplane be landed at Jorge Chavez and then flown to Cuzco. The airplane will land there, turn around, and return to Lima. Our runway specialist has already examined the conditions at Cuzco, and he is here today to provide any necessary advice or assistance," I added.

Tension eased. I felt new confidence.

The spokesman for CORPAC, the civilian aviation authority, posed a series of technical questions concerning gross weight, fuel requirements, turning radius, and overall airplane dimensions—nothing unusual.

Looking at me, he concluded, *"Hay no mucho problemas, solo el problema dañarse a la pista."*

I wanted Herb Skeels to understand the concern very clearly. I nodded to Chamote, who indicated that the problem did not seem to be large, but there was the concern of damage to the runway.

It was soon learned that when Air France had landed a full-sized 747 at Jorge Chavez the previous July, several of the runway lights had been broken by flying gravel, thrown up from the blast of the outboard engines during takeoff.

The SP had an identical wing, with a span of 196 feet, which positioned the outboard engines very close to the edges of the 146 foot wide runway. The aprons had not been consolidated, leaving loose gravel and dirt on both sides for the full length.

Skeels reviewed the takeoff operation in detail, pointing out that the SP was a lower gross-weight airplane, with the same power.

"Thus, we can hold the outboard engines at fast idle during most of the takeoff run, spooling them up just prior to lifting the nose," he advised.

Although the explanation seemed to satisfy some, I noted there was still much skepticism. Having discussed this possibility in detail back at Seattle, I was prepared to offer a dramatic solution on the spot.

"Gentlemen, although we believe the operation can be conducted without damage, as you have just heard from Mr. Skeels, Boeing will provide a written guarantee, and will reimburse you fully in the event that damage does occur," I announced.

The meeting ended on this cordial note, with my promise to deliver an official letter of guarantee the following morning. In parting, the CORPAC officials made a point for the record.

"Mr. Bauer, please be clear that our jurisdiction is only over technical matters. The authority to land must come from the *Ministerio de Transportes.*" I was uncertain as to exactly what that meant, but my confidence was high.

*"Muchas gracias!"* I said.

With telephone guidance from our legal experts at the home plant, I prepared a letter of guarantee and delivered it to CORPAC, when communications between Transportes and CORPAC mysteriously ceased.

In desperation, I made call after call to one and then the other. In the U.S. manner, I proposed a three-way meeting. Everybody resisted. It was not the Peruvian mode of conducting business. Protocol must be followed.

Certain that the Air Force could easily unplug the bottleneck, I once again called General Velazques.

"Mr. Bauer, I understand the problem very clearly, and we are discussing it. Please know that we have certain methods of operating that may be different than those you are accustomed to," he said.

My last hope was General Galindo. Surely he would want to see the airplane perform on Peruvian airfields.

Galindo was sympathetic, but claimed the matter was outside his jurisdiction. The door had been secretly closed. For reasons unknown, they had decided to keep the plane from landing in Peru.

My options had run out, and it was urgent that I get back to Quito where I had a live operation.

Regretfully, on November 19th, I delivered a letter to General Berckemeyer, canceling the program. In the letter, I extended an invitation for the Peruvians to be our guests in Quito, where we were making a last-minute upgrading to conduct a full-flight demonstration, even though I was certain that no one would come. Peru and Ecuador had fought each other for centuries and continued to live by an uneasy truce.


Boeing planners in Seattle scrambled to build a fill-in for the Lima-Cuzco cancellation. Otherwise, the entire follow-on schedule would have to be revised. Hurried arrangements were made to route the plane to La Paz.

Before leaving Lima, I learned the true reason behind the denial of landing permission in Peru. Air France's application for regularly scheduled service from Paris to Lima for the spring of 1976 was being held up by the Peruvians, who sensed an opportunity to capitalize on the runway damage. Peru was demanding that Air France pay the bill for installing surface-flush, blast-proof lights, as well as fifteen-foot-wide asphalt shoulders along both sides of the main runway. The estimated cost was $200,000, a huge sum in Peru, and if the Peruvians had allowed the SP to land and there was little or no damage, Air France would have had a basis for denying the claims.


I hurried back to Quito, where my mission had increased in complexity. Instead of bringing the plane in and out the same day, I was now faced with an overnight stay—on very short notice. I suddenly needed rooms for forty-one people!

# 12

In Quito, rumors were spreading that the Peruvians had determined that the airplane was so heavy it would destroy the runways. From Santiago de Chile, word came that "certain individuals" were cautioning against permitting the airplane to land there, even though official approval had already been received. The same disturbing news began emanating from La Paz. There was no doubt in my mind that our competitors were providing the fuel for those reports. They escalated the issue to ridiculous proportions. An article in the local newspaper even stated that "these four-engined jumbos will require entirely new landing fields throughout South America."

Thus, it was with a new sense of urgency that I hurried over to Ecuatoriana headquarters. In sharp contrast to the postponements and endless waiting at AeroPeru, the secretary welcomed me as an old friend, immediately ushering me into Colonel Banderas' office.

"*Como está? Señor Bauer,*" he smiled, testing my Spanish.

"*Muy bien, gracias, e usted?*" I replied, firmly grasping his hand.

"*Muy bien, gracias.*"

"*Asienta se,*" he said, motioning to the couch.

I took my usual place by the quaint little table carved from the magnificent jungle hardwoods, relaxing for a moment in the knowledge of how smoothly everything was going. Banderas sat down at his desk.

"We're negotiating with Pan Am for another 707," he announced, reverting to English. "This one will be a -320 Intercontinental."

"Great! It won't be long before you'll be needing the SP."

A worried expression crossed the colonel's face. His brow furrowed, and he lit a cigarette. Blowing a cloud of smoke, he figuratively tossed me a bomb.

"I think you have some problems with the demonstration," he said abruptly.

I hesitated, taken by surprise, and unbelieving.

"I thought everything was arranged!"

"It's something to do with runway damage. Colonel Suarez is concerned about it."

*The word from Peru had spread quickly.*

"Oh, the director of Civil Aviation. I see. Yeah, I had some discussions in Lima on runways."

Banderas scrubbed his cigarette into the ashtray, rose, and began pacing. "Suarez told me today that he didn't think it could be approved."

I didn't change expression, but my mind whirled. *All my carefully laid plans were unraveling.*

"I know Suarez. We took training together. I can arrange a meeting for you at four o'clock this afternoon."

Banderas peered at me quizzically.

Still in a state of shock, I could only manage, "Thank you very much!"

"I'll ask Edison to help in drafting a letter to Suarez to explain the circumstances." He pressed a buzzer to call his secretary, directing her to have Edison come up.

In a few minutes, Edison arrived, and we departed to his office to compose the letter. I was thankful for Edison—and even more thankful for the fine performance of the Boeing planes. They were the best ambassadors.

"Edison, please excuse me. While you're thinking about the

wording, I have to call Seattle to find out what in hell happened to our communications."

Hurriedly, I reviewed the master schedule. The SP was in Sidney, Australia. It was Friday, November 21st. The crew would have Saturday off, but early Sunday morning the plane would be departing for Santiago on the first-of-a-kind, giant leap over the South Pacific.

Nervous as a treed cat, I hurried back to the hotel. The standard procedure in South American cities was to place an overseas call with an operator, and then wait—often as long as four hours. *At least Quito was better than La Paz, where calls had to be placed a day in advance.*

The wait was only slightly over an hour, but it seemed like forever. I paced the room the entire time, muttering to myself, not daring to leave for lunch.

Finally breaking through, I reached Harold Hemke, who was pinch-hitting for Tom May, the regular account manager for my territory. Tom and Harold served as my communication lifeline to all parts of Boeing.

"What's up?" Harold inquired expectantly.

"I'm hearing disturbing news here in Quito."

"I thought you were all set there. What's happening?"

"I'm afraid we don't have acceptance. It looks as if the flight guys didn't follow up. I believe they sent in the standard request, didn't get a reply, and assumed that it was okay."

There was a silence. "Well, I'll be damned!"

"You better check up in a helluva hurry and get me right back. I have a meeting with the director of Civil Aviation this afternoon at four o'clock sharp to try to get it back on the track."

"Okay. By the way, Peter says there's all kinds of static down in Santiago about runway damage."

"Yeah, I think our friends down 'south' are working overtime." ("south" was our telephone code word for McDonnell Douglas and Lockheed). "I'll wait for your call."

"Hey, Gene, better yet, you hold and I'll call Jepsky on the other line."

"Right."

Tension was increasing by the minute. My palms were sweaty and I couldn't sit still. In about three minutes Harold came back on the line.

"You were right! That's exactly what they did. The wire went out on October 23rd, the same day as the one to Peru. But there's no reply here. I told Jepsky to crank out a follow-up telex right away."

"Thanks, Harold. Wish me luck. I'll be in touch."

Back at Ecuatoriana, I found Edison excited and upset. He had fallen in love with the idea that the 747SP would be coming to Quito.

"Gene, there isn't much time. Things are pretty bad!"

"How is the letter going? Colonel Banderas said you would help me write it and he would sign it."

"It's not that easy. Ecuatoriana can't take the position of promoting Boeing airplanes to the government. You'll have to write the letter to Colonel Suarez yourself."

With Edison coaching, I hurriedly composed a letter. We had continuous phone interruptions, and messengers kept running in and out.

Finally, there was the problem of getting it typed in Spanish, the extra touch that I felt was imperative. Colonel Banderas' secretary volunteered.

Between phone calls, questions, and errors, I came near to despair. Because of poor reproduction facilities at Ecuatoriana, the secretary was stuck with the old method of making five copies on the typewriter—using carbon paper—resulting in time-consuming erasures and corrections.

At last the letter was finished. I literally snatched it from the girl's hand, scrawled my signature, and rushed for the door.

"*Muchisimas gracias!*" I shouted over my shoulder as I fled for the stairs, bounding down three at a time. The elevator was too slow. On my next trip, I brought her a large box of chocolates.

Fortunately, the office of the *Dirección de Aviación Civil* was close at hand. I arrived at the lower landing at one minute to four. The elevator was stuck at number six. A quick glance at the listing showed number eight for Colonel Suarez. I made a beeline for the stairs, taking them in multiple leaps, and thanking Providence that I was a mountain climber and in top condition.

Approaching the desk and announcing myself, I presented my card to Colonel Suarez's secretary. Glancing around, I noted the front office was full of people—all hoping to see the colonel. I understood he usually left at five o'clock. I sat down to wait.

At twenty minutes after five, I was having visions of Suarez leaving by a back door and myself being told to come back on Monday—when I was ushered into his office. He was unexpectedly cordial. Perhaps curiosity was as strong a motive as any at that point. Suarez had an excellent command of English.

*Thank Heaven for small favors,* I muttered to myself. This subject was much too complex to risk with less than perfect Spanish.

I stepped forward toward the massive carved wooden desk, and handed him a copy of the October 23rd telex. He glanced at it, turned to the side, and picked up a page from a pile of papers.

"Oh, yes, Mr. Bauer, I have the message here. We've been considering your request. Our concern is that the airplane can't make the turnaround on the main runway. Our taxiways are under major repair and can't be used."

He paused, and my mind switched to overdrive, but before I could reply, he continued.

"There is also concern about the weight, it might break up the runway."

I was ready with answers, poised to give him the letter, when he delivered the blockbuster.

"I've just sent this telex to Boeing this afternoon."

He stood up and handed me the copy. It was addressed to Jepsky. Written in Spanish, it was a short message. The bottom line leaped out at me.

"Referring to the visit of the Boeing 747SP airplane, this office laments that we are not able to authorize it to come to our country because of the physical conditions of our runways in Quito and Guayaquil. It will not be possible to land there."

*Failed!*

The word boomed like a clanging bell in my brain.

*But wait, the SP is still three days away. Keep a cool head,* I told myself. *There must be a solution.*

# 13

If ever I needed to be fast on my feet with a convincing argument, the time had come.

"Colonel Suarez, I have summarized some technical information which I hope will change your mind," I said, handing him the letter.

Believing the issue was closed, he seemed ready to take his leave. Hesitating, he reached for the letter, scanned it briefly, saying nothing. Finally, he sat down, still reading the letter.

"*Asienta se,*" he said, looking up and beckoning to a chair.

I breathed a sigh of relief. I was not dead yet.

"You see, Colonel, the SP has sixteen wheels on the main gear, while the DC-10 has eight. Yet the SP weighs only one-fifth more than the DC-10. That makes the load on each wheel significantly less than for the 10. As for turning, the Boeing analysis shows that both the 747 and the SP are capable of turning as tightly as the 10. Two airlines are already operating into Quito with DC-10s and are turning 180 degrees at the end of the runway. That's why we foresee no problem."

Colonel Suarez seemed impressed. "I get your point. I'll discuss it with the staff."

I was beginning to see a little daylight.

"There's one thing, Colonel. We really need a quick solution. The airplane will be in Santiago tomorrow, and La Paz on Monday."

Colonel Suarez hardly noticed my tone of urgency. He was relaxed, unruffled, unhurried. It was the way of Latin Americans. There was always *mañana*. His mind had already shifted to the weekend at his country estate.

Instinctively, he glanced at his watch.

"Everyone will be out of town until Monday. I won't be able to get in touch with them. Give me your number at the hotel and I'll call you."

My heart sank. Mechanically, I wrote the room number on my card and handed it to him—fearful that he would never call.

There was no joy in Seattle when I phoned Harold. It was still four o'clock there.

"Right now, we have a problem, but I feel certain that Suarez will approve it," I pleaded.

"All we have here is a telex saying we can't bring the plane in," Hemke complained. "We'll just have to cut you off on Sunday afternoon and instruct the flight crew to go directly to Caracas from La Paz," he announced. "It's completely out of my hands."

"Harold, I'm dead in the water! Everybody is out in the country! We won't know a thing until Monday!"

There was a long silence. Harold apparently had some of the bosses on the other line, and they were having a small conference.

"Well, keep working on it," he said at last. "I won't be calling until Monday morning for a final shot. The big brass will wait until then to cancel you out."

"Okay. Thanks for small favors."

Sitting in the hotel room, the waiting and uncertainty during the weekend became unbearable. I had a telephone number for Colonel Banderas at his country place, and finally decided to bite the bullet and call him. *What could I lose?*

I was in luck.

Banderas was optimistic and encouraging. "I think it will work out," he said. "Don't worry."

I had learned that in South America, when they said things like that, it was usually time to begin worrying.

"But Colonel Suarez didn't feel that he would know until Monday, and that will be too late. Unless we get the turndown rescinded, the airplane isn't coming," I pleaded.

"I don't understand. Colonel Suarez doesn't have to ask anybody. He's the final authority."

On Monday morning at nine o'clock, I went directly to Colonel Suarez' office and waited. Time difference gave me a three-hour jump on Seattle. He didn't arrive until ten-thirty. One more hour and the Seattle office would give the Quito demo the axe. *Sixty minutes from sudden death!*

Unable to wait in any more reception lines, I stepped forward—ahead of everybody—greeting the colonel as he came through the door. I came straight to the point.

"Colonel Suarez, I have to tell Seattle before the hour is out if we can come in!"

He gave me a studied look.

"Well, Colonel Banderas says Boeing is pretty confident about turning the airplane around on the runway, so I think it will be okay."

"Thank you very much, Colonel. Will you do me the favor of sending a telex to Seattle? They need an official acceptance or they'll reroute the airplane directly from La Paz to Caracas."

"I'll send a telex right away."

Jubilant, I hurried back to the hotel to call Harold Hemke. *If only I can get through in time,* I worried.

Almost immediately, my own phone rang. Harold was on the line.

"I thought I'd better call before I go in to see the big brass. I know how it is there for getting through," Harold announced. "So what's the news?"

"The news is fantastic! We have the O.K.! Suarez is sending a telex right now!"

"Hey Gene, that's great! I was damned worried for a while."

"There was nothing to worry about, Harold," I joked. "We still have almost fifteen minutes before cutoff."

There was a pause as Harold chuckled.

"Gene, one more thing. We have their flight schedule. They expect to arrive at 1430 hours tomorrow afternoon."

"Okay, Harold, but please make some things clear to the crew. We've been getting cold mountain fogs the last few days. The fog rolls in about four in the afternoon and then we're completely socked in until the next morning. Tell them four o'clock is absolutely the latest for touchdown here."

"They should make it fine. The departure time from La Paz is 1230 hours, and it's a two-hour flight."

Tuesday morning was cloudy, and the fog didn't lift until noon. I went to the airport to have lunch with Alfonso Fiallos, who was in constant contact with the control tower.

At 1430 hours—the expected arrival time—the tower reported nothing. They called La Paz. The SP had taken off only minutes before. It would be 1630 hours before they arrived, even without headwinds. We would need some exceptional luck. Alfonso and I went down to the runway.

At 1500 hours, clouds began to boil up in big thunderheads around Mt. Pichincha, immediately west of Quito—towering over the city. The bright sunshine of only moments before abruptly disappeared, casting a sudden, sullen shadow over the landscape.

After all the turmoil and trouble, with success so close, I dreaded to think of the possibility that the plane would be cruising up there a few thousand feet over our heads, and never get down.

The Mariscal Sucre International Airport was without any automated landing system, relying totally on visual approach. Incoming planes made a pass over the field, then turned 180 degrees for final.

At 1630 hours, rain began to fall. The cloud cover became threateningly black. Only a small sliver of blue remained. In moments, the light breeze was whipped into strong gusts.

A few minutes later, the sound of engines reached our straining ears. Alfonso called the tower. Contact!

Suddenly, the big bird appeared up in the clear space—two miles high and straight down the runway. Headed south over the city, it disappeared in the black cloud mass. My heart sank, fearing we had been passed because of the weather.

In a few minutes, the engine sounds began to increase again, and we caught sight of the plane—this time on final—heading in below the clouds.

Landing was uneventful, as the big red, white, and blue bird touched its tires to the runway and rolled to a stop. Now the crew had to prove the 180 degree turn—the first time—otherwise, they were stuck. There was no tow truck in Quito powerful enough to move the airplane on the ground.

I crossed my fingers. It proved to be unnecessary. The number one crew headed by chief pilot Jack Waddell had the situation under control. The demonstration flight was scheduled for the next day at 1100 hours.

The storm passed during the night and the morning sky was crystal clear. The city of Quito turned out a hero's welcome in the brittle-bright sunlight. They even provided a military band, which played with *gusto* all during the boarding of the guests. I was surprised but elated with the intense enthusiasm.

Jack Waddell invited Colonel Lara to take the captain's seat. Having logged over 10,000 hours of flight time in four-engined jet airplanes, Lara still was taking his regular turns with the Ecuatoriana fleet. He flew the plane out over the coast and the Galápagos Islands, back over the mountains, and with a little coaching from Waddell, landed it like a veteran.

Meanwhile, on board during the one-hour flight, the brass from the Air Force, the airlines, the *Ministerios*, the Airport Authority, and the U.S. embassy were being presented with a slide show explaining the attributes of the airplane. As sales director, I played the role of *maestro*, introducing the various elements of our team and handling the question period.

Nobody came from Peru.

The mayor of Quito, highest ranking official on board, presented an Ecuadorean flag to Clancy Wilde, himself an ex-mayor of the city of Bellevue, Washington.

At exactly 1500 hours, Quito waved goodbye to the 747SP, as it roared down the runway and disappeared over the ridge beyond Pichincha, leaving only a lingering contrail. I could hardly contain my joy, and my expectations soared. The demo had gone off perfectly in every detail. I remained in Quito for several days, assessing the results.

The SP flew on to Caracas, Mexico City, Belgrade, Athens, Lusaka, Nairobi, and Abidjan, finally swinging back to Kingston, Jamaica, where it made its final demonstration on December 9th.

On Sunday, November 30th, I flew to Port of Spain, Trinidad, and made contact with the largest of my new accounts, British West Indian Airways (BWIA). I met with Captain Eric Mowser, Vice President of Operations, and invited him to come to Kingston. He complained about his unyielding schedule, as he was still taking regular turns flying BWIA's 707s.


Planning to meet the airplane in Jamaica, I took advantage of the few extra days, and made a quick trip back to Peru. My curiosity was strong about the reaction there. In spite of the blizzard of bad press emanating from Lima, the big bird had successfully demonstrated its performance along almost the entire Andean spine, stopping at the capital cities of Chile, Bolivia, and Ecuador, leaving out only Peru. Peter Stross handled the demos in Chile and Bolivia.

"AeroPeru was anxious to have the plane come in," General Berckemeyer lamented, when I met him in Lima. "It was not up to the airline," he added.

He said nothing about the Air France flight, and I felt the subject was too sensitive to pursue, certain that no one would be willing to admit responsibility.

"Mr. Bauer, do you suppose Boeing could make a demo early next year for us?" he ventured.

Caught by surprise, I improvised.

"I'm afraid the answer is no, as we visited what appeared to be all the potential SP customers, and separate demos are very expensive," I said. "However, we welcome you and your staff to come to Seattle to fly in it."

Our parting was cordial, and I promised to help AeroPeru in its forward planning again right after the first of the year.

"Gene, the money just isn't there," Chamote informed me when we reviewed our possible future strategies.

"I'll take another look at  refocusing the program with the long-range version of the 727," I concluded.

Giesela, always with her ear to the ground, had not changed her tune. "Gene, I told you, AeroPeru is Dooooglas. You have to get somebody who is a friend of the new *Ministro*," she said.

"I know, I know, we're working on it."


After the demo in Kingston, I remained on board the airplane, and we flew as the crow flies, straight to Seattle, with only a slight kink in the route to avoid Cuban airspace.

History recorded the round-the-world flight a little differently than it actually happened.  The Boeing *Annual Report* for 1975 had a map on its cover[1].  One detail was in error.

The map showed that the 747SP visited Lima and Cuzco, but not La Paz.  Those last minute changes had escaped the attention of the authors. Thus, the true story has not heretofore been told.

But it was branded in my brain forever.

1. *Annual Report,* The Boeing Company, 1975, Cover.

# 14

**E**arly in January, each year, was review and renewal time. It provided a brief escape from the high pressure of the road—a time of reunion with my family.

At the plant, all the frontline salesmen had come home to participate in a two-day briefing prepared by Clancy Wilde's core staff. Each salesman had submitted trip reports throughout the year, and at year-end had prepared an assessment of each of their customers, as to the probability of sales for the coming year. From these, Clancy's staff developed summaries of the past year's operations, and made forecasts for the future. Finally, each salesman was given a sales target by customer and model number for the year. We referred to these as our "marching orders."

In 1975, foreign sales had again outpaced U.S. domestic sales—for the seventh year in a row—gaining three-fourths of the $1.3 billion company total.

Europe, the Middle East, and Asia were the largest contributors. Although South and Central American carriers appeared to offer the least potential, we aimed for those crucial initial sales. By mid-decade,

Boeing had achieved a strong position in most of the Latin American accounts.

Brazilian airlines were flying eighty-five Boeing machines—707s, 727s, and 737s—against four McDonnell Douglas DC-10s.

Aerolineas Argentinas, the major carrier in Argentina, was flying twenty-three, with none from our competitors.

Avianca, the largest airline in Colombia, and South America's oldest, owned twenty-one, with none from the competition.

Lan Chile, flag carrier for Chile, was flying eight, with none from the competition.

Venezuela was the only major South American market apparently lost to Boeing. Early in the sales battle, all three of its airlines had gone solidly to McDonnell Douglas. Of the major countries, that left Bolivia, Ecuador, and Peru as the strongest targets.

In Central America, Mexico was the major market, with Air Mexico primarily Douglas, and Mexicana primarily Boeing. We had also begun to study the needs of the smaller countries in Central America and the Caribbean.


I had read the news of the "Lockheed Scandal" in the international edition of the Miami Herald in the summer of 1975. At the time, I was in Quito, busy with preparations for the 747SP demonstration, and gave it only a passing glance.

The U.S. Senate Subcommittee on Multinational Operations under the chairmanship of Senator Frank Church had begun hearings on the business practices of Lockheed. The Securities and Exchange Commission (SEC) soon disclosed that Lockheed was engaged in massive bribery campaigns in overseas markets, beginning with military airplanes, but continuing into their commercial operations.

That proved to be only the tip of the iceberg. The echoes of the revelations that followed reverberated throughout the boardrooms of some of America's largest corporations.

Other United States firms, including all of the major aerospace companies, came under the scrutiny of the Church Subcommittee, the SEC, the Federal Trade Commission (FTC), and the Internal Revenue Service (IRS). Many of these companies were eventually investigated by the Justice Department.

Responding to the SEC accusations in the summer of 1975, after months of denial, Lockheed acknowledged that it had made $22 million in payoffs to foreign countries since 1970 to get lucrative aircraft contracts—a practice it termed necessary to meet competition.[1]

The Lockheed dispute took twenty-one months to resolve, and in May 1977, pursuant to a negotiated court order, a special committee of Lockheed directors filed a report specifying how the company "secretly generated as much as $38 million for questionable foreign market practices."[2]

Interest quickly focused on the practices of Lockheed's main rivals—giant Boeing and its most tenacious competitor, McDonnell Douglas.

At the time, McDonnell Douglas reported that between 1970 and 1975 approximately $2.5 million in foreign fees, commissions, and consultants payments were made to promote sales of commercial aircraft.[3] However, they eventually conceded to making $21.57 million in questionable payments to sales agents in eighteen countries, including Venezuela, between 1969 and 1976.[4]

Boeing denied any illegal activities, and in its 1975 report to the stockholders, outlined its practice of using sales representatives and consultants, offering legitimate commissions.[5]

At our January 1976 sales meeting, the sensitivity of the bribery issue with consultants was strongly emphasized. All consultant contracts specifically forbade offering bribes of any kind. Nevertheless, we were under intense pressure to make sales.

Some Boeing salesmen had voiced their frustration about the company's scruples when Boeing would not take the extra step—matching payments that they knew were being made by competitors. Herbert Grueter, manager of Boeing's Far Eastern airplane sales between 1968 and 1973, believed that Boeing needlessly lost business by failing to fill a few outstretched hands. He cited the All Nippon decision to buy Tristars. Grueter claimed to be very aware of the payments that Lockheed was promising to the Japanese. He felt certain that one million dollars in bribes would have landed the order.[6]

Alfredo Dodds had been particularly abrasive on numerous occasions during the past year. "Gene, you have to get your ass in gear in Peru," he told me privately one day. "Chamote isn't getting the job done."

"Alfredo, I have my own conscience, and I'm committed to the Boeing tradition."

"Well, you can do a helluva lot more—maybe you should go to bed with Giesela," he had answered slyly. "I think she can get you next to the right people."

Although I was single at the time, and Giesela was divorced, the idea was foreign to my ethics.

"I have my own standards," I said, bristling.

Alfredo always had to be right, all but demanding to be greeted as *"él jefe,"* which I refused to do, and he reveled in demolishing his colleagues' positions. Then in my thirty-fourth year with the company, I had never "brown-nosed" the boss, and I wasn't planning to change.

Deciding to let the cards fall where they might, I pressed on, but I sorely missed John Broback's quiet diplomacy.

I kicked off the year with an ambitious, month-long sales trip, beginning with Lima, to Quito, back to Lima, back to Quito, on to Paramaríbo, Surinam; to Port of Spain, Trinidad and Tobago; and finally, home in mid-February.

In Trinidad and Tobago, I was starting from scratch, gearing up for a bitter battle between the 737 and the DC-9 for the island hopping and Miami market that BWIA was preparing to consolidate.

Surinam was a complete unknown, having only recently achieved the status of an independent nation, after centuries as a Dutch colony.

Consultant support would be a major factor in all of these accounts, and I needed to find candidates in both Ecuador and Trinidad, as well as a replacement in Peru, where we had let Chamote's contract quietly expire at year-end. Alfredo insisted on finding a "more aggressive" individual.

In spite of the obvious potential of Lima as a key city in the international network, the principal planners lacked the courage and initiative to move forward in developing a strong, competitive airline, with modern equipment. Another crucial element was to develop an FAA-approved maintenance base. My inability to turn them away from their buy-cheap-and-plan-short philosophy continued to frustrate me.

Returning to Lima, I found that General Berckemeyer had already been overwhelmed by multiple problems. The government, smarting from severe losses by AeroPeru, was wary of any new capital outlays. Further, dictator Velasco, still paranoid about relations with Ecuador and Chile—ancient enemies—had cozied up to the Soviets, and was buying a large fleet of fighters for the Air Force with funds that would have been far better spent on commercial airplanes.

The government demanded that Berckemeyer turn the airline around and show an operating profit—in one year.

With a perfect opportunity to commit AeroPeru to a fleet modernization, he chose instead simply to seek a cheaper lease deal.

He found the oldest—and cheapest—DC-8-53s in existence, at Air Jamaica, which had taken them out of service. He was able to lease them for a song—$35,000 a month—compared with $88,000 under the existing lease. AeroPeru canceled their lease with McDonnell Douglas, and signed a one-year contract with Air Jamaica for all three of the old airplanes.

Word of the deal permeated through the airline community like ink in a blotter. Travelers began avoiding AeroPeru flights like the plague. Where planes had been three-fourths full, they suddenly became three-fourths empty.

This lease affected me in a bittersweet way. On the positive side, postponement of the wide-body decision was in Boeing's favor. On the negative side, the fortunes of AeroPeru were headed for the bottom.

Nevertheless, the door had opened a little wider. Seizing the opportunity, I outlined an integrated plan encompassing the entire country, which we named *A Plan for Profitability*. I brought the Boeing traffic and route-planning specialists back to Lima to work out the details.

The plan proposed a combination of 747SP and 727-200 airplanes. Under the plan, 727-200 airplanes would be introduced in July 1977, replacing the leased DC-8s. With auxiliary fuel tanks installed in the body, the modified plane could reach from Lima to Miami, Rio, or Buenos Aires.

After traffic reached an appropriate level, the 727s would be shifted into domestic service, flying the longer routes, and the first 747SP would take over the international service.

The lure of nonstop capability from Cuzco to New York remained in the wings, and I kept pulling it out to center stage.

Initial SP service would begin from Lima to Santiago, Buenos Aires, Caracas, and Miami in July 1978. By mid-1980, the second SP would begin the nonstop Cuzco-New York flights, and would inaugurate service from Lima to Madrid, Paris, and Frankfurt.

Boeing backed up this ambitious proposal with a realistic economic and financial analysis. The key was to find a visionary somewhere in the tight bureaucratic organization.

Boeing traffic projections from historical data showed that modernization could attract substantial numbers of passengers from competitor airlines, and had the potential of attaining an operating profit during the first year, and be completely paid for in ten years. No subsidy would be required from the government, only a guarantee of the original loan.

General Berckemeyer showed keen interest in the proposal. However, a quick decision was too much to hope for. Leaving the airline a time for incubation, I took off for Quito.


The two-hour flight over the mountains, with its spectacular scenery, was a most enjoyable respite. I mulled over the recent events.

Resolution of the consultant situation was my major near-term goal. The campaign in Peru would succeed or fail on the ability of Boeing to find a person of influence who could straddle the gap between the *Ministros* of *Aeronautica* and *Transportes*, both now engaged in a turf battle over airline jurisdiction. With an annual parade of new *Ministros*, there was no middle road. I concluded the best policy was to gamble—playing a waiting game until the final steps of the competition.

Putting AeroPeru out of my mind, I shifted to my Ecuadorean hat. The consultant situation there was more cloudy than ever. Scarcely a month after the SP demo, there was a bloodless coup in Ecuador. General Rodriguez was sent packing by a three-man military *junta*. With Colonel Banderas claiming no consultant was necessary, and the Embassy people adamant that one was essential, I was squarely on the horns of a dilemma.

General LeBailly was scheduled to arrive the next day to help me sort out candidates.

When the phone rang in my room on Sunday afternoon, I picked it up expectantly.

"*Hola, mi amigo! Como está?*" It was Ben.

"*Bien, mi general, que pasa?*"

I invited him to come over for a strategy session.

In a few minutes there was a loud banging on the door. I jerked it open.

"*La vida está un fandango!*" Ben shouted, extending his hand in greeting.

"*Si, si, por cierto,*" I replied.

"What good words do you have from the head shed?" I inquired.

"I just came from Caracas," Ben replied.

"What's going on there?"

"I'm helping Bob Brog find a consultant for the sale of the Executive 737 to the president of Venezuela. That's a mare's nest! If you think Peru is bad, you should see that deal."

Brog was the Boeing salesman for Colombia and Venezuela. Selling an executive plane to the Venezuelan government was a critical step in cracking the McDonnell Douglas monopoly.

Ben walked over to the window and looked down at the magnificent valley below the Quito ridge.

"You're looking at the site for the new Quito airport," I broke in. "The plan is to build a new one down there about 1,500 feet lower in elevation. It'll be 3,000 meters long."

"Just right for those DC-10s to beat us out," jibed LeBailly.

"Not exactly. It's at least ten years away, and I'm not sure the DC-10 can make it all the way to New York nonstop from there either. We'll have to study it."

I joined Ben at the window. "Right now, I'm trying to figure out the consultant riddle here in Quito. I hope you have some good ideas."

"Well, for a long time I would have sworn General Montesinos was the right man. He was the most influential person in the Air Force when I was on the Inter-American Defense Board a few years back. I figured he had the inside track."

"But after Banderas crossed him off the list of demo guests, it sounds like that's down the tube."

"Yeah, I know, Banderas came right out and told me it would be better if we didn't invite him to fly. Knowing how these cats operate, he's pure poison. He's sure as hell gotten himself crossways with somebody in the *junta*. We better stay clear of him."

Sadly, I agreed with Ben. Montisenos had not only looked like a gold-plated candidate, he had presented me with a beautiful black iron-wood spear from the jungle Indians, during a previous visit. I left it in his office, promising to pick it up on my way back home.

"I'm going to miss that spear," I lamented, "but now it's onward and upward. I have an idea how we should proceed. Let's run a two-track approach. I have a meeting with Banderas tomorrow, so I'll concentrate on the airline, and you concentrate on the government."

Ben nodded.

"I'll also be seeing my good friend, Colonel Lara. Oswaldo will give me the straight scoop. He's in love with the SP, and I've been helping him with special favors like providing free flight and operations manuals for the 707 fleet. I'm bringing those new ones to him this trip." I pointed to a bulky package on the table.

"Let's watch that *mordida*, Gene! You must be up-to-date on the Lockheed story."

"Yeah, but that looks like a different ball game. Lockheed is up to their ass in alligators. It sounds as if they're literally giving away millions of dollars. Anyway, back to the plan. You proceed with your contacts, and we can compare notes later."

"Good idea. We should be able to crack this Ecuador thing. The SP is a helluva good choice for Ecuatoriana."

"Oh, one more thing!" I tapped Ben on the shoulder. *"Muy importante!"*

"Try to arrange a private meeting with General Leoro. He must have the final say on any deal, and he might drop a name."

"Good. Personally, I never knew him too well. He's a loner. Not very well liked. But I agree, he's the key man. I know the chief of staff for the Air Force. Maybe he can get an appointment for me."

"Fine. See you later for dinner downstairs."

General Leoro was one of the three members of the ruling *junta* that had taken over the government in December: Leoro of the Air Force, General Duran of the Army, and Admiral Poveda of the Navy. By mutual agreement, Poveda was top man. However, General Leoro had a free hand in Air Force matters, and it was the Air Force that determined the fortunes of Ecuatoriana. Leoro had handpicked Banderas as president. Colonel Lara was also a personal friend of General Leoro, so *the ducks were beginning to line up.*

My meeting with Banderas was cordial as usual. I had expected the coup could have changed his views regarding consultants. However, he insisted, as he had in previous meetings, that no consultant was needed— Ecuatoriana planned to work directly with the manufacturer, and he could not conceive of any other decision than Boeing airplanes.

I didn't know whether to be pleased or worried. It sounded too easy.

The veneer on the surface was smoother than in Peru, hiding the turbulence and intrigue that Ben and I felt certain were boiling underneath.

Later that day, I made my rounds with the other major players in Ecuatoriana. Colonel Lara was first.

"*Hola, mi amigo!*" I greeted, as we shook hands.

"Gene, I really loved that SP airplane. Fantastic!"

"Jack Waddell told me you were ready to fly it already."

"It's so easy, even smoother than the 707s."

"Yeah, Boeing has incorporated a lot of new technology."

"All we need now is to find some money. Wow! Forty million dollars! I can't even imagine that much money!"

"Oswaldo," I ventured. "On a different subject. Please give me your advice on consultants here."

"I don't think Boeing needs one, but I'll tell you one thing. If the situation changes, I'll be the first to let you know."

"I really appreciate that. There's no way for me to assess the situation. By the way, I have something here for you."

I handed him the package of 707 manuals I had promised—and also a bottle of Black Label.

Oswaldo's face lit up at seeing the manuals. "*Muchas, muchas gracias.* Gene, you don't know how much these will help us—and thanks for the scotch."

After taking my leave and looking in on Alfonso down on the flight line, I visited the other sensitive departments in the airline: Colonel Camacho, V. P. of finance; Colonel Pazmino, V. P. of administration; Roberto Muller, V. P. of commercial—and of course, Edison Teran, in charge of publicity and promotion.

Boeing seemed to be highly favored all along the line—except for one.

Roberto Muller, a recent import from American Airlines, was blunt.

"Mr. Bauer, I must tell you that the DC-10 is the best plane for us," he announced.

"Unfortunately, you joined Ecuatoriana just a few days after the 747SP demo. But I'll bring copies of all the documentation, and you have an open invitation to come to Seattle to fly in the airplane."

"I'm sold on the 10s."

We parted on that note. It was apparent that he would be a major force to be reckoned with. I would not have been at all surprised to learn that McDonnell Douglas was involved somewhere in the hiring of Muller.


Barriers to Ben's meeting with Leoro began springing up. Although the chief of staff was attentive in receiving him as an old friend, he was evasive concerning the possibilities of meeting Leoro. All attempts ran into devious channels and dead ended.

Still, there was no paucity of candidates to interview. Each new prospect was adamant regarding his ability to negotiate directly with the *junta*.

Ben and I had heard the stories before. "They had grown up together—they were in-laws—they had worked together on some project in the past—they were cousins—Leoro's adjutant was a brother."

After interviewing five candidates—three retired military men and two civilians—I decided to let the case rest. I went back to Lima, while Ben returned home.

1. *Wall Street Journal*, 4 December 1975, 1.

2. *Wall Street Journal*, 20 February 1979, 13.

3. *Aviation Week & Space Technology*, 8 December 1975, 15.

4. *Aviation Week & Space Technology*, 4 August 1980, 21.

5. *Annual Report*, The Boeing Company, 1975, 5.

6. *Wall Street Journal*, 7 May 1976, 1.

# 15

I will not soon forget my arrival in Lima that Sunday evening. The airport was swarming with soldiers. I learned that a recent series of bloody riots had caused a crackdown by the army, and a curfew had been imposed. The *toque de queda* was in effect, and the soldiers had orders to shoot anyone caught on the streets after 8:00 p.m.

A written pass, the *salvo de conducto*, was required to permit safe passage to the hotel. The streets were deserted—the sole traffic limited to official vehicles—with an occasional lonesome taxicab.

My cab passed through several barricades at key intersections, where I showed my *salvo de conducto* to the soldier who shined his flashlight into my face—and asked if I had any cigarettes. A nonsmoker, it was the first time in my life that I wished I had some. It was conceivable that he might shoot me if I had none to offer.

Reaching the hotel, I found the entire first floor blacked out, the front doors blasted off, and the front plate-glass windows shattered.

I pretended that everything was normal, and went on about my business. AeroPeru was still studying our proposal, and it would have been easy to take the next plane out, but I decided to stay a few days and continue the search for a consultant.

I planted a seed in the middle management of AeroPeru that we didn't intend to renew Chamote's contract. Reaction was swift. Federico Pastor, the *jefe* of long-range planning, was particularly attentive.

"Federico, as you know, Boeing hires consultants to help with sales," I volunteered. "We've been dissatisfied with Chamote because he doesn't seem to do anything."

I paused.

"*Así, así,* I know him. He is too important to talk to us. He only talks to the *Ministro.*"

"Well, if you've been a general for years, I suppose it's difficult to start conversing with planning people in the airline," I joked.

"In any case, we expect the consultant to talk to us," Federico said flatly.

"That's precisely the reason I'm bringing it up. We want a consultant who can work with the airline."

"*Por cierto!* That's it exactly!"

"So, if you have any recommendations, I'd like to hear about them."

Federico smiled, and then quickly became more matter-of-fact, putting on a feigned aloofness.

"I'll think about it," he replied curtly.

When I returned to the hotel I found a message at the desk. It was from Federico. He wanted to discuss an urgent matter. I immediately phoned.

"Gene, about the discussions we had this afternoon—"

"Yes?"

"I'd like to stop by the hotel this evening to pick you up. Say about 6:30—we can talk about it some more."

The quick response surprised me. It was an encouraging sign.

"Fine, I'll be down front at 6:30. *Hasta luego!*"

With the chief of planning getting into the act, the scenario was perfect—or, maybe too perfect. His reaction was a little out of character and I was suspicious. He was General Soto's son-in-law, and it could easily be part of a plan to dead-end the Boeing consultant effort.

In Peru, polite lateness was a half hour, but being accustomed to being early, I went downstairs at 6:20.

After an hour had passed, I began to be concerned. *Maybe he had changed his mind. How long should I wait?* There was no way to phone. I began pacing the sidewalk, cursing the pompous Peruvians under my breath. At a quarter to eight, a Volkswagen beetle roared to a stop.

Federico jumped out. "I'm sorry to be late. I hope you weren't waiting too long."

*The standard cliche.*

"*No importa, no problema,*" I assured him, smiling broadly.

"I'd like to introduce my wife, Liliana."

"*Mucho placer para conocerlas, Señora.*"

"*Iqualamente.*"

Liliana hunched forward, and I climbed into the rear seat.

"We got held up," Federico complained. "Liliana took too long." He glanced toward her. She responded with a cold glare.

"*No problema, no problema!*" I insisted.

Conversation ceased as we drove out into the Miraflores suburb, the finest district in the entire city. Federico broke the silence.

"I want you to meet my cousin. He owns the Datsun agency here in Lima. They have the franchise for the whole country. The cars come in here and are distributed to different cities. He's interested in the consultant job for Boeing."

"Good! I want to meet a number of candidates. As you're aware, I don't have the authority to make the final selection. The big brass makes those decisions."

"*Así, así, entiende, no problema.*"

"His name is Gonzalo", Federico continued. "He has an apartment here in Miraflores."

We were winding along wide boulevards with elegant lighting, the night heavy with the sweet fragrance of hibiscus, and the streets lined with well-manicured trees and shrubs. We stopped in front of a large apartment building. Federico got out. *"Un momento!"* he cautioned.

I remained in the car with Liliana while Federico approached the apartment call box. All apartments and private homes in the good districts of Lima had call boxes as part of an elaborate security system.

Federico pressed the button on the box and spoke into it.

*"Hola! Está Federico aqui!"*

A hollow feminine voice came out of the box.

*"Entre! Entre!"*

Federico went to the door, and at the sound of an insistent buzz, opened it, motioning to me and Liliana to join him.

The next barrier was the elevator. Federico pushed another button, again waiting for a signal. The procedure was repeated a third time at the entrance to the apartment.

Security measures were stringent, but necessary. Robbery, the most common crime, was endemic. Walking in the streets at night was particularly hazardous. Next to money, jewelry was the most sought object. Peruvian women were noted for wearing expensive ornaments. Thieves tore necklaces and bracelets off their unwilling victims as if they were department store mannequins, even snipping off a woman's ring finger with surgical scissors to get the diamond ring more quickly.

I was greeted by Gonzalo and his wife. The interior was breathtaking. The trappings of wealth covered every square inch. On the wall were beautiful hand-woven tapestries, and on the floor, lush carpets of llama and alpaca. Statuettes, glassware, ceramic figures, ornate Peruvian copperware and mirrors dazzled my eyes.

*"Hola, mi amigo!"* Gonzalo greeted, extending his hand. Informal, and friendly, he quickly added, *"Yo no hablo Ingles—solo Español."*

I gave him a disarming smile. *"No importa, yo hablo Español suficiente."*

*"Quiero un pisco?"*

*"Si, si, gracias, pisco está muy delicioso."*

Gonzalo rang for the maid to bring the *piscos.*

A redistilled white wine made from *pisco* grapes, native only to Peru and Chile, *pisco* was the national alcoholic beverage, even more popular than imported Scotch. Two *piscos* were sufficient to make lively conversation, and after three, a novice would be completely drunk. The delicacy of its flavor made it easy to forget its potency.

The maid brought the *piscos* and we settled into a discussion concerning our consultant program. Gonzalo expressed keen interest in used airplanes, knowing the propensity of the airlines to buy cheap, and I reemphasized our goal—to sell new machines exclusively.

When I indicated the fee would be 2.5% of the sales price, Gonzalo smiled. *"Será muy difícil para vender con tan poco comisión!"*

I shrugged. *"Hay no otro posibilidades, la Compania Boeing está muy, muy conservador."*

Seeing the impossibility of negotiating the fee upward, Gonzalo quickly capitulated. *"Pero es* okay," he replied, half in English.

I declined to go beyond two *piscos*, resisting the persistent urging of both Gonzalo and Federico. Anyway, it was time for dinner, and Peruvians serve sumptious meals.

In Peru, shrimp are plentiful, including a fresh-water variety from the rivers of the southern part of the country, so shrimp cocktails are the usual *entrada*. As a second *entrada, cebiche* is usually served. No dinner is complete without *cebiche*, a South American delicacy consisting of raw fish marinated in lime juice. Served with sliced raw onion, cabbage, and coarse-kerneled corn, it was not one of my favorites; however, I ate whatever was offered when a guest in a foreigner's home—with *gusto*! A basic rule!

The main dish was *corvina en mantequilla negro*, a delicate sea bass cooked in dark butter.

Peru is famous for its potatoes. They originated there, and did not appear in Europe until after Pizzaro. Now, with the military dictatorship controlling the land, they were in short supply in their native country. I suspected the potatoes I was served were from Idaho.

The other vegetables were steamed cauliflower and broccoli, both Peruvian favorites, served with tasty sauces. *Ensalada* was a mixed fresh vegetable salad similar to those in the U.S.

Wine served with meals is the custom, and Peru had several local wines of excellent quality, particularly the red *Tacama* and the white *Ocucaje*. However, Peruvians seemed to prefer imported wines, mostly from Chile and Argentina. I was served a white *Undurraga* from Chile.

Peruvian desserts have few peers. *Flan*, a sweet caramel custard, is the most common and a universal favorite.

As dinner progressed, my anxiety increased. The *toque de queda* had been relaxed to take effect at eleven o'clock, but the rules were still the same for anyone caught in the streets.

Frederico noticed my uneasiness.

"Don't worry," he said, looking at his watch. "We plan to get to the hotel on time. The rule applies to everybody, and we have to go home from there. They can shoot us too!"

With extravagant phrasing, I thanked Gonzalo and the *señora de la casa* for the magnificent hospitality, promising to keep in touch directly with Gonzalo.

We hurried back to the hotel. The streets were filling with soldiers, and the main intersections were dominated by armored vehicles with 20mm guns.

I was not only relieved to reach the comparative safety of the Sheraton Hotel, I was doubly glad that I would be leaving Lima the next day, for a month. Maybe things would be settled down by the time I returned.

At the hotel, there were several messages waiting at the desk, three from someone named Percy.

It was always the same the last day of my visits. Somehow, word got around. I decided to postpone answering until morning. I had been in bed a few minutes, when shooting began outside.

In the morning, with time short, I concentrated on Percy. Saturdays were much better on the phones, and there was no delay.

He was positive. *"Eugenio, usted necesita mi ayuda,"* he announced boldly. I knew full well that I needed *"ayuda"* from somebody, but it was damned difficult to decide who could help. All the candidates for consultant claimed they were buddies of people in high places, all the way to the *Ministros*.

I found myself casting around in the dark, operating on intuition alone.

"What can I do for you?" I inquired, testing if Percy spoke English.

"Why don't we have lunch together, and I'll talk to you about some important matters. We can't talk over the phone."

"I have a reservation on the eleven o'clock plane to Quito, and I'm not packed yet."

"Can't you postpone that until tomorrow?"

"No, the planes are fully booked."

"Let me come by the hotel for a few minutes right now. I must talk to you about something very important. I'll talk while you pack."

"Okay, but you'll have to hurry! I leave the hotel in about an hour."

"I'll call from the lobby. *Hasta luego!*"

"*Hasta luego!*"

I began to rush. Things became more frantic when it was time to leave. I started to stuff my document case. Before I could finish, the phone rang.

"This is Percy. I'm down in the lobby."

"Come on up! The door is open."

I went quickly to the door, opened it wide, and hurried back to my packing.

In a few minutes Percy arrived. With him was a thin, hungry looking companion, whom he introduced as his partner. We exchanged business cards. Percy, ebullient, intense, and with a pleasant countenance, was president of a small import firm, dealing in aircraft parts and instruments.

"I'm running out of time, so let's move along."

"I only need a minute," Percy said confidently, as he closed the door. "We have to be careful, you know." He glanced around the room. "That's why I came over. The phones are all bugged. Government spies listen to everything."

I knew about that. Using a code when calling Seattle, I never mentioned prices or terms, particularly concessions—and never a word about consultants.

"*Asienta se,*" I invited.

We sat around a little table, pulling it up close to the bed so the third man could sit on the edge.

Percy was all business, explaining how important it was to have connections in the government, claiming to have the best.

"The next time you come to Lima, I'll take you to meet some important people," he offered, smiling.

"For example?"

"To start, the president of *Banco Nacion*, but I'm also a personal friend of the *Ministro de Transportes*. Let's just call him Harry. If you don't mind, I'll send you some information by airmail that will prove that we have good relations with him."

Percy's partner said nothing, simply nodding and smiling all the while.

I was getting interested. Percy sounded like the kind of person we were looking for, with connections and a good grasp of aircraft technology—a difficult combination to find. Then he threw me a curve.

"I'm the master of B and C," he announced.

"B and C?"

"Yeah, bribery and corruption."

I raised an eyebrow. "I don't understand those terms," I replied starchily. "Boeing doesn't deal on those terms. We are a very conservative company."

"I know, I know—but you want to sell airplanes, no?"

"Of course. But we have strict rules. You would have to sign a contract that commits you to steer clear of bribes and payoffs."

"Okay, *no problema*, we only deal with friends. Everybody in Peru has friends. There's no other way to do business."

Percy's partner was nodding more emphatically.

I glanced at my watch. "I have to run for the airport. I'll look forward to hearing from you. We'll not make up our minds in a hurry, probably not before the end of the year. AeroPeru isn't going to buy anything right away. If fat turkeys were selling for five *soles* each (about two cents), they couldn't afford to buy a single butt."

Everybody laughed.

"You're right about AeroPeru, but just remember we need time to pave the way with the government and the banks." He extended his hand.

"*Muy bien viaje!*" he said.

"*Gracias, y buena suerte por ustedes,*" I replied, shaking hands with both men.


I was off to Paramaríbo, Surinam—and started taking malaria pills.

I had routed myself via Quito, as Colonel Banderas had an open door, which I took advantage of to keep up on the fast-moving events. Alfonso Fiallos, Edison Teran, and Oswaldo Lara had become my close friends, and on every visit, I invited each of them with their wives to dinner at the Colon Hotel.

Alfonso and his wife, Susanna, were becoming like family. They invited me into their home, where I met their two little girls, Selma and Saskia, seven and eight years old.

When I mentioned mountain climbing to Alfonso, his ears perked up.

"Gene, you know how attractive our mountains are for foreign climbers, and I have many friends who climb," he confided one day. "But we only have primitive equipment, and we can't afford those fancy boots."

"Alfonso, I have an idea," I proposed "Let's plan on climbing Cotopaxi as soon as the best season arrives."

"I've never climbed, and Cotopaxi is over 19,000 feet—I think a little high for a start."

"Okay. Let's plan on going up Pichincha. It's not quite 16,000 feet. We can do it on a weekend."


Relaxing on the flight to Caracas, on the way to Paramaríbo, I congratulated myself on the good relations which were developing in Quito.

# 16

There were no direct flights to Surinam. International traffic from South American countries was being funneled through Caracas, a frighteningly congested airport, bursting at the gates with travelers. There was no possibility of getting through the same day, and with the Caracas hotels geared to large tour groups, the prospects of obtaining a single room for one night were poor.

My Pan American flight from Quito arrived late in the evening, and it was past ten o'clock when I reached the downtown hotel.

"Mr. Bauer, we're sorry, but we don't show a reservation for you," the clerk announced, with a sad face.

My trip itineraries were planned in advance from Seattle, including guaranteed payment for late arrivals, and the Boeing travel office always included copies of confirmation telexes in the envelope. I opened my briefcase and handed him a copy of the confirming telex, which was dated three weeks before.

"*Un momento,*" he said, disappearing into the back room. After a rather long wait, he came out, a big smile on his face.

"Oh, yes, Mr. Bauer, please forgive us—we just mislaid the confirmation. We hope you have a pleasant stay."

I had resigned myself to this familiar scenario, but I found Caracas to be far worse than the others.


It was Wednesday, February 4, 1976, when I arrived in Paramaríbo, Surinam, for a two-day visit to meet airline executives and explore the airline's potential.

Meeting with Mr. K. C. de Miranda, the director of Civil Aviation the next day, the setting was almost comical. He had no office, and we met in an old, one-room shack with white-washed walls. I believe it was a garage, but all I could think of was the chicken coop back on my father's homestead in Montana.

Mr. Miranda sat behind a battered wooden desk, bare except for a telephone and a scratch pad. The only other furniture in the room was a small stool, where I was invited to sit.

"My apologies for these modest facilities, Mr. Bauer," he said, "but my office is being remodeled."

Surinam had only received its independence from Holland the previous November, and change was the order of the day.

"I understand. Office facilities are not so important. In an airline, it's the airplanes that count."

Miranda winced.

"Actually, Mr. Bauer, we don't have an official airline right now," he said, with a pained expression. "We're still in the planning stage."

"But I have a flight schedule."

"Oh, that! We have a pool agreement with KLM. They come in twice a week with a DC-8. Then there's Antillian Airlines, a subsidiary of KLM. They fly DC-9s in here from Curaçao five times a week."

"Have you considered the Boeing 737-200 in your plans for domestic and regional service?" I questioned.

"We know about the 737. Air France flies one in here twice a week from Port of Spain, but we're not considering short-range airplanes—we want to begin with long-range—for international service. What we really want is a cargo version of your SP airplane."

Amazed, I glanced around the chicken coop, groping for words.

"Unfortunately Mr. Miranda, a cargo version of the SP is not in Boeing's current plan. We would need a sizeable order to launch a program. But we're working on a longer-range version of the big 747, with the main deck divided to carry both passengers and cargo."

Undeterred, Miranda continued. "Well, we're not talking about needing planes right away. We want to develop a free port here in Paramaríbo to tie European cargo markets with the Far East, and provide a gateway to all of South America."

I was impressed by the audacity of the program—but I was from Missouri.

"You have an excellent idea there. I would be pleased to bring you a copy of our study of worldwide cargo movements, and Boeing's forecast for potential growth."

"Oh, thank you very much, that's very kind of you."

"I'll put it in the mail as soon as I return to Seattle next week."

The following Sunday, I took an Air France 737 to Port of Spain Trinidad, to visit British West Indian Airways (BWIA), which everybody referred to as simply *BeeWee*—my first account in a country with an English heritage. *Life should be a little easier.*

Waves of crimson swept over the jungle green below "Fat Albert" as it made its landing approach. The mystery of those crimson waves was soon solved when I learned that they were huge flocks of scarlet ibis moving restlessly from place to place in the Caroni Swamp, adjacent to Piarco International Airport.

My mission to the twin-island country of Trinidad and Tobago, which we referred to simply as Trinidad, was to rescue a dead-ended sales campaign with BWIA, the government-owned international flag carrier. The airline served the Caribbean, flew north to New York and Toronto, and east to London.

Run by a loosely knit group of managers who reflected the diverse elements of a society of severely striated ethnic groups, BWIA had suffered through a series of ill-considered decisions.

As a business entity, its government ownership caused the most insignificant details to be thrown into the argumentative arena of Parliament, and the temper of the Press, resulting in no action except through committee and public debate, the worst possible climate for an enterprise seeking profit in perhaps the most competitive of all undertakings, an international airline.

Splitting off from the old British Overseas Airways (BOAC) after the country's independence in the '60s, BWIA found it difficult to operate. To save the airline from total disaster, the government purchased 90 percent of the equity, sold the old Britannia airplanes, and purchased 707s. It was a good start.

A few years later, the rejuvenated airline purchased three new 727-100 airplanes from Boeing, ideal equipment for the short island hops and the nonstop run to Miami. As traffic grew on these routes, lack of professional leadership led them to sell the 727s and to purchase additional 707s to increase capacity, under the mistaken idea that "standardizing" with a single model would bring additional profits. However, they soon learned that the four-engined 707s were unsuited for their island-hopping routes. A much better plan would have been to buy twin-engined machines.

They immediately began to lose money, and the government belatedly decided to seek professional help from the Europeans, hiring Mr. Eric Svanberg, a manager from Scandinavian Airlines (SAS), as chief executive.

Svanberg was faced with pressures from all sides of the multifaceted, politically oriented airline. He had to choose between going back to the 727s, a favorite of the pilots, or buying the 737-200 or DC-9 twinjets. He decided to consider only the twins.

Unknown to me, while I was preoccupied in South America preparing for the SP demos, competitive proposals had been submitted by both Boeing and McDonnell Douglas over a year before I arrived on the scene. The airline had selected the DC-9.

Faced with the reality of that decision, the BWIA pilots' association had staged an eleventh-hour revolt, refusing to fly the DC-9s if the purchase was carried out. The united voices of 130 pilots were impossible to ignore. The government was left no choice, except to terminate the contract negotiations. They announced the launching of a "new, detailed reevaluation to get all the facts from the two competitors and then to purchase the airplane with the most favorable attributes."

Mr. Svanberg was personally convinced that Boeing was the behind-the-scenes culprit in the pilots' revolt and laid the blame directly on Bob Brog, who was the regional sales director at the time.

It was part of the salesmen's cross to take responsibility when airline management perceived that things were going wrong, and they were losing confidence. That was a major reason for shifting accounts. *New faces had a germinating effect to foster new outlooks. I represented that new face.*

To be certain my mind was not clouded with previous events, Boeing management had not told me about the sales history.

I had arranged an appointment with Mr. Svanberg for Monday morning, the 9th of February, to begin the delicate campaign of winning back the confidence of BWIA, not only in the integrity of the management of Boeing, but also to convince them that the 737-200 was the best technical and economical choice.

It was a tailor-made assignment for me, an incurable optimist—honest, hard driving, open faced—and at once believable. The meeting with Svanberg was intense and direct. I listened patiently for over an hour about the problems, plans, and goals of the airline. He was courteous, but brisk and accusative. I felt like a student being lectured by a stern master.

"Mr. Bauer, there is one thing that I must make very clear," he concluded, piquing my attention. "That is the manner in which the campaign was conducted. I was shocked at the way Boeing worked behind the scenes through the pilots, without ever bringing the case to the attention of top management."

He gave me a hard look, his huge frame and intense demeanor confronting me as a juggernaut of determination.

"The decision was at the board level when the Pilots' Association came in with an official statement against the DC-9. It was extremely embarrassing!"

There was only one possible response.

"Mr. Svanberg, I'm here to assure the management of BWIA that whatever happened during that campaign, if it was not done in accordance with the most ethical of business practices, it definitely did not have the blessing of top Boeing management."

I paused.

"Everybody has friends, particularly in such a campaign. It's easy to develop loyalties. We're convinced it was through such loyalties that some actions may have been taken not conducive to the highest ethical standards," I concluded.

Svanberg seemed relieved. "Yes, I understand perfectly, and I'm pleased that Boeing has sent you down here to start things on a new note."

"Our policy is to come through the front door," I stated flatly. "You can count on it. I will personally see to that. My contact will always be through the office of the president. Anyone who comes here from Boeing will be announced through me."

"Thank you very much, Mr. Bauer. I think we understand each other. The government has decided to appoint a Trinidadian to take my job. I'm going back home to SAS in about thirty days, and the new man, Mr. Peter Look Hong, will assume responsibility. I would introduce you now, but he's in Europe taking executive training courses. We expect him back the first of March. Naturally, there will be a transition period, and then on the first of April he'll be on his own."

"I see. It sounds like a tough job for Mr. Look Hong. Boeing will do its best to help him."

"True, it will be difficult. But he has extensive experience in the airline. He started as station manager at the airport twenty-four years ago and worked up through the marketing organization. We're also bringing in a strong executive as board chairman, Mr. John Scoon. He's a very successful banker here in Trinidad. I think we'll have a good team."

"Our analysts are updating the 737 performance study for the BWIA

Caribbean route network that you requested. I'll bring Roger Wynne with me the first week in March to present that data."

"Oh, yes, good. I know Roger—a fine chap. He's been a great help to us in our route analysis. Please give him my regards."

Svanberg was leaving, but his influence appeared to be substantial. "Your planning has been very thorough," I observed. "I'll be looking forward to meeting Mr. Look Hong next month. Thank you for devoting so much of your valuable time to these discussions."

"It was a pleasure to talk to you."

Svanberg was finally smiling, and his pleasant, round Nordic face with the keen blue eyes left me with a quiet confidence—indeed regrets that he would be leaving.

# 17

**B**ack home, during the next few weeks, I devoted myself to an intensive education program.

Trinidad and Tobago had gained their independence on August 31, 1962, a time of impending international crisis. Britain refused continued economic aid after the independence, putting the island nation on its own, and only ten days later, announced the decision to seek admission to the European Economic Community (EEC), causing doubts about the future of traditional exports from the islands.

A month later, President Kennedy, in a somber speech, alerted the world to the Cuban missile crisis, raising the spectre of nuclear war and heralding unrest in the Caribbean community of nations.

Geographically, the two islands are insignificant. Trinidad, 1,864 square miles in area, the southernmost in the Caribbean, lies within sight of the Venezuelan coast. Its smaller companion, Tobago, only 116 square miles, is located twenty miles to the northeast.

Together, Trinidad and Tobago had slightly over one million people at the beginning of the '70s, with Port of Spain, the principal city and seat of government, claiming fully one-fourth of the total. The ethnic mix was as varied as any part of the world: consisting of 43 percent Africans; 37 percent East Indians, mostly Hindu; 2 percent Europeans; 1 percent Chinese; and the remainder other nationalities. Roman Catholic was the predominant religion.

The government was patterned after the motherland, with a Parliament. Representatives were elected for five-year terms by universal adult suffrage. Members of the Senate were nominated by a governor-general in consultation with, and on the advice of the Prime Minister and the leader of the Opposition. The governor-general was appointed by the Queen of England during the period that the country remained part of the Commonwealth. However, that power was eliminated in September 1976, when Trinidad and Tobago declared itself a republic.

In the ten years after independence, a number of crises deepened throughout the world, with ripple effects for the multiracial country. Serious racial problems developed among Asians within their own countries in Malaysia, Singapore, Bangladesh, and Ceylon; between Africans and Asians in Guyana and East Africa; between whites and blacks in Rhodesia, the United States, and the United Kingdom, with sharp undertones in Canada; and between Catholic whites and Protestant whites in Northern Ireland.

Growing conflict was apparent between the developed and developing countries in terms of trade and foreign ownership of their natural resources—particularly in respect to oil in the OPEC countries and bauxite in Guyana, Jamaica, and Surinam.

Originally a land of sugar and coconuts, oil became the catalyst for economic progress in Trinidad and Tobago.

Offshore exploration was promising, geologists reporting the structure to be a continuation of the Venezuelan fields. In the early '70s, large quantities of natural gas were proven in offshore wells. A liquified gas plant and pipeline were under construction. With the anti-refinery climate in the United States at the time, Trinidad also offered sites for additional refineries, providing further stimulus to the economy. The

GNP per capita of $866 in 1962 rose to $1,275 by 1974, a compound annual rate of 3.5 percent, excellent growth for a developing country for such a sustained period.

The words of Prime Minister Eric Williams on independence day in 1962 continued to be true:

"There can be no Mother India for those whose ancestors came from India—there can be no Mother Africa for those of African origin—there can be no Mother England and no dual loyalties—there can be no Mother China even if we could agree as to which China is the Mother—and there can be no Mother Syria or no Mother Lebanon. A nation, like an individual, can only have one Mother. The only Mother we recognize is Mother Trinidad and Tobago, and Mother cannot discriminate between her children."

The intermarriage among the races in Trinidad and Tobago created a Trinidadian, who began to be recognized as such, and a national culture, which found its own niche in the world. Perhaps more than any other one thing, the music built around the unusual qualities of the "pans," the descendants of plain steel oil drums, had welded a nation of individuals into a true community.

The second force for nationhood was the remarkable staying qualities of Dr. Williams himself, who remained in power nearly five terms, dying in office on March 29, 1981, at the age of sixty-nine. Brooding over his people like a mother hen, he knew when to spoon-feed them, when to jolt them, and when to listen.

It was not until the second visit that I began to size up the physical attributes of the islands—and the infrastructure that would support a modern airline. The facilities at Piarco were dismal. Airplanes were loaded and unloaded by hand, unshielded from the sixty-four inches of annual downpours. Uncaring laborers tossed the bags onto the cement dock, often causing them to burst like ripe watermelons.

Passage through customs would have been hilarious except for waiting in long lines in the oppressive heat, always lurking around 100 degrees in the summer. Customs agents, reveling in the authority of their newly won badges, repeated an endless litany of irrelevant questions. Two hours was about the minimum for elapsed time between deplaning and getting a taxi, and four hours was not unusual.

The natives, famous for calypso, limbo, and pan music, also had a talent for jesting. BWIA, which had more troubles than one could imagine, was a favorite butt of their jokes. "Believe it When It Arrives," and other colorful phrases were used to lampoon the airline. Even the tiny commuter airline, Trinidad and Tobago Air Services (TTAS), which flew only between Port of Spain and Crown Point, did not escape their attention. A favorite jest was, Take a Ticket And Suffer."

Piarco Airport was seventeen miles from the hotel, connected by a two-lane highway, a road choked with automobiles, trucks, and oxcarts. During the busy periods of the day, an hour and fifteen minutes was necessary to make that traverse. The picturesque trip was fraught with danger. I subdued my fears by diverting my attention from the road to the unfolding countryside. On rare openings in the stream of traffic, the drivers zipped in and out, taking our lives in their hands every time. Statistics in the morning newspapers justified my fears. I adopted a practice of sliding over to the left side of the right-handed-steering cars, thinking at least I would avoid the center of impact.

The road wound through fields of sugar cane, nurtured and harvested by hand. Oxen, plodding through the fields next to the airport, pulling wooden carts, were in sharp contrast to the modern jet airplanes parked on the apron.

Considered to be an expensive boondoggle by the local populace at the time, the road—a winding, deeply rutted oxcart path—had been converted during World War II by the occupying U. S. Army.

In early 1976, belatedly recognizing the need for modernization, the government embarked on an ambitious project to widen the highway to four lanes. My arrival coincided with the first bulldozers—and the worst was yet to come.

Already accustomed to frightful telephone systems, I could hardly have imagined anything worse. The phone lines were often dead, particularly during the rainy season, when they would be completely out for days at a time. BWIA had long since capitulated—setting up a short wave radio system to communicate between their downtown offices and the airport.

Trinidad had neither the geographic location, the climate, nor the mood to be a place of business. It was a lazy, lovely island that lulled its captives into complacency. The idyllic retreat of Tobago, habitat of Robinson Crusoe, was even more tranquil.

Perhaps tragically, the shape of the economic world surrounding them, and the blessing or curse of abundant oil, demanded that they be dragged reluctantly into the mainstream of the twentieth century.

The Trinidad Hilton, situated on a hill above the city of Port of Spain, overlooks a beautiful harbor. Historically, its calm tropical waters were hosts to pirates, explorers, and merchantmen alike, but now it sat heavy with oil tankers. The Hilton was billed as the world's only "upside-down" hotel. With the access road terminating at the crest of the hill, the lobby is on the top of the building, the remainder hanging down the slope, resting on the shoulder of a ravine below. The twelfth floor is at the very bottom.

The first week of March, Roger Wynne joined me as I kicked off the intensive sales effort. Our meeting with Mr. Svanberg was cordial.

"Mr. Bauer, I'm pleased to introduce you to Peter Look Hong," he announced. "He's taking over at the end of the month, and I'm going home."

"I'll be needing a lot of help!" Peter exclaimed, stepping forward to greet us.

"You can count on Boeing whenever we have something to offer," I assured him, as we shook hands.

"My director of long-term planning, Glenn Castagne, will be doing the analysis, and you should work closely with him."

After introducing Roger, we departed for Castagne's office. BWIA had established a target date for introduction of new medium-range planes in just fifteen months, so a decision would be necessary by June to allow time for manufacture.

"Welcome back to Trinidad," Castagne said with a big smile, shaking hands with Roger and looking expectantly toward me.

"It's my pleasure to meet you," I offered, extending my hand. "I'm the new sales director from Boeing."

Castagne motioned us to his conference table, while he called the secretary to bring coffee.

I had not made an advance mental picture of Castagne, and was surprised at his youth, barely past his twenties. He appeared to be of European descent, with a fleeting mixture of more than one other ethnic group. Expecting a person of devious nature, I was relieved at his open candor.

In spite of the pleasant reception, I knew that he preferred the DC-9, and suspected the ground rules had been preweighted in its favor. An industry joke referred to that method as "picking an airplane first and then designing the route system around it." If so, we were simply aiding him in driving nails in our coffin.

"We're happy to be here, and we'd like to start at square one," I said. "Roger has completed the performance analysis in accordance with your ground rules."

Roger took several copies of a formal document from his briefcase, and handed a copy to Glenn.

"Fine. We're well along."

We listened to Glenn's overview.

"What about economics and fleet planning?" Roger inquired.

Glenn gave a disarming smile. "We're only requesting performance, price, and maintenance costs from all the competitors. We'll do our own route planning and economics."

Uneasy, but deciding not to pursue the issue further at the moment, I took my leave and hurried over to the office of Captain Eric Mowser, manager of flight operations, leaving Roger to discuss the performance details. Later in the day, I met with the other middle managers.

Mowser, a veteran RAF pilot from World War II days, appeared to be a confirmed Boeing advocate when he declared, "Look, Gene, we're firmly on the Boeing tree. It would take a very traumatic thing to change that now!"

Nevertheless, he was preoccupied with keeping the 707 fleet in the air, and seven operational airplanes were a full-time job. Therefore—

like all of the other managers—he was merely playing a waiting game for the "Castagne Report." For BWIA, but particularly for Boeing, that was a perilous approach. I decided on a strategy of designating a specific Boeing individual to interface with each of the managers in the airline—matching like disciplines. *We would cover them like a wet blanket—and also play the consultant card.*

BWIA had strong ties with Canada as a result of its common heritage, and thus it was convenient for us to utilize our Canadian consultant in Toronto, Ken Patrick. Ken had assigned a portion of his potential 2 percent commission to Bruce Procope, a local lawyer in Port of Spain.

When I returned to the hotel in the evening, there was a call from the lobby.

"Hello, Mr. Bauer, this is Bruce—Bruce Procope. Ken Patrick told me you were here."

"I'm pleased to hear from you. Why don't you drop down to room 723 for a chat?"

In a few moments, I answered the knock on the door, and Bruce appeared. A round, robust black man with shining eyes, he was a bundle of energy, too much in a hurry to sit down.

"You're well acquainted here, and know where the bones are buried," I said. "But I'm very concerned by the way the evaluation is being conducted."

Bruce looked at me sharply. "You mean Castagne?"

"Right, it looks as if we're playing right into his hands."

"Don't worry, Mr. Bauer—Gene—may I call you Gene?"

*The signal to begin worrying,* I thought.

"Of course. We don't have any reason for formalities."

"Gene, let's let Castagne play his games. I know Peter, and I'm sure he'll be watchdogging the progress of the planning. Anyway, the government will make the final decision."

"I met Peter today. He seems very tentative—not sure of himself—is he Chinese?"

"Partly—his father is from Taiwan—and he married a local. Everybody here is a mixture. He's a quiet chap, but I think capable. The problem is the government wants a true Trinidadian to be in charge, and there's not much choice. Mowser is far better qualified, but he's not a native. They're depending on Scoon to give Peter a little backbone."

"Do you have access to the prime minister?"

"Certainly. Eric is a friend of the family."

"Bruce, please keep your ear to the ground. We don't have much time. With the decision set for June, I expect Castagne's report will be due in May."

"I understand."

"Please call me direct in Seattle, at the slightest indication of the way the wind is blowing. And, by the way, try to find out what our competitors are doing."

"Don't worry."

I winced.

TTAS, operating the Trinidad-Tobago, half-hour commute with two old DC-6B airplanes, served under the same board of directors as BWIA, and Peter Pena, its president, whom I met the next day, was poles apart in his equipment requirements. Further, Pena proved to be a capable analyst, and had no intention of rolling over for the strong-minded chairman.

TTAS had received a proposal from Hawker-Siddeley for an HS-748 turboprop the day before I arrived, and was in the middle of an evaluation.

Pena was informal, knowledgeable, incisive—coming straight to the center of the issue.

"Gene, we only have thirty days to respond to Hawker-Siddeley. I want Boeing to evaluate this proposal and tell me how it stacks up against the 737-200," he said.

"Fine, we'll get right at it."

"But I need a document in my hands next week. I've got a lot of convincing to do."

"We can do it. I'll telex the proposal to Seattle this afternoon, and we'll send a messenger down with the analysis. You'll have your document, and we'll be back here for a presentation to the board of directors before the end of the month."

The politically charged, biased climate at BWIA was proving to be only the tip of the iceberg. Our options were clear—fold our cards, or step up to a costly, balls-out campaign.

# 18

Boeing decided to bite the bullet in Trinidad, and I had orders to spend as much time as possible in Port of Spain during April and May.

I was beginning to feel like a juggler with six pins in the air at the same time: Faucett, AeroPeru, Tame, Ecuatoriana, BWIA, and TTAS were all on the front burner.

Besides, I had promised an early visit to Guyana Airways in Georgetown. Fortunately, Pan Am flew daily flights, and I decided to take a quick, one-day hop to introduce myself to Guyana Airways.

I found a country of abject poverty. Gaining independence from Great Britain in 1966, Guyana quickly fell into the Castro camp, the only country in South America to do so. Georgetown was dirty and run-down, teeming with robbers.

Captain Chana-sae, manager of flight operations, picked me up at the hotel, insisting it was dangerous for a foreigner to walk down Main Street—even at high noon.

"What about the police?" I inquired, noting there were a number of uniformed officers on the sidewalks.

"Oh, they don't pay any attention," he laughed. "You must look out for yourself."

"We're very sorry, but Mr. Abrams, our president, was nearly killed in an automobile accident," he continued.

"Terrible! I talked to him on the phone from Port of Spain on Tuesday—just the day before yesterday! And how is he now?"

"Well, he'll be out for at least a month, so we'll struggle along. But there are a couple of things we'd like to talk about."

Chana-sae introduced me to Mr. Loy, the chief engineer, and we discussed the airline's equipment plans.

With one old, poorly maintained DC-6B flying cargo from Miami representing their total fleet, they had visions of purchasing a convertible jet, and they had heard about the 737.

Operating on a shoestring, there was no way they could finance a purchase. Nevertheless, I agreed to develop a route analysis and a forecast of cargo traffic. The country contained the world's largest deposits of bauxite, and it was conceivable the economy could be turned around over the next few years. I promised to return when Mr. Abrams was back in the saddle.

The next morning, I arose before dawn for the forty-mile trip over jungle roads to the airport, a traverse which had seemed never to end the night before.

A sump pump groaned and hissed beside the road as it labored to keep ahead of the rising water from a sudden shower. Soon, water rose to the road level and began washing over it. Sections of the roadway were jammed with pedestrians and horses, with an occasional oxcart creaking along on wooden wheels. Goats loped unconcernedly between the cars, and squawking chickens fluttered to the safety of the ditches.

This was not an unusual season, nor the aftermath of a rural catastrophe; rather, it was perfectly normal—so normal that the populace was conditioned to accept it without complaint.

The taxi coughed and sputtered, threatening to die by the wayside at any moment, as I kept glancing anxiously at my watch, counting the minutes until flight time.

Finally reaching the airport, already exhausted from the two-hour ride, I hurried to the door of the terminal building, which I was barely able to push open. The inside was packed with wall-to-wall humanity. I was a full hour early, but I broke out in a cold sweat a few minutes later, when the loudspeaker blared, "Pan Am Flight 905 is now boarding."

*My flight!*

An error, I reflected, unable to see the departure gate over the massed crowd. I scanned the walls for a clock to check my watch. None! *Probably stolen the day after the terminal was opened.*

There was no time to exchange currency, and I plowed forward to reach the check-in counter. Twenty minutes passed in a flash. Then I fought my way to the immigration checkpoint. Quickly, it became clear that nine-tenths of the people were not going anywhere at all; they were family members who had come to say goodbye, clinging to the passengers' clothing until the last second.

All the while the speaker intoned the impending departure of the flight. Finally, a flight attendant appeared and the passengers began boarding.

Parked on the apron was the big jet, resplendent in silver and blue, its powerful engines ready at the touch of the pilot's finger to bring thousands of pounds of thrust into action.

Once on board, I had time to reflect on the airport atmosphere, the jungle environment, and the new nation struggling to be born.

The change in scene from gate to loading stairs was dramatic. I had literally passed through an invisible "technology curtain"—a curtain separating two worlds. On board, all was cool efficiency. Outside, dispatchers waggled their signals. Mechanics made their last-minute checks. The captain strolled casually under the wing, peering upward to spy any unusual condition. Everywhere there was calm and confidence.

The stifling heat and oppressive humidity bowed to the

air-conditioned interior. I plumped down in a magnificently engineered seat, and listened to music played over a transistorized system. Departure time arrived—and passed.

Everyone on board waited impatiently for the Third World over there in the terminal—on the other side of the technology curtain. Scarcely 100 yards away, the primitive methods, broken-down machines, and poorly trained personnel were still sorting out the last of the passengers.

Lima and Quito, Caracas and Rio, and many other cities had inadequate facilities, but nowhere else had I found such a profound lack. It seemed clear that a market for new airplanes in Guyana was indeed somewhere beyond the horizon.


Returning to Port of Spain, I spent most of the time by the hotel pool, keeping track of the McDonnell Douglas salesman. It was a deadly serious game, each trying to outwit the other. When one of us disappeared from poolside, the other began to make inquiries to determine if he was meeting with airline or government executives. Geoff Paterson, manager of public relations for BWIA, proved to be a Boeing disciple, and a series of quick, short visits to his office kept me posted.

My next demand date in Trinidad was at TTAS the first week of April, and I headed back to Seattle to get ready for another swing to Lima and Quito.


Reverberations from the Lockheed scandal, which had burst upon the international scene in the summer of 1975, quickly spread. American news media, still fresh from their Watergate bonanza, welcomed the unfolding drama, exploiting and sensationalizing each new disclosure. On the cover of its February 23, 1976, issue, *Time* announced "The Big Payoff, Lockheed Scandal, Graft Around the Globe." *Newsweek* printed a feature story. Many newspapers, including the *Washington Post* and the *New York Times*, embarked on a series of overblown editorial comments.

Outcries in the Congress were becoming more strident, and the wheels started turning slowing toward a law addressing itself to the problem.

I was ready for the road toward the end of March, and a visit to Lima was overdue—nearly two months since I had left.

In Peru, the grapevine was very much alive. Percy called before I had finished packing.

"*Hola, me amigo, bienvenida!*" he exclaimed.

"*Hola, que pasa aquí?*"

"Gene, there's nothing going on now. The government is in some turmoil. But it's important to keep working on the inside. I can help."

I paused.

"Are you still there?" he inquired.

Boeing had decided not to retain Percy as a consultant, as even Alfredo was reluctant to recommend him in the light of the latest SEC investigations. I decided to stall.

"Percy, we haven't made up our minds about a consultant. Maybe we won't hire anybody—but we'll be in touch."

My meeting with General Berckemeyer was cordial, but he was pushing everything off on the Peruvian government.

Federico Pastor was feeling glum. "Things are pretty bad. The load factors are way down."

"Have you been in contact with Gonzalo?"

"He says the 747SP is too big, and too expensive. And he's certain they'll only buy used."

"I see. By the way, please give my best to him—and the Señora. We haven't decided about a consultant yet. Tell him the big brass is still thinking about it."

"There was a lot of interest in the L-1011s, but we can't talk to Lockheed anymore," Federico announced.

I perked up my ears. "Yes?"

He reached over to the side and held up a copy of the February 23 issue of *Time*.

"Lockheed representatives aren't welcome," he said emphatically.

*One competitor down,* I mused.

"How are the DC-8s doing?"

"AeroPeru has a new rule—employees are restricted from flying on foreign airlines. We have to fly the 8s."

"So what do you do?"

Federico looked sheepish.

"Well, I go on days when we have no flights—and book on Braniff."


Giesela was glad to see Lockheed out of the picture, but was still warning me of "Dŏŏŏŏglas."

"I don't foresee any progress by AeroPeru for the next year or two," I said. "So I'm currently concentrating on helping our people with Revoredo's campaign to get another used 727-100."

General Revoredo had made an urgent inquiry to Boeing to find a used 727-100 convertible airplane to handle Faucett's growing traffic to Miami. We had exactly the right airplane for him, but alas, due to U.S. tax laws, a lease to a foreign carrier would result in exorbitant fees to the lessee, and Faucett had no money to purchase it. The Peruvian government was still refusing to guarantee loans from American banks. The only way out was to find a third party willing to put together a lease/buy deal.

Such an individual appeared in the person of James "Jim" Matthews, a retired Eastern Airlines captain, who had recently formed International Flight Research Corporation in Miami, specializing in such deals.

Used airplanes were handled by the inventory sales department at Boeing, entirely by correspondence—thus I took on the task of providing liaison assistance in Peru.

During the preceding months, Revoredo and I had become good personal friends, talking at length about his early exploits in the little Stinsons.

"General Revoredo, I want to write your story," I told him one day. He had laughed and put it off as nothing. Nevertheless, I was doing free-lance writing, and had been quietly taking notes. The time seemed right for more discussions.

I had not met Jim Matthews, but knew he was staying at the Crillon Hotel. We needed to work together, so I called him.

"Hello, Jim, this is Gene Bauer, the Boeing guy. How is the Faucett deal going?"

"Oh! Gene—it's great to hear you. Well, we expect the deal to be completed any day. Maybe on the 29th. You know, they're celebrating the anniversary of Revoredo's flight."

My heart sank. "Who?"

"Everybody. The Air Force is doing a show at Jorge Chavez, and Faucett is putting on a big bash. The actual anniversary date is the 27th, but they decided to do it on Monday."

"But it's only the 39th anniversary! My God, I didn't bring a single gift! We generally plan for this type of occasion way ahead of time, and we were looking at the 40th."

"Well, you know the general is seventy-nine years old, and I believe they thought he might not make it for another year."

Now, I *was* near panic. After all the attention I had paid to the general's accomplishments, I would arrive at Faucett empty-handed! *Gifts are fundamental in Latin America!*

"Boy, am I in trouble. When I get home I'll be hung, drawn, and quartered!"

"Don't worry, Gene, I brought a huge trophy—it's enough for both of us," he offered. "I'll see you at Faucett on Monday."

Numb, I hung up the phone.

In the afternoon, I visited Faucett. Elsa greeted me cordially, but had a sad look.

*"Que pasa, mi amiga!"* I exclaimed. "You should be happy with the celebration."

Elsa wiped away a tear. "It's about the general," she wept. "He's dying of cancer."

Now I was certain that I would write his story. But the lack of a gift was weighing even more heavily.

"The General is not here today, but you'll see him at the celebration."

I cringed.

Back at the hotel, I racked my brain for something appropriate. *What to do in the face of the prestigious Matthews gift?*

Revoredo had told me one day that he had also done free lance writing, even sending an article to the United States for publication. It was the story of Jim Faucett, American barnstorming air pioneer and founder of Faucett airlines. He had submitted the story to the *Readers Digest* for their feature, "The Most Unforgettable Character I Ever Met."

I decided to write a poem about the General's life. After all, I had two days—*plenty of time to reinvent the world!*

The urgency increased when I read *La Prensa,* Lima's leading newspaper, the next morning. Dominating the front page was a salute to General Revoredo.

The announcement read in part:

*". . . invites all employees and all retirees to the airline headquarters, at 11:00 o'clock on Monday, to pay tribute to Sr. Mayor General (R) FAP Armando Revoredo Iglesias, on the occasion of the 39th anniversary of his historic nonstop flight from Lima to Buenos Aires. "[1]*

1. *La Prensa,* 27 March 1976.

# 19

I hardly left the hotel on the weekend, poring over my notes and composing the poem. Late on Sunday afternoon, it was ready. There was no place to get it typed, so I lettered it by hand on Boeing stationery.

Lima, Peru
March 29, 1976

General Armando Revoredo, Managing Director
AeroFaucett
Aeropuerto Jorge Chavez
Lima, Peru

Dear General Revoredo,

On the occasion of the 39th anniversary of your historic flight over the Andes, on behalf of all your good friends at Boeing, I extend our most sincere good wishes.

It has been our fervent hope that your 727 airplane purchase would be completed long before this date, but perhaps, even today, we will achieve that success.

On this occasion also, I must add a personal note. When I first came to Peru as a Boeing salesman in August of 1974, you were the first airline official whom I had the pleasure to meet. In looking back, I regard this association as the most interesting, helpful, and pleasant of any that I have made since.

It is difficult for me to determine what is most appropriate to do on an occasion such as this, since your accomplishments rate among the very highest of the world's air pioneers in the history of aviation.

I have therefore taken up my pen to write a poem, which I call "Ode to a Flier," which I hope you will enjoy.

> Kindest personal regards,
> Eugene E. Bauer
> Regional Sales Director, S.A.

I wrote the poem in English, then translated it into Spanish. It didn't work! Poetry just doesn't translate. So I went back to English, hoping Revoredo would understand.

Monday, March 29, 1976, was a day to remember. At Faucett headquarters, a brightly festooned podium on a raised platform had been constructed for the featured speakers, with rows of hastily built bleachers half encircling it. A military band played the national hymn of the Peruvian aviators, a poem written by Revoredo's beloved wife, Maria, and set to music.

*"Up, always up . . . owners of space,*
*Of the earth and the sea.*
*We will never die. . . ."*

Overhead, a squadron of the Peruvian Air Force rolled and dived their Russian built MIGs in a dazzling display of power.

To the side, resplendent on its permanent pedestal, *Él Chico*, Revoredo's little single engine monoplane, shone in the bright sunlight—where it had stood since that historic flight.

Crowds were gathering—all of Faucett's 300 employees, its retirees, government officials, Air Force brass, U.S. embassy representatives, and members of the press, flashing their cameras in everybody's faces.

Expecting to merely hand the letter with the poem to the general in an envelope, my anxiety peaked when Revoredo personally invited me to a chair among the honored guests!

When the band finished, Gustavo Aspillaga, vice chairman of the board, stepped to the microphone as the master of ceremonies.

As was the custom in Peru, he delivered a ringing speech—a testimonial to the accomplishments of General Revoredo—presenting a beautiful bronze trophy with a tiny replica of *Él Chico* mounted on the top, on behalf of the airline employees.

Next came Ambassador Robert Dean of the U.S. embassy in Lima. Dean spoke briefly, also presenting a handsome trophy, with an inscription attesting to the importance of Revoredo's accomplishments in furthering commercial aviation.

Jim Matthews followed with a short speech, hoisting the huge trophy up for the photographers to get a good view.

The butterflies were really fluttering in my stomach when Aspillaga finally turned to me. I stepped to the microphone.

"On behalf of all your good friends at Boeing, I salute you," I said, shaking hands with the general. "I have written a little poem which I shall read, entitled "Ode to a Flier." Please forgive me for writing it in English, but as you know, being a poet yourself, there is no way to properly translate it."


ODE TO A FLYER


To all men, both strong and bold,
The skies called for them to come;
The story, through the ages told,
For there at last they could feel at home.

Then came one, above the rest,
And fixed his gaze beyond the mountains;

Much higher than the eagle's nest,
From where there sprung the river's fountains.

Forbidding mountains, they grimly stood to wait,
Their rocky faces thrusting up;
To dare mere mortals who would penetrate,
And their solitude disrupt.

But he, with stout, courageous heart,
Steered his plane in steady flight;
Never wavering from the start,
Through mist and storm and dark of night.

And through life, the course he steers,
To run a true and steady race;
He helps to fight against man's fears,
With scalpel, pen and words of grace.

Now he sees before him darkening skies,
He hears the distant thunder, and feels the fierce winds blow;
On every side the lightning plies,
But somewhere in that storm he sees a pathway show.

When comes the time to take the stick once more,
When he hears the call from far above the mountaintops;
He will fix his compass on that distant shore,
And set the throttle at its forward stops.

After finishing, and turning to Revoredo with an embrace, I saw the tears in the old man's eyes. I believe he valued the poem more than a thousand trophies.

The conditional contract for the used airplane, which Faucett had signed on February 28th, was completed shortly thereafter, and another 727 joined the fleet.

In the ensuing months, I continued to take notes, and one day Revoredo consented to a taped interview. In December 1979, the story of his life was published in *Aerospace Historian*.[1]

A small portion of that story is reproduced here:

"At precisely a half hour past midnight, on the fog-shrouded night of March 27, 1937, a single-engine Stinson monoplane took off from Limatambo, an unimproved airfield long since buried beneath the sidewalks of the great city of Lima, Peru. The blackness was broken only by the flickering lights of a few oil-soaked torches that had been stuck into the ground at the edge of the runway.

"The tight little group who watched from the eerie darkness milled around nervously as the tiny airplane labored and strained to become airborne. Using all but a scant few meters of the runway, it finally lifted into the fog-laden air, rose with agonizing slowness, barely clearing the rooftops of the sleeping city, and was swallowed up in the black void.

"And so began—what some consider to have been the most daring and perilous flight since Lindbergh flew the Atlantic in 1927—a nonstop flight over the forbidding Andes Mountains from Lima, Peru, to Buenos Aires, Argentina.

"Alone at the controls, disdaining even a parachute in favor of fuel, was a grimly intense young airman of the Peruvian Air Force who was destined to become known as the Eagle of Peru, Lt. Cmdr. Armando Revoredo Iglesias.

"After taking off from Limatambo, Commander Revoredo turned immediately south along the coast, taking as precise a bearing as his crude instruments would allow on his destination, 3,300 km away, beyond the unconquered *cordillera* of the Andes.

"There was no opportunity for Revoredo to comment during his hair-raising takeoff since those were the days before radios in the cockpit. However, he no doubt would have simply remarked, 'The runway was exactly the right length.'

"Rejecting easier routes, Revoredo had fixed a compass course between the two cities. No mere stunt, he had set his mind on demonstrating the feasibility of commercial flights.

"The first great hurdle was the 1,000 km across the open ocean in the dead of night. And then the Andes. He had chosen to cross at their widest place.

"Known for their fierce storms which could rise from a benign sky to full fury in less than a half hour, blanketing out any visual link to the ground and replete with murderous turbulence, cross currents, and drastic temperature drops, the Andes seemed to be more than a match for the little *Chico*. Revoredo needed a lot of help from the weather, as he would be spending at least four crucial hours over that dangerous area. Within a short distance of his chosen path were a half-dozen peaks which exceeded the 5,426-meter ceiling of his plane.

"Early in the morning he sighted the coast of Chile over Iquique, and as a bright sun rose on the eastern horizon, he headed into the *cordillera*. The snow-capped mountains glistened in the clear dawn, with the jagged 6,186-meter peak of Auncanquicha nearest on his left. He kept a steady course, passing Cerro Palpana and Salar de Chalkviri in quick succession, and finally 6,225-meter Cerro Pilar.

"At 10:05 a.m., he left Chile behind, but still ahead in Argentina stood two of the Andes' mightiest mountains, Nevado de Cachi and Cerro Galan. Revoredo's route took him between the two peaks.

"His anxiety mounted as a thin layer of wispy clouds began to form in the distance, with *Él Chico* traveling at full speed, still needing two more hours to be safely through. But that day, Revoredo's guardian angel was riding beside him in the cockpit. The weather held. An hour later, he was passing Nevado de Cachi, rising nearly 7,000 meters above the plain, about twenty-five kilometers to his left. Terrifyingly beautiful, he had caught it naked in the sunlight without its treacherous robes of clouds, and he began to feel a surge of elation and a growing certainty that he would succeed.

"Around noon, as Cerro Galan, the last major hazard, passed by his right shoulder, the terrible tension drained from his body and he relaxed in the seat for the first time since he had taken off. Before him lay only the pleasant plains of Argentina.

"At 3:00 p.m. he reached *Él Palomar*, the airfield of his destination, where people had been scanning the skies for a first glimpse of OA-BBQ since sunrise."

Revoredo never told anyone then, but later he confided to me— "No one ever knew the size of my fears."

1. E. E. Bauer, *The Eagle of Peru*, <u>Aerospace Historian</u>, December 1979, 208.

# 20

When I returned to Port of Spain on Sunday, April 4th, Peter Pena had already studied the HS-748 versus 737-200 analysis that Roger Wynne had delivered a few days earlier.

"Listen, my man, this proves my previous thinking," Peter announced. "The 737 will do the work of four of the Brits."

"Great! I told you they wouldn't have a chance of a fart in a windstorm."

Peter laughed.

"Now, what I need right away are some firm numbers on price and delivery."

"No problem! We can crank that out by the end of the week."

"My strategy is to hit 'em where it hurts. The board is pretty damn sensitive to the noise from Parliament, and we really peak in July and August when everybody runs over to Tobago on vacation. We need a June delivery next year."

"Right on! June should be easy. Our cycle is about twelve months— but we'd need a decision by the first of May."

"That's our big if. I need to get on Scoon's back tomorrow."

"You can tell him that Boeing will meet the peak traffic if we can get a "go" by May 1st."

Peter had a reputation for moving decisively—and fast.

On Monday afternoon, Pena called.

"Listen, my man, Scoon decided to let the British proposal expire, and go for a jet."

"Our lucky day!"

"But, don't celebrate yet. He still has the BWIA problem to solve. The plot is thicker than ever."

"Peter, hold your ground. Maybe we can improve your position still further if we can find an interim airplane to handle the peak this summer."

"Good show, keep me posted."

On April 9th, Boeing was able to offer a one-year lease of a New Zealand 737-200, available immediately, and on the 15th I delivered the proposal for a new airplane for June 1, 1977.

TTAS was now in the position of the tail wagging the dog, and the McDonnell Douglas salesman had not even bothered to talk to them.

Back in Seattle, overconfidence was beginning to set in, as the performance of the 737-200 on the island hops clearly left the DC-9-50 in a weak second place. Primary to this superiority was the nonstop capability from either Piarco or Crown Point, all the way to Miami.

When BWIA requested a proposal from Boeing for three airplanes, two 737-200 passenger models and one 737-200C convertible passenger/cargo model, McDonnell Douglas began to feel the pressure.

Though my confidence increased, there seemed to be something strange about Peter Look Hong's position. He never gave an opinion on either airplane, continuing to lean on the as-yet-to-be-released "Castagne Report."

The technical evaluation at BWIA was solidifying toward Boeing, particularly as a result of Captain Mowser's support, and the new-found ally in Peter Pena.

Boeing offered a combination first class/economy configuration with 101 seats, providing comparable seat spacing, aisle width, and passenger accommodations as a DC-9-50 configuration at 115 seats. However, on the prime run—nonstop to Miami—the superior takeoff and landing characteristics of the 737 assured a full load of passengers, plus 4,000 pounds of additional freight. By comparison, the DC-9 could carry only 96 passengers—*leaving nineteen unusable seats!*

Seeing the cards beginning to fall against them, McDonnell Douglas decided on a dramatic new move to refocus interest in their machine.

The opportunity came when a Finnair airplane, ready for delivery, was not urgently needed by the airline. Negotiating a later delivery with Finnair, they offered a live demonstration in Port of Spain.

The countdown quickened. Peter Look Hong requested a firm price and delivery schedule for the three 737s by May 10th.

"Gene, I want to complete everything at the government level by the end of May," he announced in our latest meeting.

Normal Boeing strategy was to delay final price proposals until just before the decision time, in order to avoid insiders passing numbers to the competition. *By then, I was certain that Castagne had been bought off, continuing to delay his report to gain additional time for neutralizing our advantage.* Up to that time, only study prices had been submitted. There was always a bottom line at the end which could include "concessions," such as additional crew training, maintenance training, spares support, and technical post-delivery field service.

There was no way to stall on Look Hong's request, and we complied.

I kept pulling in additional technical personnel, and our contingent in Port of Spain grew to seven.

Boeing management, confident in the performance of its airplanes, was cool to spending money for demos in the four corners of the world. Further, new or nearly new airplanes were difficult to find. All units in the Boeing assembly line were under contract to specific buyers.

Thus, when I returned to Seattle—pleading for a demo to match McDonnell Douglas—I had to appeal directly to Clancy.

"Gene, you can forget a demo down there," Clancy told me, puffing on his pipe. "But you can invite the BWIA people up here, and we'll do a demo in Seattle."

"Clancy, that's not enough—but if that's the word, we'll do the best we can."

I prepared an official letter request, estimating the cost to be $10,000, the principal element being fuel.

Obtaining immediate approval, I called Peter Look Hong with the offer.

There was a brief silence at Peter's end.

"But Gene, we have the government problem. I'm sure Scoon would want to bring a contingent, and time is so short."

It was a polite turndown.

McDonnell Douglas, with the bit in their teeth, accelerated their own schedule, moving it up to April 21st, a full week earlier.

Trapped by this change in schedule, I was still in Seattle when Bruce Procope called.

"Gene, the DC-9 demo was a smash hit! To add to the pizzazz, they even brought along Pete Conrad, an Apollo astronaut. That's the kind of thing that impresses these people. We've got to do something drastic!"

"But Bruce, just yesterday you told me not to worry, Boeing had the inside track. What happened?"

"Gene, you don't know these people like I do. They're like a bunch of children."

"Bruce, there's a hardening of the arteries up here. I'm out of ammunition. I want you to put all the details you can in a telex and get it up here within the hour."

"Good."

"As soon as I get the ball rolling here, I'll be on a plane to Port of Spain."

First, I composed a letter to Clancy Wilde, which stated in part:

"I have concluded that the demo in Seattle could not bring the message to enough of the right people in Trinidad, and currently feel that an executive demo in Port of Spain, followed by a pilot's demo to the short fields of St. Lucia and Grenada, are essential to securing the sale of the three 737s to BWIA, and one to TTAS."

Adding an estimate of the total cost, which would include leasing an airplane from a South American carrier and flying it up to Trinidad for two days of demonstration flights, I came up with $50,000.

Later in the day, the reinforcing telex arrived from Bruce.

"McDonnell Douglas demonstration of DC-9 materially changed outlook for future Boeing sales. Visit was skillfully handled and got attention of politicians, board, and management. Emphatically recommend 737 visit to Trinidad in addition to inviting BWIA and TTAS executives to visit Seattle. To upstage McDonnell Douglas' use of astronaut, suggest we feature popular local Trinidadians, such as Carnival Queen, top Carnival band leaders, leading sportsmen."

Clancy approved "the whole nine yards" with barely a blink of an eye.

With so many elements of Boeing involved in such an undertaking, there always had to be an "it" man—and I was it.

Tom May was given the task of finding an airplane, preferably in our own region, close to Port of Spain. Brazil was the prime candidate, and the nearly new 737 machines that we sold to Cruzeiro the year before were not being highly utilized. They jumped at the opportunity to gain some quick cash.

Dolf Rischbeiter made the arrangements with Cruzeiro, and I put together the flight crews, maintenance support, and the myriad elements of the people/time/place management for the two days in Port of Spain. We included technical presentations, both on the airplane and in the board room, to cover all detailed questions.

The whirlwind program was set in motion for May 18th and 19th, with a grand cocktail party cresting the activity on Wednesday evening and a special banquet for board members and management of both airlines. The Boeing team had grown to eleven.

I departed for Port of Spain a week ahead to make the advance preparations, arriving on May 11th.

The main Boeing team came on Sunday night, headed by Mr. Brien Wygle, vice president of the Boeing Customer Support organization. That evening, a Cruzeiro 737-200 airplane flew in from Belem, almost new, and in excellent condition.

On Tuesday morning, May 18th, the caravan of cars moved out of the Hilton bound for Piarco Airport for the technical presentations to airline executives and engineers. Then a series of demo touch-and-go flights were made over a period of four hours in the afternoon, allowing BWIA and TTAS flight crews to take the plane off, fly, and land it. The runway at Crown Point, barely 6,000 feet long, with both ends bordering the ocean, was the acid test for the pilot demos.

Wednesday, May 19th, was the biggest day. The Boeing party departed for Piarco at 7:30 a.m., to be ready for the first executive demo flight at 9:30.

Bands of sunlight and shadow moved over the airport scene as the "Little Giant" from Cruzeiro sat proudly on the apron, beckoning to its guests. I paced around, checking details, worrying about rain.

After briefing the stewardesses, I loaded the brochures and the giveaways. Roger Wynne departed for Tobago on the 9:00 a.m. TTAS flight to greet the guests as they deplaned there, as well as inviting Tobagonians who wished to fly to Piarco to come on board. TTAS had volunteered to take them home afterwards in a special flight. At 9:30, the guests began arriving: Ministers of Finance, Industry, External Affairs; the director of Civil Aviation; presidents of major banks and principal industries; Tourist Board members; BWIA and TTAS boards of directors; managers and staff of the airlines; technical, maintenance, and engineering personnel. There was barely room for the U.S. ambassador and his commercial attaché.

The Boeing public relations manager arranged for broad news coverage, holding a press conference after the flights.

A glittering cocktail party on the West Terrace of the Hilton Hotel that evening was a big event, with rum punch, a Trinidadian specialty, running like water. I lost count, but estimated that 225 guests were in attendance.

For high-ranking guests—John Scoon, Peter Look Hong, Peter Pena, and several board members—I arranged a special banquet.

Food, wine, and speeches were the order of the evening, with John Scoon, Chairman of both Boards, monopolizing the discussions, adroitly evading our efforts for clues concerning their choice of airplanes.

There was no doubt that the demonstrations and technical presentations had evoked high interest, and based on general remarks, my confidence for the sale rose substantially. Some "insiders," self-appointed experts from the news corps and hotel public relations staff, were already saying that Boeing had won.

The following day, the local newspapers were expansive in their coverage and liberal in their praise.

The *Evening News* reported that "many experts see the comforts of Boeing," and ". . . it was instant pleasure to fly across to the sister island of Tobago. The 737s have solved a quite a few problems should BWIA decide to acquire several of these aircraft."[1]

The *Express* had a front page photograph inside the airplane and a noncommittal story.[2]

The *Guardian*, the major morning newspaper, quoted Mr. Mahabir, minister of industry, as "highly impressed by the performance of the aircraft, and found it to be comfortable and spacious."[3]

Officially, as the "Castagne Report" was being evaluated, there was only silence. Informed that a final review was due by the board of directors at the end of May, I arranged a one-on-one meeting with Peter Look Hong to discuss manufacturing schedules. The meeting took place on May 30th.

"You know, Peter, our proposal for the 737s expires tomorrow, and the delivery date of June 1977 will be in jeopardy because we must commit the first parts to the line in less than thirty days," I advised.

"Perhaps you would be willing to make a conditional acceptance, subject to government approval. Many airlines take that approach to protect delivery dates."

Peter chuckled.

"Here in Trinidad it's not a good idea to make any public recommendations until the government makes up their minds. The prime minister himself may get involved."

"O.K., I'll be available. You can call me collect at any time. Bruce is also here to provide assistance."

I was optimistic, particularly since the personal connection between Bruce and Prime Minister Williams might prove to be the final factor.

When I returned to Seattle, Bruce reported that Boeing was very much in the thick of contention.

"The government will decide in a few days," he concluded.

Boeing international salesmen never spent much time in Seattle, and I was due back in Quito.

1. *The Evening News,* 20 May 1976
2. *Express,* 20 May 1976
3. *Trinidad Guardian,* 20 May 1976

# 21

The axis of activity for my sales world had now swung to the north. Whereas I had been commuting between Lima and Rio a year before, I now found myself on the Port of Spain/Quito merry-go-round. Peru remained in my action book, but its status had been reduced to a holding operation. The country was nearly bankrupt, its financial position in the world of nations tied with Bangladesh for last place.

In Ecuador, Ecuatoriana was gearing up for a full-blown wide-body competition. Small in comparison to most of the world's international flag carriers, it had become a dynamic organization under the leadership of Colonel Banderas. Without a subsidy from the government, they realized a profit during the first year of flying the Boeing airplanes.

In fact, I found stirrings all through the ancient, mountain-bound country. Sparked by oil exports, the economy was healthy. Optimism pervaded the air. By South American standards, the people were energetic. Newspapers carried the call to opportunity— *"Buenos Dias, Pais! Ecuador si puede!"*—Good Morning, Country! Ecuador is able!

I felt confident about sales prospects, primarily at Ecuatoriana, but also domestically, and it was time to make contact with the domestic airlines. Ecuador was served by three small carriers. All three had much in common, they were poor and had worn out equipment. Nevertheless, the country was highly dependent on air travel, having few roads and only one railroad—Quito to Guayaquil.

Of the three domestic carriers, TAME had the advantage. It was owned by the government and operated as an extension of the *Fuerzas Aereos Ecuatorianos* (FAE), whereas the other two were privately owned. After visiting each one, I found TAME to be the only logical target.

On a previous visit to Quito in February, the morning of the day I arrived, one of TAME's twin-engined Avro 748s crashed in the mountains on its way to Loja, killing everyone on board.

Feeling it in poor taste to appear at the TAME president's door the day after a fatal crash, offering to sell airplanes, I had postponed my first visit.

Colonel Bolivar Mora, a friend of Colonel Banderas, was a young, enthusiastic leader, eager to move into modern jet operations, but like many others, had focussed on the 727-100, primarily because of availability—at attractive prices.

"Colonel Mora," I proposed early in our first meeting, "you need to take a hard look at a new 737-200."

"But Mr. Bauer, look at the price comparison. How much did you say a 37 would cost?"

"Something over $8 million."

Mora reared back in his chair. "That's more than two used 727s!"

"Colonel Mora, we hear this comparison quite often, but it's a short view. We can show a definite advantage in profitability over the long range."

"How about some numbers?"

I reached in my briefcase, pulled out a document, and handed it to the Colonel.

"I want you to study this comparison of the two machines over a ten-year period. We took your current system, using identical traffic growth scenarios. By the end of the period, you would have a higher profit from the 737, with 30,000 hours on the airframe, and your used 727 would have about reached its economic life expectancy of 60,000 hours."

"Very interesting."

"Of course, this study needs to be fine-tuned. I'd like you to work with our analysts to update costs and revenues, and refine the economic projections."

"Fine. That's what I want to hear. You know there's no way I can sell the idea to the government without a pretty airtight case."

"Of course, that's why Boeing is in the business. If it's O.K. with you, we'll send in our man next week."

Returning to Seattle, I learned that the lieutenant governor of California, himself of Trinidadian descent, had made a rush trip to Port of Spain to visit Prime Minister Williams, to argue the importance of the DC-9 sale to employment at the McDonnell Douglas factory in Long Beach.

I called Bruce Procope immediately. He reported that Mr. Mahabir, minister of industry and commerce—who had flown on the demo—personally favored the 737. "Mahabir has more clout with the prime minister than anyone," he said.

That same day, Castagne made a rush trip to Hawaii to visit both Aloha and Hawaiian Airlines. Aloha was operating 737s, and Hawaiian, DC-9s. On the surface, this development sounded positive for Boeing, as our information from those airlines showed a superiority of the 737s on the inter-island hops.

Castagne didn't tell us what he had concluded, merely saying that he had "found some very interesting things," and would be including an addendum to his report.

On June 1st, New Zealand Airlines withdrew its lease offer, having received a firm bid from another airline.

On June 9th, Bruce stated categorically, "I am fully confident that the 737 will be chosen."

Tobago traffic was hitting the summer crunch, signalling an all-time high, and Cabinet pressure was imposed on BWIA to introduce jet service to Tobago by mid-July. There was no mention of the latest role of TTAS.

Ken Patrick, our consultant in Canada, called, informing us that McDonnell Douglas had submitted a lease offer for a new DC-9-50 on very attractive terms. Boeing started a new worldwide search for a suitable lease airplane.

On June 16th, a long conversation with Bruce indicated everything was still on track for a 737 selection. "Gene, I think you worry too much," he said.

*There it was again!*

I was not satisfied, and called Peter Pena.

"How are we doing with the 737?" I inquired.

"Look, my man, I only know what I read in the papers," Peter chuckled. "You know how it is here in Trinidad."

"You must have some idea—"

"No, only rumors—the wildest one is that BWIA has signed up with Douglas, and they're working on a lease deal."

"That doesn't sound good."

I decided it was time to get back to Trinidad—fast!

Alfredo accompanied me, feeling compelled to get closer to the action. The next day we met with Castagne and Look Hong to discuss an interim lease. We had determined that Pacific Western, a Canadian carrier—and a good Boeing customer—was willing to spring an airplane loose for a year.

The atmosphere was hurried, but cordial. Peter was surprised that Boeing had located an airplane so quickly.

"We are definitely interested," he said quietly.

"I understand you have a representative out at the Long Beach plant discussing a DC-9 lease?" I asked guardedly.

"Yeah, but no commitments have been made. We do need a fairly new airplane. How old is the Pacific Western?"

"About five years old."

"That's pretty old. We need a new one—for, ah, passenger appeal—you know how touchy the people here are about image on the Tobago route."

"Does McDonnell Douglas have a new one?" I was fishing.

"That's what they claim. Apparently Finnair has two on order and one is complete, but Finnair is not ready for it. McDonnell Douglas is doing them a favor by delaying the delivery."

"Let me check whether Pacific Western will let one of their newer ones go on lease."

"O.K., but we need to move fast."

I glanced at the calendar. "Today is Friday, the 18th. We can get back with you on Monday afternoon."

The proposal was telexed at noon Monday. I put the package together, wrote a transmittal letter, and it was ready to deliver by midafternoon.

Look Hong was incredulous. When he vacillated, my suspicions mounted. I feared he had already committed to McDonnell Douglas.

"The airplane is available for inspection in Vancouver, B.C., at any time. The plane is commuting in Western Canada, and Pacific Western only needs eight hours notice. It's nearly new, less than 10,000 hours on the airframe."

"I'll pass the proposal to the board. It's up to them now. We'll advise you on the timing for the inspection team."

I began making detailed arrangements by phone to Seattle. Pacific Western was very cooperative. The plan was to bring the BWIA team to Seattle, fly them up to Vancouver, and help to negotiate terms.

Boeing offered additional incentives. Pilot training could begin immediately for an alternate BWIA crew, and Boeing would send four technicians to Port of Spain for several months to help get the airline started. The engineering service representative, normally provided on the pro forma at delivery, would be accelerated and should be on station in Port of Spain by September. In the meantime, Boeing maintenance specialists could be on a twenty-four-hour-call from Miami.

On Wednesday, no word had been received from Look Hong. Having a nervous breakfast in the hotel, I was startled by an announcement on the front page of the *Trinidad Guardian.*

"According to a BWIA spokesman, maintenance training for the DC-9-50 will commence very soon at Piarco."

I called Peter. He was very upset—or putting on a good act.

"Gene, no decision has been made. I don't know where the rumor came from. We can never find out anything from the newspapers about their sources. That part about receiving information from a BWIA spokesman is false."

The next day, I arranged a dinner meeting with Peter Pena. "Well Peter, what are the latest facts in this strange competition?"

Peter smiled. "BWIA has had a lot of problems. When they made the decision for the DC-9 last summer, and the pilots revolted, they went underground. We both know Castagne is 100% Douglas."

I nodded.

"We have assumed that all along, but what about Mowser and the others?"

"They were too busy to get involved. Mowser left his part up to his assistant, Ted Webb, and Castagne just snowed him. Eric didn't know any of the details of the evaluation until the final report had been signed, sealed, and delivered. And, of course, it recommended the DC-9."

"We figured that, too, but after the 737 demo, we expected the government to take an objective look."

"What can they do? They're not experts. They have to take the technicians' word for it. I don't think the planning group did an objective evaluation at all. They merely justified the original decision by shaping the results to favor the DC-9."

"Damn!"

On June 23rd, Bruce learned for the first time that the BWIA board of directors had actually recommended the DC-9-50 to the government, just as Pena had told me. On the same day, Alfredo and I were having lunch with Errol Pinard, manager of engineering and maintenance for BWIA, and during the conversation, he mentioned the "extra seats" that the DC-9-50 offered.

Later in the day, we submitted a letter to Peter Look Hong, copies of which were made available to government officials, which included circle range charts from Trinidad to Miami showing the serious performance deficiency of the DC-9: 96 passengers and nineteen empty seats, compared to a full load of 101 passengers and 4,000 pounds of extra freight for the 737. The letter also pointed out the even more serious deficiencies in the event nonstop Tobago to Miami flights were included.

On June 24th, the cabinet met and we learned that the recommendation for the DC-9-50 had been accepted, subject to "clarification." Nothing was announced officially, and Look Hong indicated that Mr. Mahabir had requested the BWIA Board to meet with him on the following afternoon, June 25th. Peter then requested an extension of the Boeing proposal to June 30th.

I did not plan to give up without a last ditch fight. Calling Glenn Castagne at his home on Saturday morning, I asked for an urgent meeting, a highly unusual request. BWIA did not normally work on Saturday. Nevertheless, Glenn agreed to meet me in his office. Edginess showed through the thin veneer of his cordiality.

I reviewed the Boeing computer runs on takeoff performance. Glenn countered by pulling out the McDonnell Douglas computer runs—my first look at them. Where Boeing numbers showed 96 for the DC-9, the McDonnell Douglas document showed 112. Shortly after, they had sent a letter that claimed three additional seats from "increased fuel efficiency." That got them to the alleged 115.

Comparing airplanes strictly on the basis of numbers of seats was hazardous. The real test of profitability was the payload—passengers and cargo that could actually be carried on a customer's routes, taking into account all the technical factors such as field length, field elevation, ambient temperatures, and winds. Every route in the world is different.

"Glenn, I find it difficult to accept the McDonnell Douglas data.

We've run their airplane through our computer a dozen times and it comes out the same."

Glenn's reaction was to become angry. "Why should we believe the Boeing data over the McDonnell Douglas data?" he retorted. "And as far as the Tobago/Miami thing is concerned, we'll always stop at Piarco. So it's immaterial."

At last I had proof that the evaluation had been rigged. Castagne had the numbers to prove it. The rules were set up to fit the airplane that had already been selected a year before—the DC-9. I feared there was no way to get that decision overturned, but still was not yet ready to throw in the towel.

I called Seattle to have the numbers checked and the OEW (operating empty weight) of the DC-9-50 verified. On Sunday, Seattle confirmed the numbers and referred to a Douglas report which listed the OEW and other airplane parameters. I requested a telex laying out all the numbers and rules, suitable to present to BWIA management, which I received late Sunday afternoon.

That evening, I arranged via Bruce to have the performance telex delivered to Mr. Mahabir and other officials of the government, still clinging to the idea that there was a court of fairness somewhere in the hierarchy. Somebody must be willing to stand up and be counted for the best plane.

On Monday, I met with Peter Look Hong, delivering the proposal extension and leaving a copy of the telex. He agreed to restudy the numbers.

Glenn had not yet arrived, so I met with him later. He was clearly angry at my persistence.

"Glenn, what I'm showing you is of crucial importance. Don't get suckered in. You'll be flying nineteen empty seats to Miami."

With that, he excused himself to attend another meeting.

Meanwhile, Bruce delivered copies of the extension letter, as well as the performance telex, to government officials.

There was nothing more we could do.

On Tuesday evening, June 29th, I called Captain Mowser at home.

"Yes, we picked the DC-9," confirmed Mowser. "The best airplane."

"On what basis?"

"First, the maintenance people went for the DC-9."

"Oh?"

"Also, the `9 will fly a little faster, an advantage on the long routes. Besides, McDonnell Douglas offered fourteen more seats."

"You don't want to fly empty seats. On the Miami run those seats will be empty—plus five more."

"Is that so? Not according to McDonnell Douglas data!"

"Have you verified the numbers with your own studies?"

"Of course not! We took the official data at face value."

My sick feeling returned. Final proof. Castagne had engineered the entire evaluation.

On Wednesday, June 30, 1976, headlines appeared in the *Guardian*. I didn't know whether to curse or cry, so I did both.

"BWIA CHOOSES DC-9."

The article said that the airline planned to purchase two passenger planes and one convertible freighter, and would lease an airplane for one year to begin service on the Tobago route by the end of July.

I requested an "independent analysis" from Bruce, and scheduled a debriefing meeting with Peter Look Hong, which also gave me the opportunity to discuss their future planning schedule for wide-body airplanes.

The next day, I returned to Seattle to plan a 747 campaign for BWIA. And the work in Ecuador had barely begun.

# 22

The summer of 1976 brought a unique honor to Trinidad. The country rocketed to international notice on the swift feet of Hasely Crawford, world's fastest human, who won the gold medal in the 100-meter sprint at the Olympic Games in July.

Vacationing in Montreal with my wife—my first vacation in three years—I witnessed those flying feet. By the luck of the draw for ticket assignments, we sat close enough to almost touch the runners as they crouched at the starting blocks.

July was also the month for delivery of the DC-9-50 airplane leased to BWIA while they waited for the new ones to be manufactured. It was promptly named the *Hasely Crawford*.

Shortly, the *Hasely Crawford*, with a sleek sprinter painted on the side of its cockpit, started regular service. Almost immediately, information began to filter out of BWIA on its performance—even a little worse than the Boeing predictions.

When I revisited BWIA in August, I made a special effort to find out the true facts about the DC-9 performance, meeting with Geoff Paterson, who had been so honest and helpful in the past.

He had been solid Boeing from the beginning, and was eager to share the details.

"Geoff, I know the inaugural flight is history, but we're still interested in the numbers—it's helpful for future campaigns."

He smiled a difficult smile.

"We reconfigured the plane to an all-tourist pitch, giving us 135 seats—and the flight was a fiasco."

"So what actually happened? I understand you stopped for fuel."

"Well, let me tell you. As you know, we were suddenly on the map with Hasely's victory in the Olympics. So, the original plan was to do a "look at us, world" full load, nonstop flight directly to Miami. But it was soon obvious we couldn't do it  and stay within the FAA fuel reserve rules."

"Yeah, we knew that."

"The powers that be decided to take a one-stop instead, putting on fuel at Antigua. A refueling stop meant more payload, and the bigger the load, the more publicity."

"So that's why the reconfiguration?"

"Of course! Maybe I shouldn't say this, but it would make the BWIA board appear to be oracles in their selection."

I chuckled.

"So—fat, dumb, and happy—we loaded the airplane up with 135 bodies and normal baggage. Everybody wanted to be on the inaugural, so we had a lot of BWIA people and media."

"Sounds like a circus."

Geoff nodded.

"But I recollect the one-stop numbers. I think the number was 121 max, even by Douglas calculations—wasn't it?"

"Gene, you're exactly right. But we didn't want to believe them, figuring maybe we'd get an advantage in headwinds."

"Well, I'm sure you made it to Antigua all right."

"That's where the trouble started. The captain recalculated his flight plan on to Miami, and then things hit the fan. I was sitting in my seat, waiting, when he announced that the airplane was too heavy, and suggested that some passengers might want to volunteer to off-load their baggage. "We'll bring it along on another plane," he said. Everybody jeered—'Believe it When It Arrives!' You couldn't hear yourself think."

"And what next?"

"Finally, it was agreed to put off a number of BWIA people, mostly the PR types, but I got to stay on. Then, halfway to Miami, the captain came on again and said he would need to land at San Juan for still more fuel. So we did, and that's the story."

Geoff threw up his hands.

"I can just see the scenario. The government investigating the captain for falsely reporting the fuel," I joked.

He laughed out loud.

"Yeah, there was talk of that, but in the end it was decided to put the whole mess behind us."

Somehow, I obtained a copy of the official Castagne report. True to my suspicions, the technical evaluation was leveraged to favor the DC-9-50. However, it was a professional job, and it took an expert to highlight the subtle shadings that were used. The technique was to list a series of attributes for direct comparison, weighting each item, and then listing multiple subitems in those areas where the DC-9 was superior. Thus, the DC-9 received a larger numerical rating in positive attributes. The alleged fourteen-seat capacity advantage was highly emphasized.

I also learned that as soon as Boeing announced the date for the 737 demo, the Castagne report was accelerated by a full week, and the demo was never a factor in the evaluation.

How McDonnell Douglas was able to quote performance figures for fourteen more passengers nonstop from Port of Spain to Miami was never explained. It remains a riddle.

For me, it proved once again that the best airplane does not always win. It was clear that Boeing would need better consultant support for the 747/DC-10/L-1011 competition that would be starting soon at BWIA.

Information began to leak out about payoffs, and the Trinidad newspapers suggested that BWIA officials were involved. The *Trinidad*

*Guardian* reported that a representative in Parliament stated that "a BWIA official had been presented with the gift of a sailing boat, by Douglas Corporation for 'conducting such good negotiations.'"[1] Although the official was unnamed in the newspaper, I learned of Castagne's new sailboat from local sources, and also noted that he had begun construction of a new home in the most fancy district of Port of Spain.

Not until the SEC investigations in the United States were completed, and a special review committee appointed by McDonnell Douglas made its report several years later, were the full facts behind the selection of the DC-9-50 airplanes revealed. The committee determined that McDonnell Douglas had made $575,000 in questionable payments during that campaign.[2]

In Trinidad, such payments were know as *boobol*. The "bite" had proven to be the most powerful sales tool of all.

And so ended the Boeing effort to sell medium range airplanes to BWIA. I had been in the frontline trenches in the struggle between two giant U.S. corporations, each with a different management philosophy, demonstrating day by day their corporate conscience.

Nevertheless, I took heart, as the SEC spotlight was becoming public, and future payoffs—at least by U.S. corporations— would be less likely.

Technical problems with the integration of the DC-9, internal turmoil within the airline, and arguments in the Parliament all combined to produce a postponement in the wide-body competition. In September, Peter Look Hong notified me that it would not begin until December.

I decided not to wait. We needed all the time we could get.

Castagne's duplicity had not yet been addressed, and he was again in charge of the evaluation team. However, Peter Look Hong instructed all his department heads to take a personal role. *Perhaps we could have a fair fight.*

Nevertheless, I began a search for additional consultant assistance. Alfredo was personally acquainted with Phil Kelshall, retired general manager of BWIA, and we signed him on. We decided also to continue with Bruce Procope, in order to keep our government liaison intact. Together, their commission equalled 2.25%.

Postponement of the evaluation allowed me more time to plan a deliberate campaign—no panics. I included plant visits, demo flights, and the use of our own computer programs to do the performance and economic analysis—denied by BWIA previously.

The Trinidad competition promised to be tough. BWIA traffic demand would not nearly justify the 443 passenger 747-100 until about 1982. The SP was closer to the correct size, but still pretty large.

With essentially sea level airports at all of their potential ports of call, BWIA did not need the takeoff performance of the SP, which gave it such an overwhelming advantage in the Andes countries, and the three-engined trijets had significantly lower airplane-mile operating costs.

Thus, our sales approach was based on growth, emphasizing future requirements. The 747 had the lowest investment cost per seat for the three competitors, as well as the lowest seat-mile operating costs of any airplane then flying in the world. We counted heavily on its outstanding passenger appeal to fill the seats.

Sending invitations to all BWIA managers to visit the Boeing factories in Seattle, I zeroed in on Captain Eric Mowser. If I could get him to fly the 747 demonstrator, I would be halfway home.

I was pleased when I received his acceptance to visit Seattle the third week of September, promising also to bring his wife Elizabeth. She was a singer and choir director and had common interests with Beth, also a professional singer. It was exactly the kind of personal chemistry that I needed.

I had developed an easy relationship with Mowser, and toward the end of August we had a candid conversation.

"How do you see this new equipment plan evolving, Eric?" I inquired.

"We're sure as hell going to take a hard look at all the numbers. My man Ted Webb will review everything."

His blue eyes twinkled. "Let's just say we don't want any surprises on performance on this one."

I knew the salaries of the crew were tied to a general formula, which took into account the size, complexity, and weight of the airplane, with size the most significant factor. Eric would be the first to move up to captain in wide-body equipment.

"We have many factors to consider. Performance may be the most important, but commonality is critical, too. That's why we probably would not consider the L-1011."

That statement piqued my attention.

"Are you saying the L-1011 won't be included?"

"That's damn near right. I can't see a small airline like BWIA operating three types."

I felt some comfort in his words, but no complacency. It would be easy to argue that the mix could be reduced to two by simply phasing out the 707s.

"I think your big concern should be competition with British Airways, when they start coming in with their 747-100."

"But we don't have to meet them head to head. While we're still flying the 07s, we can restrict them to equivalent loads out of Trinidad."

"I see. But that advantage won't last, and there's also pressure from other European carriers such as KLM, who fly through here."

"You bet. We need the best. I really want to fly the 747, and Liz will be looking forward to the September trip."

Back in Seattle, I directed attention to every detail of the Mowsers' visit. Beth and I met their plane at SeaTac on Saturday evening, September 18th, and escorted them to the Washington Plaza Hotel, the most modern in the Queen City, where the skyline had completely changed in a single decade.

For Sunday, I arranged an outing on Puget Sound, chartering the Monte Carlo, a sleek fifty-five-foot luxury cruiser. We were fortunate to have one of those rare, crystal clear days, with a light puffy breeze, barely sufficient to riffle the water. We went to Blake, a wilderness island in Puget Sound, where a replica of the old longhouse of the Duwamish

Indians stood in the shelter of towering Douglas firs. Inside, modern-day Indians were baking salmon over an open fire, just as their ancestors had done for hundreds of years.

The next day, Eric was exposed to the technical side of Boeing; fleet planning and economic methodology, a review of the 747 program, a tour of the passenger cabin mockup, and an hour in the flight simulator.

That evening, we took the party to the Space Needle, the revolving restaurant atop a 600-foot-high spindle of steel, built for the 1962 World's Fair.

Tuesday morning, Paul Bennett, chief 747 pilot, met us at the flight line and introduced Eric to RA 001, old Number One 747 off the line. Beth and Liz spent the day touring Seattle.

After a general briefing on board, Paul motioned for Captain Mowser to take the left seat. They started the engines. Eric seemed hesitant when Bennett told him to taxi out. Sitting thirty feet above the ground was quite different from the fourteen feet of the 707 cockpit. For a moment it appeared as though he would steer the airplane directly into the side of the hangar, but the big ship started coming around, and he straightened her out almost exactly on the taxiway centerline.

"Good going," Paul observed.

"Thanks," Eric remarked, glancing sideways. "I was a little antsy about that building for a minute."

"You're doing fine—see how easy she handles."

I had a crow's nest seat directly behind Eric, and I watched, fascinated by the quickness with which an experienced pilot could master the details of flying the 350-ton giant.

Eric took the plane off, headed south from Boeing Field, and pointed her nose toward Mt. Rainier, a huge pink ice cream cone in the morning sunlight. A few miles south of the field, Bennett steered him eastward, and we headed for Moses Lake, a Boeing test base about 150 miles away over the crest of the Cascade Mountains.

Reaching Moses Lake, Bennett instructed Eric on the use of the autoland feature, and locked it in.

"Now take your hands off the wheel entirely. You don't need to do a thing until you're down. Then when you're into the roll, apply the brakes. You even have a choice; if you want, the airplane will put on the brakes."

The plane settled into a perfect glide slope, flared out, and landed soft as a feather. Eric could not believe how smooth it was. We stopped halfway down the runway.

"Wow! This is an old man's airplane. It flies itself."

"Okay, take her off!" Bennett commanded.

"Are you kidding? From here?"

"Sure, go ahead. I want you to see her climbing ability."

Eric was unsure, but he applied takeoff power, released the brakes, and away we went, lifting out with runway to spare.

We were about 200 feet up when Bennett reached over and pulled number one throttle back to idle. He looked at Eric. "You just lost number one!" he announced.

The plane made a slight jerk, and then quickly smoothed out on three engines. Eric was incredulous.

"I wanted you to see how well she does on engine-out during takeoff."

"Fantastic!"

It was the same reaction that Colonel Lara had in the SP in Quito. Love at first sight. Once in love with the plane, it would be hard to divorce it.

That's exactly what happened. After the Seattle visit, Eric spread the word within the airline and to the government officials in Trinidad, becoming our best salesman for the 747.

1. *Trinidad Guardian*, 27 November 1976.

2. *Aviation Week*, 4 August 1980, 21

# 23

W hen I returned to Peru, there had been still another mini-coup, the second since Velasco had been deposed only a little more than a year before.

Conditions in the country were worse than ever. Inflation was out of hand, the international debt had rocketed, and one newly appointed financial minister after the other succeeded to the unforgiving task of bringing order out of chaos.

My first order of business was to meet with Federico Pastor for an update on the consultant discussions. Boeing had decided to drop further consideration of Percy, but had a favorable inclination toward Roberto.

Elizabeth was surprised when I asked for Federico.

"Mr. Pastor doesn't work for AeroPeru anymore," she announced. "This is Raoul's office, and he's not here right now. Why don't you call later."

I could not believe my ears! The last time I talked with Federico, he seemed on the verge of a promotion.

Raoul Seminario had taken over planning. I knew him well, as the previous director of Finance. We were good friends, and he was a good head—but this development was terrible! *I feared that the inside connection had been lost, and I was back at square one!*

"Look, Elizabeth, I'm coming over to wait in the office. I have important business to discuss with Raoul. *Hasta luego!"*

I put the phone down before she had time to object.

Leaving the Sheraton, I started down old Union Street toward Cailloma, headquarters for AeroPeru; past the tumbled down adobe walls of earthquake damaged buildings; past the polished ebony doors of the *Tambo de Oro,* an anachronism amid the ruins; past the beggars and the fruit and vegetable carts. Summer was coming to Lima, and the hot, breezeless air attacked my nostrils with a mixed smell of stale urine and overripe fruit. The crumbled sidewalk, scarcely a meter in width, forced pedestrians into the street, filled with honking, speeding automobiles and broken-down buses, all belching black smoke from their scorched engines.

The most recent mini-coup had done nothing to change the lives of the Peruvians. Perhaps the poverty was even a little deeper. The people's faces were etched with fear and hunger.

I dodged in and out among the street hawkers with their wares spread on the sidewalks of Avenida Pierola. Walking briskly in spite of the oppressive heat, I quickly reached AeroPeru headquarters on the top floor of the thirteen-story building.

"Meeester Bauer, how are you?" Elizabeth cooed. "Deeed you bring my candy?"

I smiled.

"Of course." Opening my briefcase, I brought out a box of Russell Stover chocolates, handing it to her. A tiny box, only four pieces, but she clutched it to her breast, as if it was the best and last candy in the world.

"Thank you, Meeester Bauer."

Candy continued to be my ticket for successful meetings. I always brought five or six pounds on my trips—usually a dozen small boxes and two or three larger boxes.

Elizabeth dialed a few numbers, speaking rapidly in Spanish.

*"Asienta se!"* she said, smiling and motioning to the sofa. "Raoul will be here in a few minutes."

Raoul seemed particularly friendly, inviting me into his inner office.

"We really appreciate the Boeing study on a plan for profitability," he volunteered. He reached for the document with the brilliant red cover and Inca logo, holding it up. "Personally, I like your approach— but things aren't easy here—too many difficulties in the government."

"And how is your current planning horizon?"

"Well, as you know, we still have those leased DC-8s, and the lease expires in July 1978."

"So AeroPeru will need to make a decision soon. That's only about eighteen months away."

"We're working on it."

"By the way, you're probably aware that Federico had recommended Roberto as a candidate for consultant. Do you think he's a good man for the job?"

"Oh, yes, the Datsun dealer. We all know him. I believe he's person- ally acquainted with General Berckemeyer."

"Maybe I'll recommend him to the brass."

"Well, that's your business."

Later, at dinner with Raoul and his wife, we discussed family matters and economic problems, and engaged in small talk, including the birth- days of his young son and daughter.

My gift list was growing.


It was time to nail down a consultant in Peru, and I recommended that we offer Roberto the job. Alfredo concurred, and we drew up a contract, with the same commission as our old agreement with Chamote.


Back at TAME, Colonel Mora had reviewed our updated study, and concluded that the 737 was the right airplane. Their route system was expanding and would soon include several flights a week to the Galápagos

Islands, the Darwinian jewels located 650 miles off the coast of Ecuador. Tourists from the United States and Europe in large numbers were discovering Ecuador, particularly Quito and the Galápagos.

There was reason to be hopeful that the airline could pay for the airplanes without a government subsidy. The *sucre*, national unit of currency, was strong, holding constant at twenty-five to the dollar.

Traffic had been growing at a 16.9 percent annual rate for twelve years, considerably higher than the world average. Realistic growth projections indicated a need for the first 737 in January 1978, and a second machine a year later.

Based on those optimistic indicators, TAME requested Boeing to conduct an updated route plan and a new economic forecast, to convince the Air Force that the 737-200 was indeed the proper choice.

Meeting once again with Colonel Banderas, I inquired on the fleet status, suggesting Ecuatoriana must be feeling a shortage of planes. He pointed proudly to the model of the 707-320—one I had given him on an earlier visit—perched on a pedestal near his desk.

"We'll shift the -320. We're planning on purchasing a third 720B, hopefully with a main deck cargo door. That'll handle our traffic expansion for the next year or so."

"And what's your latest feeling about wide-bodies?"

"Oh, they're a few years away, certainly not before we expand our routes to Europe—but it's never too early to begin planning."

"I'm pleased to hear that. I believe the SP will be exactly right for your routes."

"Of course, we prefer Boeing airplanes, but I have to tell you one thing."

His face clouded.

"McDonnell Douglas has been here all the time lately. I don't know how to get rid of them. They're driving me crazy!"

I laughed.

"I understand. But can't Ecuatoriana do as it pleases?"

Banderas frowned.

"We weren't able to. They complained to the U. S. embassy about unfair competition—claiming they weren't being allowed to compete fairly. We had to pass a national decree this fall, allowing Ecuatoriana to do its own negotiations."

"Good. That brings me to a rather important question. Have you changed your views about local representation—consultants?"

Banderas looked surprised.

"Oh, we'll deal directly! No other way! There's no need for consultants here."

I was relieved to hear Banderas restate his position in such positive terms, but still confused by contradictory opinions from reliable contacts in the embassy. I decided to wait a little longer.

Banderas confided that McDonnell Douglas had offered a package deal of DC-8 and DC-10 airplanes, while helping Ecuatoriana sell their Boeing equipment.

"We're not at all interested in the McDonnell Douglas airplanes. It makes no sense to be changing the fleet."

I recalled the meeting with Colonel Lara right after the SP demo, when he said emphatically, "Ecuatoriana is married to Boeing."

Back at Seattle, I set the wheels in motion for a kickoff traffic study for Ecuatoriana, looking toward delivery of a 747SP about sixteen months later.

When I returned to Quito, I brought the Boeing analysts to TAME to present the route plan and economic forecast that Colonel Mora had requested. The study concluded that they could easily finance and pay for the airplanes, showing a positive cash flow after the first year of operations.

Clearly, it was time for a bold equipment decision. Colonel Mora was not a visionary, but he recognized the economic soundness of Boeing's recommendations. Further, McDonnell Douglas was not a competitor, since the DC-9 could not match the takeoff and landing performance of the 737 on the short, high-altitude runways of the mountain country.

Taking his case to the Air Force, Mora was successful in winning their support, and was given the green light to proceed. It was only necessary to obtain concurrence from the board of directors.

Since the board had interlocking directors with Ecuatoriana (shades of BWIA/TTAS), including Colonel Banderas, jurisdictional rivalry quickly developed.

Banderas preferred a merger of the two airlines—under his control. Colonel Gudino, successor to Colonel Suarez as director of civil aviation, had different ambitions—to combine the three domestic carriers, increasing his own power base.

The board voted the only way they could agree—for postponement.

Progress continued at Ecuatoriana. The purchase of a third 720B from Pan Am had been completed and the airplane was undergoing refurbishment and installation of the main deck cargo door. It was scheduled to go into service early in 1977.

I had sealed a brother-like relationship with Alfonso, using our common interest in mountain climbing as a thread to keeping communications open later in the campaign when things heated up.

It was now my standard practice to invite him and his wife, Susanna, to dinner at the hotel on each visit. This time I brought along a package, which I stowed under my chair.

The conversation quickly drifted to mountain climbing.

"What about going up Pichincha this weekend," I suggested.

"Well, I don't have any boots—you know how it is here—we can't get good boots."

"Really! What about these?"

I reached under the chair and picked up the package, handing it to Alfonso.

I'll never forget the expression on his face when he opened it.

"They look expensive. I don't think I can afford 'em."

"You must have a birthday soon. They're for your birthday."

*"Gracias! Gracias! Muchas gracias!"*

Susanna was beaming, as Alfonso tried on the boots.

They cost $52, not much more than a bottle of whisky. Nevertheless, I worried a little that the SEC might classify them as *mordida*.

The next day, Sunday, we headed for the 15,910-foot mountain, less than twenty-five kilometers from the airport.

Before sunup on the clear morning, we reached the plateau by jeep— at the base—about the 12,000-foot level. In good weather, the summit can easily be achieved before noon, and we embarked in happy spirits. Patricio, an experienced climber, wearing only tennis shoes, was with us to show the way.

Toward midmorning, a cold fog suddenly enveloped the mountain, and we were socked in. Hunkering down to wait for the fog to clear, I began to feel a certain uneasiness and a responsibility for Alfonso, since it was initially my idea to climb. Patricio was very confident; however, we had not brought ropes, as climbers of Pichincha did not consider them to be necessary.

Alfonso and I decided to work our way back down and Patricio disappeared in the fog, to continue the climb. Late in the afternoon, having made a fast rush to the summit, he joined us as we waited at the base of the mountain.

We were disappointed, but no less enthusiastic, and began planning for a climb of 19,700-foot Cotopaxi, world's highest active volcano. Personally, I much preferred the glacier climbing that we expected on Cotopaxi, to the rock of Pichincha.

The next twelve months witnessed a dizzying parade of presentations and fast trips between Quito and Port of Spain, with no direct flights connecting them. The choice was on Ecuatoriana to Panama, staying overnight, and then on KLM to Port of Spain via Curaçao in the Netherlands Antilles, or to take Viasa or Iberia via Bogota and Caracas. The most frequencies were via Caracas, jumping-off point for Madrid, Paris, London, and Amsterdam. The Panama option was only available once a week. Thus, I usually traveled the Caracas route, taking a local Venezuelan domestic flight from there.

I was due back in Port of Spain soon to make advance preparations for the first stage of our wide-body campaign, but having a hard time getting away from Quito.

The first week of December is a festive time, the anniversary of the city's founding. The occasion is observed with a famous fair, one of the most exciting events in the Americas. Donkey caravans loaded with handicrafts pour in from every province, as the fair is a showcase for Ecuadorean artistic craftsmen. There are songs, contests, parties, parades, and bullfights throughout the week. People joyously welcome the festival, the most carefree of the year.

After the TAME presentation, my week was crammed with meetings, and I was rushing to be on my way on Saturday. Then on Friday morning, I received an unexpected call from Alfonso, inviting me to the bullfights—that very day. At first, I tried to excuse myself because I was waiting for a call from the director of Civil Aviation for a meeting schedule, but upon finding that the *corridas* always took place between noon and 2:30—*almuerzo* and *siesta* time—I accepted with enthusiasm.

The combination of a bullfight and a Friday afternoon was almost certain assurance that no business meetings could be arranged anyway. Fascinated by stories of bullfighting, I looked forward to my first opportunity to experience the real thing.

As we entered the *plaza*, Alfonso explained the classic division of the bull ring. You can sit on the sunny or shady side, in *sol* or *sombra*, among the rabble or the bourgeoisie. The more expensive seats, in the *sombra* where the official's box—a draped balcony—is located, are closer to the action.

Alfonso had purchased the tickets in the *sombra*. Arriving late because of parking difficulties, he had to summon the authorities to shoo the inevitable squatters out of his reserved seats—amid loud protestations and unearthly scowls. However, once the fights were in progress, I noticed that no one paid any attention to their seats, since the drama of death in the ring riveted their interest from the first *clarin* sound to the final echo of the *olés*. The thousands of seats were filled with chattering, cheering, singing *aficionados*.

*Él Toro* is one of the fiercest and bravest of animals. He will meet any foe and fight him to the death. He had come a long way from his native Andalusian fields in Spain to meet his destiny in the cadenced, clocklike ritual that dates back to Roman times.

The men who would shortly appear on the stage of death were lined up behind the closed gate on the opposite side of the ring. I admired the richly embroidered dress capes which they wore over their left shoulders and tightly wrapped around their waists. They appeared uneasy as they squinted into the sun, smoking a last cigarette, impatient in expectation of the bugle which would relieve the terrible tension of those last agonizing moments.

The anxiety of the bullfighters was well-founded. I learned that since the year 1700, over one-third of the major *matadors* had been killed in the ring.

The assets of the bull are his power, speed, and courage, his fearless instinct to attack any other creature in sight. His weakness is his tendency to charge in a straight line once he has picked his target. This is the handicap upon which all the *matador's* work is based, by directing the bull's attention away from himself and toward the *muleta.*

We watched the fascinating drama in the ring, all carefully programmed from the official's box by the sounds of the *clarin.* As each *matador* finished off his bull and took his final bow, he walked triumphantly around the arena, hoping to be rewarded with the ears of the dead bull. *Sombreros* fluttered down from the stands. The horses came to drag the body of the bull away.

The ritual continued for the alloted time to finish off six bulls. Chattering and gesturing excitedly, the *aficionados* filed out to return to their late afternoon tasks.

I invited Alfonso to join me for lunch. We chose a restaurant close by, ordering ox tail soup and beef tongue—the specialty of the house.


Arriving in Port of Spain early Sunday morning, with no appointments until the next day, I decided to take a tourist-type excursion.

The most popular tour was to the Caroni Swamp, a four-hour combined car and boat trip into the Caroni Bird Sanctuary, where the Caroni River runs into the Caribbean near Piarco Airport. Incoming planes flushed out great clouds of scarlet ibis, egrets, blue herons, spoonbills, and kingfishers.

Guides loaded the tourists into large scows with outboard motors, for the trip down the slow-moving river.

Gradually, the cane fields gave way to clusters of mangrove trees, isolated by interlacing streams, which themselves became larger until there was more water than forest. In the center of that mass, choosing certain large trees for reasons undiscovered, the birds flocked to their branches by the thousands, covering them with waves of white and crimson.

I was informed that the flaming crimson of the ibis was the result of eating the tiny red land crabs which proliferate on the Caribbean beaches. The Venezuelan coast, scarcely forty miles away as the ibis flies, was their daytime habitat. Every morning, at first light, they formed into great flights to make the journey, there to feed on the teeming masses of land crabs. Each evening they returned, never varying in their choice of roosting trees.

Around six o'clock in the evening, flocks of birds began to arrive. The flocks grew to streams, the streams to clouds, until the air was filled with thousands of screeching birds, circling and diving in restless spirals, preparing to settle down for the night.

The Caroni Swamp excursion was a memorable event. I wondered how long the birds would tolerate the noise that reverberated through their roosting place. The technology curtain had opened more than a crack on the pristine swamp, splitting it wide with a crescendo of jet blasts. Perhaps one day the birds will decide to leave, their natural cycle disturbed, then slowly waste away and disappear. Relentlessly, time was pecking away at the jungle's heart, and sometime—before mankind could catch its breath—it would all be gone.

Early the next morning I made the rounds of BWIA executives to finalize February 1st as the date for our team to kick off the wide-body campaign at BWIA.

With all in readiness, I went home for Christmas—my second in a row.

# 24

My plane was scheduled to leave from SeaTac just after midnight on the 27th of January—the red-eye to Miami. Night flights were part of the normal routine for Boeing salesmen, and I had booked a connection with the BWIA DC-9 flight out of Miami the following afternoon.

Beth had the flu, and I was running late, worried about getting a cab out to the boonies, when my neighbor, Bob Wells, volunteered to take me to the airport. He roared down the empty highways in record time with his wife's new toy, a two-seater Datsun sports car, whistling and skidding around the curves.

I was burdened with baggage, including three boxed 1/100 scale plastic desk models of 707-320 airplanes.

Flight NW26, Seattle to Miami, with stops in Chicago and Atlanta, was on time. In Chicago the temperature was -8° F, the middle of the snowiest winter in 100 years, and snow had reached all the way to Miami, the first in its history. I arrived near noon and checked into BWIA. The big board showed "delayed."

Departure was finally posted for 2:30 p.m., then 3:00, then 3:30, and at last the airline reluctantly admitted that the plane had not yet arrived from Port of Spain. "Believe it When It Arrives" was proving its accuracy. Finally, at 4:00, we began boarding. The official reason for the long delay was that the plane had encountered "unpredicted head winds." We departed at 4:30, arriving in Port of Spain near midnight. Customs officials were nasty, charging the maximum duty on my models.

On Saturday, I met with Mr. Aguiton, the banquet manager of the Hilton, to verify my previous reservations.

In the afternoon, I met with Glenn Castagne. He was barely cordial.

"When did you arrive?" he inquired.

"Oh, about midnight—your plane was late."

Castagne looked startled.

"You mean our scheduled eight o'clock arrival?"

"Your fantastic DC-9 couldn't make it from Antigua. Something about head winds."

"Or maybe we had an overload."

I twisted the knife.

"No, only 113 passengers—it's performing like we predicted. They stopped again in San Juan for fuel."

"Oh, but the one we're getting next summer has bigger engines—JT8D-17s instead of the -15s."

"Great, and that means more fuel consumption."

"Yes, but it has another tank in the body."

"Yeah—like I said."

Castagne scowled.

Seeing that I was ruffling his feathers, I changed the subject, and gave him one of the 707 models. It was beautiful in BWIA colors.

He finally smiled and offered his thanks.

I delivered a model to Captain Mowser, but Eric was out flying and I left it with his secretary—with the usual little box of candy.

"Thank you, Mister Bauer, my chil'ern look forward to your arrivals."

In the evening, I invited Phil Kelshall, our new consultant, and his wife to the Chinese restaurant in Tiki Village, to discuss our latest strategy.

On Sunday, I slept late for a change. I was a jogger, but found it dangerous to run in the streets, so I had taken up rope jumping and usually did about 400 jumps in the mornings.

In the afternoon, Phil and Rosalie invited me to join them for a quick visit to Maracas Beach across the ridge of hills from Port of Spain. A small cove, then a public beach, perhaps one mile of stark white sand, was sandwiched between two steep cliffs. The beach was a mecca for the upper class, mostly Caucasians from Port of Spain and their guests, as well as tourists. I was surprised that there were no blacks. There was no prohibition against coloureds, but apparently an ancient unwritten tribal custom had simply edicted a separation. The coloureds went to other beaches.

The well-heeled people frequent the beaches during midday on Sundays. They stand around, chatting in the shade of the palm trees, meeting friends, and drinking rum punch. The sand blows in their faces, and there is no place to spread their lunches except on a blanket on the sand. It would be much more comfortable at home around their swimming pools, but it was a ritual to go there—every Sunday. A few ventured briefly into the surf, and all scurried for their cars upon a sudden shower.

For me, Monday came all too swiftly. The night before, the Boeing team descended on Trinidad from all directions, but with a common purpose.

Our team was headed by Alfredo Dodds, and included Upali Wickrama, manager of traffic forecasting and market predictions; Dave Sepanen, analyst for passenger traffic; Don Nelson, analyst for cargo traffic; and Roger Wynne, analyst for performance and fleet planning.

The Blue Emperor Room, which I had reserved in December for the presentation, was the most elegant of all the banquet rooms. I had planned the smallest detail for the big show on Tuesday morning, but had not reckoned with Murphy's Law.

Late Monday afternoon I passed Mr. Aguiton in the hall. He was hurrying, and deathly pale.

"How are you, my man?" I greeted him, adopting a Trinidadian expression.

"Do you really want to know? The Blue Emperor Room is flooded!"

I flinched.

"Flooded! How in hell? It isn't even raining."

"Not rain, man, water pipes."

Sometime during the night, the pipes in the wall had burst, and water flooded into the room, rising to eight inches deep. It was not discovered until morning, when it began seeping into the hallway.

"So what are you doing about it?"

"We're drying it out, but I'm afraid it won't be ready for tomorrow."

*Damn. There goes the presentation down the tube, and after such meticulous preparation!* Somehow I wanted to blame the competition for engineering the whole bloody affair.

"Don't panic," Aguiton said, and seeing my anguished expression, laughed out loud.

"Hey, my man, this is serious. What do we do?"

I knew every suitable room in the hotel was booked. There was only the Scarlet Ibis Room, which I had already reserved—for lunch. Finally, we were left with no choice but to partition it with a hurriedly constructed plywood wall.

The next morning, Murphy's Law worked to perfection. The signs directing the guests had not been changed, and the hotel bulletin, printed in advance, was incorrect. Worse still, with no activity expected until noon, the room had not been prepared.

Like a wounded bull, I charged around to unwind everything and set them on a new course.

After completing the rearrangement, I was horrified to discover that the Grand Ballroom, adjacent to the Scarlet Ibis Room and served by a common hallway, had a women's singing festival scheduled for the same time. Small groups were already congregating in the hallway outside the closed doors for their final tune-ups!

*What else could happen?*

The coffee and rolls were erroneously sent to the Blue Emperor Room—as previously scheduled.

At the appointed time of 10:00 a.m., the guests began to arrive. Suddenly, as if on cue, the room darkened, the sun disappeared in a twinkling, and a tropical downpour drenched the arriving guests. What a welcome!

Working against the handicaps of the singing in the hallway, the noise of setting up the tables, and the laughing and joking of the workers behind the thin partition—besides the audience sitting in wet clothing—the team launched bravely to the task. Somehow, it all worked out.

Peter Look Hong was gracious in his praise of the coverage and depth of the studies, and his favorable impression of the 747 airplane family. Well received! The meeting ended on a high note, with cocktails and an elegant lunch to top it off.

The next day was reserved for the big brass. Bruce Procope had invited Mr. John Scoon and another member of the board, Mr. Francis Prevatt, for lunch with Alfredo and me.

I had scheduled all three to come to Seattle for a visit to the Boeing plants. They departed the following Saturday, with Alfredo accompanying them on the flight and conducting a personal tour.

February was not a good time to do business in Trinidad and Tobago. The country went mad for the Carnival Festival, which stretched to a week of frenzied singing and dancing.

My Trinidadian friends had been urging me to visit Carnival, and I finally succumbed, making reservations for Beth and me at the Hilton for the following year.

With the principal players scheduled to be off to Seattle, I finalized plans to revisit Guyana Airways in Georgetown. I had scheduled my visits to once a year—sufficient to keep my finger on the pulse of that slowly evolving airline—and once every two years for Surinam.

I was delayed by one day due to important business at BWIA, and sent Don Nelson ahead to finalize the meeting arrangements.

With my plane an hour late, I touched down in Georgetown at four o'clock on Friday afternoon. Speeding to the hotel, I saw Don standing on the front steps.

"You better hurry," Don blurted, "I set up the meeting with the president for four o'clock!"

I pointed to my watch. "But that's impossible. It's already fifteen to five!"

"I told him your plane was due at four. He said to come over as fast as you could."

I didn't need to check in, Don had already handled it. I grabbed the key and leaped up the stairway three steps at a time. The temperature was 95 degrees and the humidity 85 percent. *Thank heaven for air conditioning!*

I arranged my notes, put on a clean shirt and tie, and was bounding back down the stairs in less than ten minutes.

Mr. Abrams had returned that very day, after more than a month in the hospital and many months of rehabilitation. He had moved so quickly that Guy Perry, his stand-in, had not yet vacated the office. I had called Perry from Port of Spain only the day before, fully expecting to meet with him. But on Friday morning, Abrams announced his decision to return, and simply grabbed his wheelchair and came over.

Abrams had improvised a desk in a small building behind the main office building, itself a ramshackle, two-story frame structure; paintless, parched, and pitiful. It had no air conditioning, poor lighting, and one telephone.

The bare room in the back reminded me of the white-washed "chicken coop" at Paramaríbo. A plain desk occupied the center of the tiny enclosure. The desk top was clear except for an ashtray and a copy of the *Guyana Chronicle*.

Mr. Abrams was a tall, strongly muscled man, wearing blue-tinted glasses and a kindly expression, and puffing clouds of blue smoke from a big cigar.

We shook hands and exchanged cards.

"Please excuse our modest surroundings," Abrams apologized, directing us to sit down on a wooden bench. "You already know the story."

"We're certainly glad to see you back in circulation," I said. When I was here before, things didn't look very good."

Abrams smiled. "Yeah, nobody thought I was such a tough son-of-a-bitch."

"Well, on that visit, I talked to Captain Chana-sae and Mr. Loy. They expressed interest in cargo traffic, and Don here has made a detailed study of world flows, with an emphasis on the Caribbean sector."

Don handed over several copies of a document he had prepared, explaining the details. The bottom line was a profitability forecast, utilizing a 737-200 cargo plane. As I watched, I couldn't help thinking how the scene would appear to an uninitiated observer.

*Ludicrous! Mr. Abrams seated in a wheelchair, his first day in office in nearly a year, intensely discussing the acquisition of a $9.9 million airplane. The airline probably could not afford to pay cash for a new car.*

Regardless, the game of selling demanded that the smallest of leads be taken seriously, nursed carefully, and pursued diligently—even to a bitter conclusion.

When we said goodbye to Mr. Abrams, I did not realize it was the last time I would visit Guyana. Before the year was out, the fluidity of the sales organization had called for another realignment—I had too many accounts. Guyana and Surinam were transferred to Bob Brog.

Our patient efforts in Guyana were not in vain. In October 1980, Guyana Airways began flying a leased Boeing 737-200 airplane.

# 25

It had been scarcely a month since Avianca, the flag carrier of Colombia, announced the lease of a 747-100 and was beginning negotiations with Ecuador for landing rights. Ecuatoriana would be dramatically affected, and I headed for Quito.

I dreaded the trip back through Caracas. An endless hassle! The hotels catered to large tour groups, sniffing at business travelers. Even though my reservation at the Macuto Sheraton had been confirmed to our Seattle office for Saturday night, I expected the usual excuses.

I bounded up to the desk as if I owned the world, plunked down my Boeing card, and with a big smile, I said, *"Está todo bien?"*

The clerk looked up, took my card, and headed for the back room. *"Por favor, un momento,"* he said over his shoulder.

He came back with a sour expression.

"Sorry, Mr. Bauer, we don't have any rooms."

I handed him a copy of the confirming telex with the reservation manager's name at the bottom.

He studied it, shaking his head.

Since being nice was not working, I turned aggressive.

"I'd like to talk to the manager!" I shouted. "This happens to me all the time!"

There was a long delay, and finally the manager appeared from the back room.

"I think you got canceled out," he announced, before I could speak. "Maybe we'll have something around six."

I looked at my watch. "Canceled out! It's only four-thirty! Our telex guarantees the first night payment."

He shrugged. "I'm sorry, you'll have to come back at six."

I cooled my heels, walking around the hotel. Time dragged.

At six the story was the same, and at eight, no change. I knew there would be no room, so I curled up on the sofa in the lobby.

Tiring of the fitful naps, I left early for the airport. The terminal was under construction, overcrowded and reverberating with the noise of jackhammers—full of choking dust. Lines of passengers wound among the piles of debris, and there was no place to sit. I stood, half asleep, for nearly three hours.

Arriving in Quito on Sunday afternoon, I relaxed, taking a short nap in the cool tranquility of my room—a good cure for the slight head-ache from the altitude.

I called Alicia early in the morning.

*"Hola Alicia, como está!"*

*"Bien! Bien! Senor Bauer."*

"I wonder if it would be okay if I come over this morning to see the Colonel?"

She hesitated. "I'm sorry, Mr. Bauer, we have a problem. Colonel Banderas had so many requests for meetings, he had to set up a formal schedule. I'll try to arrange for you tomorrow afternoon—or sometime Wednesday."

*Something drastic had happened.*

"What's causing all the activity?" I asked.

"I don't know, but all of a sudden, Lockheed, Douglas, and a bunch of engine manufacturers have their salesmen here. Besides, there's a lot of government people."

"Okay, thanks. I'll wait for your call. *Hasta Luego!*"

I never worried about Alicia forgetting to call back. She was dependable—and always qualified for one of the large boxes of chocolates.

In the meantime, I scheduled meetings with Colonel Palmer, military attaché at the U.S. embassy, and Colonel Mora at TAME, holding Tuesday afternoon open. Then I went back to the airport to chat with Oswaldo and Alfonso, who had adjoining offices. Oswaldo was on a flight.

They were always very receptive and informal, so I never bothered to announce my coming—just popped in.

"*Como está, mi amigo!*" I greeted, appearing in the doorway.

Alfonso leaped up with a big smile and a back-slapping greeting.

"We're getting the 320 ready for the inaugural flight to Los Angeles."

"And when is that?"

"Well, we hope by the end of the month. Colonel Banderas is going along—and I think Muller and Camacho."

"So, it's a big tour."

Alfonso turned a little a sad.

"The Douglas people have invited them to take a plant visit at Long Beach. I wish they wouldn't fool around with Douglas."

"So it seems like Banderas is being overwhelmed with visitors—according to Alicia."

"Yeah, the Avianca announcement really changed things. They're negotiating a bilateral—and Air France is talking about starting service through Quito with a big 747 soon. Everybody's here."

Alfonso suddenly brightened. "But Oswaldo won't see 'em. He just told Lockheed and Douglas that he didn't have anything to discuss— came right out and said his choice was the SP."

"So, let's forget business for a bit, and you and Susanna come to the Colon for dinner one night this week."

"Thanks, Gene, Susanna always enjoys the dinners. Maybe Thursday will be okay?"

I took out my appointment book, and added a quick note. "It's in the book for eight o'clock."

I found Colonel Mora a little disappointed.

"My financial people are worried about the Boeing traffic forecast," he confided. "I've asked our accounting department to go over everything once more. I'd still like to find a way to get that 737."

"Good, keep pushing. Is there anything else Boeing can do to help?"

"Well, no, our people are very conservative. Even though our last twelve years of traffic history have been positive, they're afraid of the investment—and would much rather buy a used 727-100."

He paused in a gesture of futility.

"We'll have the new study finished in March, and then we'll go back to the board."

"Okay, Good luck! Let me know if we can help."


Colonel Palmer advised me that political infighting between Guayaquil and Quito was intensifying. The *costenos* were insisting that Guayaquil be designated as the official international gateway for the big airplanes. The *serranos* were even more vocal—since Quito was the capital. There appeared to be no middle ground.

"And what about the consultant equation?"

"Well, I haven't changed my views on that. We see it all the time. Rigged deals. It seems that the *junta* is involved in a lot of details."

"Maybe I'll capitulate, in spite of what Banderas says. What about Lockheed and McDonnell Douglas?"

"I know Lockheed has a representative here, and I believe McDonnell Douglas has also. I guess you knew that McDonnell Douglas appealed to the embassy about competition. They said Boeing was running a monopoly here."

I laughed. "I know you can't take sides, but I do appreciate keeping up-to-date on the political developments."


When I returned to the hotel on Monday afternoon, there was a message from Alicia. Tuesday at two o'clock was okay for Banderas.

"I've been hearing all kinds of new developments," I ventured, as I entered the familiar surroundings of Banderas office.

He was charging around, nervous and agitated. Stubbing his cigarette in the ashtray beside me, he immediately pulled out another. Stopping for a light, he stared hard at me.

"Mr. Bauer, we're going to need wide-body operations here a lot sooner than I thought. I'm sure you know about the Avianca discussions."

I nodded.

"We need to start service to the U.S. in two years, and to Europe the following year."

"Great, that timetable fits right into the schedule I've already proposed back at the plant."

I unrolled a flow chart with the important milestones for our 747 presentations to the airline and the government. "I need your concurrence on some of these dates."

We studied the chart, and firmed up the dates.

"I understand you'll be starting Los Angeles service with the 320 soon."

"Next month at the latest."

"And visiting our loyal competitor in Long Beach," I joked.

Banderas looked annoyed. "I wish they'd quit bothering me," he lamented. "But what could I do? We'd be on the flight anyway, and it would be bad manners to turn them down."

Then after a long drag on his cigarette, he turned to me and pointed his finger. "Mr. Bauer, I want you to work closely with Edison. He knows all the details."

"Okay. Good luck with the 320, we'll be in touch," I said as I departed.

I invited Edison Teran and his wife for dinner on Wednesday evening. He was worried.

"We've got a lot of problems here, Gene," he confided. "There's a splintering of opinion. I guess you know Muller is a DC-10 advocate— and Oswaldo won't even talk to Douglas. Pazmino hasn't said, but he's a maverick—could jump either way. Camacho is too busy worrying about finances. He'll probably lean to the lowest price."

"Well, Edison, I appreciate being able to stay on top of things—and Banderas seems pretty rock solid for Boeing. I haven't spoken to him lately about consultants—what do you think?"

"Maybe it would be a good idea."

With the Boeing traffic analysts due into Quito in early March to work with the airline, I went on to Lima.


In December, we had learned that General Berckemeyer was on his way out as president of AeroPeru. General Oswaldo Cabrera, from the Peruvian Air Force, would be taking over. Further, a special commission had been formed to review the AeroPeru organization and operations.

With the uncertainty of the political and economic status in the country, Boeing had shifted course from a vigorous selling campaign to one of being helpful in solving the technical problems of the airlines.

In the fall of 1976, at the request of the *Ministro de Transportes*, we had sent in a team of runway experts to evaluate the landing fields in Peru, and I was bringing the results.

I delivered the study to the *Ministerio*, and also shared the results with the airlines.

General Cabrera didn't waste any words.

"Mr. Bauer, the government has decided to delay trying to solve our long range airplane requirements, and first get our domestic problems solved."

"Fine. Boeing can help. I just delivered this report to the *Ministerio de Transportes.*"

I handed Cabrera a copy. "I want to take this opportunity to review a number of items which are extremely important in your evaluation of the domestic fleet."

Cabrera laid the copy on the desk while I continued.

"Our team reevaluated the runways in twenty-three of your cities, for suitability of 737 operations."

"Well, Mr. Bauer, you know our main concern, ingestion of foreign objects from the runway. Those engines are so damn low to the ground—they just suck up everything."

"Exactly. That's why we developed the special kit for unimproved fields. The report covers all the details and includes results of the demos we flew in nine countries in northwestern Africa—on all types of terrain: sand, coral, gravel, and grass."

"I remember how well the 37 did here back in 1972—before AeroPeru bought the Fokkers."

"There's no doubt of the airplane's superior takeoff and landing performance over any other model, from those short, high fields. For operating out of gravel fields, the kit incorporates two main features. First, air deflectors are installed on the lower forward engine cowls to blast the debris aft, as the plane's wheels kick it up during braking. The other feature is a special gravel deflector for the nose wheel."

Cabrera began leafing through the document.

"We compared the results in Africa with the runways here in Peru, and the 737-200 with the kit will operate out of them all!"

"And how many without the kit?" he inquired quickly, the first trace of excitement in his voice.

"The kit increased the total from thirteen to twenty-three. Ten more cities!"

"Excellent! Maybe we have something here. But we're going to spend whatever time is necessary to do an independent evaluation."

"One more thing, General. Take a look at some Pratt and Whitney data in the back of the report. FOD (foreign object damage) is dramatically lower for the 737 with the kit installed than any other airplane. The average number of takeoffs per premature engine failure due to FOD was 28,000 for the 737 compared to 19,000 with the DC-9."

"Amazing. I wouldn't've believed it. With the 9's engines up on the tail and the 37's only a few feet from the ground."

"Well, that's their data, and P&W is pretty reliable."

Cabrera stood up and offered his hand. "Mr. Bauer, thank you very much for this report—and the work your team did here."

I took a taxi to the airport to meet with Hernando Vasquez, maintenance manager for AeroPeru. The airline still didn't own a hangar, servicing the airplanes from ladders or with the mechanic standing in the back of a pickup truck. I noted one of the Fokkers parked on the ramp, with mechanics removing the engine cowls.

Hernando's door was always open.

"*Mi amigo, Hernando, como está?*"

"*Bien, bien, asienta se.*"

"I see one of those great Fokkers out there being worked on."

Hernando laughed. "They call those airplanes. Our mountains just eat 'em up. They're in here for unscheduled maintenance all the time."

"And how is the 727 doing?"

"It's never down, except for regular checks. We're about ready for a C check. But we won't do that ourselves. We'll send it to the FAA-approved base in Bogota."

"Oh, so you've got a deal with Avianca?"

"Yeah, ever since the delivery. They do a good job."

"I'll ask our tech rep there to look it over when it's in for the C. By the way, I just came from a meeting with Cabrera—gave him a copy of the runway evaluation." I handed a copy to Hernando.

"Let's get together for dinner. How about the chicken house?" I suggested.

"No, Gene, you always take us to those fancy places. It's our turn. Martha wants you to come to our place. The kids want to thank you for the Christmas gifts."

"*Da nada! Es una placer.*"

Hernando lived in San Isidro, one of the fine districts of Lima, and I always enjoyed dinner with the family.

After a reunion with General Revoredo, who was approaching his eightieth birthday but still managing the airline on a daily basis—in spite of his growing cancer—I met with Francisco Arteaga, operations manager.

"Francisco, how are you doing with the second 727-100?" I inquired.

"Gene, that's a very reliable airplane. We've got it on the Miami run—carrying freight. But we need more lift. I think the general is going to ask the government for permission to buy a 707-320C for the Lima-Iquitos-Miami operations."

"Yeah, I just talked to him about that. We'll find out who has 'em for sale, and I'll report on my next visit."

Francisco took me on a tour of their modern hangar, in sharp contrast to the uncovered ramp at AeroPeru.

"I wish the government would let us operate," he said, as we toured. "There's money to be made if it's done right."

I couldn't agree more. But that was not the way of the government bureaucracy.


Back in Seattle, in the center of my desk, I found an official telex from Ecuatoriana, outlining the new policy.

"Due to a very high work load, and increased interest in a wide-body airplane, we regret that we can no longer accept uninvited visitors. Please don't call us, we'll call you."

It was signed by Colonel Banderas.

Now I understood why Banderas had steered me to Edison. At least Boeing would have eyes and ears into the airline without officially calling for an appointment.

# 26

All through my sales world, demand dates were stacking up. It took me five weeks to make everything ready for the road again. This was my longest stay at home—ever!

In Peru, the fortieth anniversary of Revoredo's historic flight would be celebrated, and I needed something special for the anniversary. Further, I owed him a list of available 707-320s.

In Ecuador, we would be presenting the results of the traffic forecast to Ecuatoriana, and supporting Colonel Mora's recommendations to the government for a 737.

In Trinidad, the financial and economic studies were scheduled to be presented to BWIA.

First things first. I arranged to have a handsome plaque made of walnut, mounting it on a bronze plate, inscribed with a salute to General Revoredo from all Boeing employees. Then I requested our inventory airplane staff to scour the world to find any and all 707-320 cargo planes for lease or sale.

I was also constantly on the lookout for available 737 airplanes—suddenly hard to get. Orders began to balloon in 1977, partially as a result of the airplane's spectacular performance in Africa, but perhaps more significantly, the Little Giant was beginning to be recognized as a money-maker all over the world.

Even in tight markets, occasionally a customer would suddenly lose its financial support, perhaps not until the airplane was well into the production cycle. Those lame-duck airplanes gained the name "white tails," in recognition that there was no airline logo on the tail when the airplane rolled out of the factory.

In reviewing the production schedule, known as the "firing line" at Boeing, I found two which were due to be delivered in June, with the buyer looking pretty shaky. I put together a letter of advice for Revoredo.

The Ecuatoriana and BWIA presentations were scheduled to follow each other in lock-step, separated by the Easter weekend, and I had the daunting task of getting across the continent on Easter Sunday. The air traffic would be at its highest of the year, and I made a special effort to get my flight itinerary confirmed well in advance.


Arriving in Lima on Sunday, March 27th, my first call was to Elsa on Monday morning.

"Hello, Elsa, how are you? And how is the General?"

"I'm just fine. The General is pretty weak, but he comes to work every day. Will you be attending the celebration today? It's not fancy like last year. Only the employees are involved."

"Of course, I'll be there, and I hope he can join me for lunch at the *Tambo de Oro* tomorrow."

"Hold on, I'll ask him."

The *Tambo de Oro* was all that remained of one of the finest *haciendas* in all of Peru. Located on Union Street, in old Lima, it had gradually shrunk as the city grew, finally being reduced to the front courtyard, the main residence, and the garden. The entrance was through two giant, black ironwood doors, with huge brass knockers, and a stone fence surrounded the entire complex.

The main building had been converted to a restaurant, rated as the finest in Lima.

"He sends his regards and says fine. What time?"

"Let's say one o'clock. And perhaps he would like to bring *Señor* Aspillaga along."

"Okay, I'll tell him."

The restaurant was only three blocks from the Sheraton, so I walked over. I had scheduled lunch there on many occasions, and they knew me. "Yes, Mr. Boeing, we have a nice table in the courtyard for you," the receptionist said.

Later in the morning, I grabbed a taxi and headed for Faucett headquarters.

When I embraced the old General, a feeling of sadness overwhelmed me. His body felt like a sack of bones.

The celebration was simply a big buffet laid out on tables on the lawn in front of the headquarters building. No bands, no zooming airplanes, and no ceremonies. Perhaps the Air Force was too poor to fly.

*Señor* Aspillaga read a testimonial, a representative of the employees presented a gift, and I presented the plaque. When it was over, Revoredo invited me to come into the office with *Señor* Aspillaga, and we reminisced a little about better times gone by. I gave Revoredo a list of the 707-320 cargo planes available—for sale—but none for lease.

"But I have good news on the 737," I announced.

"Yes?"

"There are two white tails coming up for June delivery. They'll need a little customizing for Faucett, but we could have them ready by October."

Desire exuded from Revoredo's face. The old fire in his belly momentarily flared up.

"Wouldn't I love that." He gazed out the window toward *El Chico*. "We'll give it a try. Go ahead and send us a proposal for one of 'em."

The next day at the *Tambo de Oro*, we talked mostly of poetry, poverty, and past. I had spent several hours taping interviews over the last year, but I always learned something new from Revoredo.

After touching bases with General Cabrera, Raoul Seminario, Hernando Vasquez, Francisco Arteaga, Giesela Plenge, Roberto Carrion—even arranging cocktails with Federico Pastor—I hightailed it for Quito on Ecuatoriana's Sunday afternoon flight.

After several postponements, Ecuatoriana had made their inaugural 707-320 flight to Los Angeles late in March. On board were Colonel Banderas, Colonel Camacho, and Roberto Muller. While there, they took a tour of the McDonnell Douglas factory.

Banderas came away highly impressed. Where he had been holding them at arm's length for years, he now embraced them completely.

The main factor in the turnabout was an offer to accept payment for the airplanes entirely from Ecuadorean commodities. *No cash!* Camacho was incredulous. A commodity deal would make him appear as a financial wizard, eliminating the need for wrangling with the government. On the surface it was all roses.

Following the plant visit, McDonnell Douglas executives met with Banderas and Camacho in New York a week later to discuss details of the commodity proposal.

Thus, in early April, I approached my friend Edison Teran, during lunch at the Colon Hotel, for advice on how to continue the highly effective personal meetings with Banderas. He confided that the Colonel did not feel it was prudent to make Boeing's access any easier than the others, but he had an idea.

Banderas had just returned from the New York meeting. A four-day Easter holiday was in the offing, and Edison used his influence to arrange a meeting at the Banderas home.

Banderas was expansive. He had suddenly become enamored with the DC-10, dazzled by the "commodity carrot." Knowing the history of failures of that approach, I was not unduly alarmed. Banderas would soon find out for himself that the idea would not work. I listened to his plan for the future.

"Since we met last, two things have become clear," he announced. "First, we must have a wide-body flying by January next year."

"That's tight—only nine months—you'll need an interim lease."

Banderas nodded. "And second, we want a total package, including the lease deal."

The wheels were turning pretty fast in my head. McDonnell Douglas, experiencing a slump in sales, would have several unsold airplanes coming off the line, which could easily be made available for lease to fit the Ecuatoriana timetable.

On the other hand, Boeing, enjoying brisk sales, had sold out the line all the way into the spring of 1978, with nothing to lease.

"I need all the wide-body presentations to be completed in May," Banderas continued. "Then we'll take thirty days for review, and we'll sign a contract by July 1st."

"Boeing can do it!" I stated boldly. "The only hard part is the leased airplane, but we'll bust our balls to find one."

I sat down with a piece of blank paper from my briefcase. "Here's our target: We'll make our presentation the first week of May. It'll consist of four parts: an eight-year traffic forecast, a fleet plan to meet the forecast, a 747SP performance analysis on your route system, and a financial analysis with a cash flow and amortization schedule."

Banderas clapped his hands. "Great!"

The cards were beginning to fall in place. Now the most difficult hurdle was to get home base to concur in the tight schedule. All the salesmen were making demands on our overloaded staff.

Later, in a meeting with Edison, I learned there was much more to the new urgency in Banderas' timetable than simply a result of increased competition and increased flights of wide-body airplanes into South America. More significantly, the ruling *junta* had promised to turn the government back to a constitutional body, with national elections, by late 1977 or early 1978. Banderas wanted to have a contract signed, and if possible, an airplane flying in the country before the change in government, concerned that a civilian leadership would look less kindly upon a purchase subsidy.

"We need to do something special for Banderas," I ventured. "Maybe an SP model with a new logo?"

"That's good."

"We could have our vice president present it to Banderas at the luncheon after the main meeting."

"Hey, Gene, I have a great idea. Let's get the public into it. We'll hold a contest in the local schools, and offer a cash prize for the most artistic effort. Think of the publicity!"

"Edison, I love your idea. I wish we could do it—but there's a big problem."

"Yes?"

"Banderas' schedule. The school process is too slow. We'll have to go commercial."

"I'll think about some candidates."

"Good. This weekend I have to leave for Port of Spain. We have a big presentation on Monday. I'll call you from there."

My last contact in Quito was with TAME.

"Well, we finished the study again in March, and it came out like you said," Mora reported.

"And?"

"And I went back to the board."

"You don't look happy."

Mora sighed. "We were so damn close!"

He snapped his fingers.

"It went all the way to General Leoro. He sided with Banderas. Ecuatoriana got the nod to modernize as a first priority—we're second."

"And what about airplanes for TAME?"

"We didn't take it sitting down. I emphasized how risky it was to keep flying the old airplanes—with major maintenance costs—and the increased odds of a fatal crash."

"Is there any possibility of going back again?"

"No chance. The board was unanimous. We have to suffer with the Electras two more years."

The TAME story did have a happy ending. In 1980, fully four years from the time I made the first contact, TAME became a Boeing customer, purchasing a new 737-200.

# 27

L eaving the task of finding a local artist to Edison, I prepared
to leave for Port of Spain to continue my marathon competition at BWIA.

With a four-day holiday in Quito, I suddenly found myself unable to
reconfirm my flight to Caracas on Iberia Airlines. I had been too busy
scrambling around during the week, and there was no answer to the
phones on Saturday.

My ticket had been validated all the way through, and although I was
concerned, I tried to put it out of my mind. The main team would be
arriving in Port of Spain on Sunday, and the presentation to BWIA was
set for Monday morning.

On Sunday morning I rose at 5:00 a.m. I was due at the airport at
seven, with an eight o'clock scheduled departure. Outside my window, a
rooster's raucous cry fractured the morning stillness. A horn honked
impatiently in the street below. Suddenly, dogs barked everywhere, and
the faint roar of automobiles increased to dominate the sounds. The
day came quickly, the light cutting the dark sky and transforming night

into morning in the span of minutes. As there is no twilight at the equator, neither is there a dawn.

On the ridge at the edge of the city, the silhouettes of the eucalyptus trees stood frozen against the sky. Cayambe's mighty volcano loomed in the distance, its commanding bulk dominating the scene. It was morning in Quito.

Suddenly the air was filled with the sound of church bells. *Easter Sunday! I longed to be home.* I quickly packed and headed for the airport.

My spirits sank when, after struggling through the surging crowds of Easter travelers, I finally reached the check-in counter and was confronted by the news that my name was not on the confirmed list.

After a few minutes of rechecking, the attendant reported. "Mr. Bauer, your name was canceled when we didn't receive a reconfirmation."

*Terrible news! I had to be on that flight! There must be a solution.*

"Please call the manager, this is a serious situation."

The manager was pleasant enough. After double-checking and conferring with the attendant, he gave me the bad news.

"We're sorry, Mr. Bauer, but the flight is sold out. You'll just have to stand by."

The airplane was a DC-10-30, booked solid—all 276 seats. I continued to argue—trying to convince him the airline was unfair, since their ticket office was not open on Saturday, and I had been confirmed two weeks previously.

Finally, after talking to the attendant in an aside, he came back to me.

"Mr. Bauer, you're lucky, I'm giving you the last seat."

I almost collapsed with joy, and checked in.

My usual practice during check-in was to leave my briefcase on the floor with my foot on top of it, but this time, I also had my suit bag and so I parked them both beside a pillar about five feet away. I kept glancing over to see if they were okay, but in the heat of the discussions, I lost track.

Now, as I turned to pick them up, I was aghast. Both had disappeared!

This was the worst moment in my five years on the road. I broke out in a cold sweat—in the 90–degree heat!

*What could I do?* In the briefcase were all my sales notes, my expense accounts, travelers checks, calculator, appointment book with irreplaceable phone numbers, names, and addresses.

I had nothing but my ticket, my passport, and a small amount of local currency.

*It was like cutting off my head! The remainder of the trip would be impossible! How could I operate in Port of Spain?*

I rushed around frantically, looking behind the posts and other people's baggage. Then I had an idea. If anyone could help, it was the Ecuadoreans. I ran over to the Ecuatoriana counter. I was acquainted with some of the people there, attendants and baggage handlers whom I had befriended. Everybody shook their heads.

*The robber would be far away by now.* I visualized my briefcase laying in a ditch, discarded by an irate thief who had found no currency inside.

I tried calling Alfonso—in the maintenance building only fifty yards away. *Murphy's Law was working overtime!* The cursed line was hopelessly busy.

I rushed back to the Iberia counter, making another thorough search. Nothing!

Distraught, I sat down on a bench, trying to settle my nerves. The terminal was abuzz with noise and milling people. Abruptly, I felt a calm. The flight announcements became clear above the din. Thank heaven, I understood Spanish!

The announcement was for a TAME domestic flight leaving through Gate #2. For reasons unknown, it drew my attention, and I glanced toward the gate.

The line of passengers was already beginning to move, and I spied my briefcase and suit bag! A young man, at the end of the line, was carrying them, glancing nervously around, and pushing to hurry.

I yelled out, *"Mi maleta y mi vestidos!"* and rushed toward him as one possessed.

Seeing the wild-eyed *gringo* charging toward him, the Ecuadorean quickly sought a way out of what had become a serious dilemma.

*"He hecho guardado su maleta y su vestidos,"* he blurted, smiling wanly.

Guarding my briefcase and suits? Like hell he was! He was stealing 'em!

*"Gracias! Gracias!"* I pounced on my belongings like a hawk on a June bug.

The thief, still with a weak smile, gladly gave them up. I never thought I would feel grateful to a robber. It was a bargain for both of us. I collapsed in a nearby seat to collect myself.

There seemed no doubt that my rescue was an act of Divine Providence. There could be no other answer. *I silently thanked my God, who was watching over me on that Easter Sunday.*

We departed a half hour late, already threatening my afternoon connection to Port of Spain in Caracas.

The plane refueled in Bogota. I made a mental note. *A fully loaded DC-10-30 could not make the Quito-Caracas run nonstop—valuable information for the Ecuatoriana campaign.*

A 747SP could carry a full load from Quito all the way to New York or Los Angeles. *It should be no contest!*

I was pleased to arrive in Bogota without losing any more time. The Caracas connection was still barely possible.

The plane was quickly refueled, and the passengers from Bogota began boarding, when the operation abruptly bogged down.

I noticed a passenger standing in the doorway, arguing with the flight attendant. *The airline had oversold in Quito!*

There was one more passenger in Bogota than there were seats. The loudspeaker began announcing names.

"The following passengers please identify themselves—" I listened, casually at first.

"—Eugene Bauer." *Startled, I gave no sign of recognition. I had to be in Port of Spain in the morning.*

Activity came to a halt on the airplane. Nobody stepped forward. Then the count started. A half hour passed. The speaker began calling out names again. Nobody stirred. Finally, the Captain announced that the airplane would remain in Bogota until somebody got off.

I maintained silence. Then a commotion began in the forward part of the plane. They were putting off a couple from the first-class section—amid loud protests—who were the last to purchase tickets in Quito.

I relaxed in my seat. *Thank Heaven!*

Nevertheless, I missed the connection in Caracas. Iberia gave me vouchers for a room in a flea-trap hotel, dinner, and breakfast, and I counted my blessings. *Better than fighting with the Macuto Sheraton!*

I spent half the night calling Port of Spain to leave a message at the Hilton that I would not arrive until Monday—with no luck.

I was on the first VIASA flight out in the morning, worrying my way every step, until I arrived at the Hilton.

At the hotel, I sensed a relaxed mood—not at all like Monday—even for Trinidad. Inquiring, I learned that Monday was a holiday!

All that sweating for nothing! I didn't know, but in lazy Trinidad, the day after Easter is taken as a "rest up" day. That made a total of five days for the Easter holiday.

*What a relief!*

I decided to use the unexpected opportunity to call Edison Teran over in Quito, to see what was developing on the artist project.

"Right after you left, I called a very fine local artist, well-known—actually famous—who is willing to do the painting," Edison announced.

"Great! How much does he want for the job?" I inquired.

"He suggested one thousand dollars."

I froze, but recovered quickly. "You're out of your mind, Edison. Did I hear you correctly? Did you say one thousand dollars?"

"Look, *mi amigo,* he is one of the most famous of all artists in Ecuador, maybe in South America."

I could see why Edison was so successful in public relations.

"That's impossible. I'd be fired if I committed to that price! It might even be illegal."

"Well, what do you want me to do?"

"I'd say drop it. It would be great for Banderas, but that's too much money."

There was a silence, and still in love with the idea, I considered a new strategy.

"I have a thought. Why don't you tell your artist friend that Boeing changed its mind—but I could easily offer him a hundred dollars. I wouldn't need approval. I can authorize it myself."

"You're not serious! My man would be insulted."

"Okay, I guess the project is dead. I'll call you when I get back to Seattle next week and maybe we can think of something else."

"*Hasta luego y bien viaje!*"

"*Mismo para usted!*"


After the Boeing team completed the 747 story for BWIA and we returned to Seattle, I called Edison Teran again.

"*Hola mi amigo, que pasa?*" I greeted.

"*Bien, bien, gracias!*"

"Edison, I called about the painting of the model. Any new ideas?"

"My friend says a hundred dollars is okay. He's going ahead with the design."

"Splendid! I'll bring the blank model on my next trip. We won't have much time. I arrive on Sunday, May 1st, and we want to present the model on Thursday. Our vice president, Brien Wygle, will make the presentation."

"Don't worry, we can do it. I'll be taking it down to Guayaquil to the *Pacha Camac* Studio. They're world famous."

"That sounds like a close schedule. I'll keep my fingers crossed. Mum's the word. By the way, do you have a name?"

"*Si! Él Pichincha!* Colonel Banderas was born in Pichincha Province. It will be a very emotional event for him."

"Outstanding! I'll call you as soon as I arrive."

I was excited about the model, but I didn't tell Brien about it.  I wanted it in my own hands first.

Realistically—although such special efforts could make a difference—I knew we would need more punch for the campaign than little favors, even with a better airplane.

I had learned that McDonnell Douglas had retained a local representative in Quito who was the son-in-law of the mayor and was beginning to get audiences at high levels. Lockheed had started wheeling and dealing through a lawyer who was reported to be a relative of Colonel Banderas.

Before I left Seattle, Alfredo gave me a parting shot.  "Gene, pay attention to the importance of power in high places," he urged.

"Alfredo, I just have to find the right person, in spite of what the competitors are doing."

# 28

ollowing the Lockheed scandal, and the continuing investigations by the SEC, Boeing made a complete review of consultant practices in foreign sales and, as a result, tightened the rules still further.

In reporting to the stockholders in the spring of 1977, "T" Wilson, Boeing chairman read the following statement:

"In August 1976, the board of directors approved an updated policy statement and implementation instructions relating to sales consultants, political contributions, and financial records, formalizing requirements and procedures designed to assure the company that in conducting its business it will continue at all times to be in compliance with applicable laws, and that the nature and extent of all payments made by the company with respect to foreign sales will continue to be accurately recorded in the accounts of the company."[1]

In searching for a person who would agree to our stringent rules as a consultant, I surveyed other organizations within Boeing with dealings in foreign countries other than airplane sales, and discovered that our Aerosystems group, responsible for logistics, had already retained a consultant in Ecuador.

Aerosystems had responsibility for airport planning, landing control systems, and cargo handling systems. The studies for the new international airports in both Quito and Guayaquil were struggling forward
against a bureaucratic tangle of red tape. Nevertheless, there was per-
ceptible progress.

Having good reports on the capabilities of Aerosystem's new consultant, I decided to attempt to arrange a contract with the same individual. His name was Ricardo—a young businessman— son of a promi-
nent civic leader of long-standing in Quito who had extensive financial
holdings and considerable influence with leaders of the government. I
had not yet contacted him in person; however, to save time, I drew up a
boilerplate contract while still in Seattle.

In reading the old contract, I was startled to note that the name was
Francisco, not Ricardo. Curious, I called the director of Aerosystems.

"Oh, that's no problem," he laughed. "They're cousins—and inter-
changeable."

*A little strange for a formal contract.*

"I guess it figures. These things are often family arrangements. Okay,
we'll go ahead with Ricardo."


Arriving in Quito on Sunday, May 1st, I delivered the airplane model
to Edison early the next morning, to allow a maximum time for the artist
to transfer his design.

"Great, *mi amigo,* I'll send it to Guayaquil on this afternoon's flight.
We should have it back on the eleven o'clock flight on Thursday."

"Boy, is that close—but it's in your hands."

*"No te preocupes, Gene."*

That's precisely when I began to worry.


The next order of business was to locate Ricardo. He answered my
first call.

"Ricardo, you don't know me, but I'm the Boeing regional sales director for Ecuador, and we're working on a 747SP sale to Ecuatoriana."

"Oh, yes, Mr. Bauer, I know about that, what can I do for you?"

"We need a consultant here, and Aerosystems says you're a good man for the job. What do you think?"

"Fine, fine, we can do it. I don't spend much time on Aerosystems anyway. No problem."

"Can you meet me for lunch at the Colon? We can discuss some of the details."

"No problem, what time?"

"How about one o'clock in the lobby of the Colon? I'll be wearing a green suit.

"Fine, *gracias.*"

Every country in South America has a period of polite lateness. In Ecuador it was a half hour, the same as in Peru.

At precisely 1:30, Ricardo arrived in the lobby, and we went in to the dining room.

Over lunch, I explained Boeing's rules about consultants, showing him the wording of the contract.

"Please note in particular that you must agree not to engage in illegal payments."

"*Así, Así*—I mean yes."

"It's okay, I can understand Spanish."

"And what is the fee?"

"That's another important point. This is a contingency contract. There's no advance. The fee is payable only upon completion of a sale. I think it will be about 2 percent, but I'm not authorized to negotiate that. It's up to our area director, Alfredo Dodds. He'll be here later in the week and you can meet with him."

"Okay, good."

"Ricardo, my main mission here this week is to head up our technical and marketing team for a major presentation to Ecuatoriana for a 747SP sale. I'll be busy on that, and as soon as Mr. Dodds arrives, I'll ask him to call you."

May 1977 was a pivotal month for the campaign at Ecuatoriana. Teams from Boeing, McDonnell Douglas, Lockheed, General Electric,

Pratt & Whitney, and Rolls Royce were staying at the Colon Hotel that first week. We all knew one another.

Sales success depended to an unsettling degree on the effectiveness of competitor spying, a crucial component of a consultant's task.

However, as salesmen, we also worked through friends in the airline, the hotels, the embassy—anywhere there was an opportunity for learning the details of plans and proposals of the competition.

In setting up the presentation, I noticed both the McDonnell Douglas consultant and salesman hovering close to the action. They had reserved a corner room near the dining area, which immediately adjoined the intersection of the hallway and the entrance to *Los Carabeles*, the banquet complex where our meetings were being held.

Through louvered panels, bits of conversation could be heard among those coming and going to and from the Boeing meeting. They sat the entire morning, ordering endless rounds of soft drinks and coffee, hoping for a few scraps of worthwhile information.

As the time for lunch approached, I left the meeting room to check with Edison Teran and the model. At eleven o'clock, the appointed hour, there was no sign of it. I went back in, and when the diners were approaching dessert, an uneasy feeling came over me, as of an impending bust. Continuing to glance toward the door, I suddenly saw Edison, motioning for me to come out.

Little miracles did occasionally happen, and maybe this would be my second miracle in Quito.

*Edison had the model! It was a creation!*

Painted in brilliant colors were Mt. Pichincha, the rising sun, rare mountain birds, the ocean, and the jungle, all put together in a dazzling montage. The design would fit well into Ecuatoriana's unique color scheme, the only one of its kind in the world, where each airplane had its own individual motif.

I handed the model to Brien Wygle, who presented it to an unsuspecting Colonel Banderas. He was completely surprised and emotionally captured.

That day was a smashing success. The response to Boeing's

technical and economic studies was highly favorable, and Colonel Banderas requested a repeat presentation to be made the next day at the Air Force base near Quito.

McDonnell Douglas had made their proposal three days earlier. Included was an offer to deliver a new airplane five months sooner than Boeing.

Lockheed requested more time for a definitive response.

I was sitting in the catbird seat, the result of having many friends in the airline, and was able to get my hands on a copy of competitor's proposals the day after they were made.

During the same week, an article appeared in *El Universo*, the principal Guayaquil newspaper, with a headline that caught my eye.

"*Aeropuerto de Quito no es apto para los jumbos—747.*" The lead-in line was even more spectacular.

"*Destrozaria la pista.*" (The runway will be destroyed.)

It was a repeat of the old story that emerged in Lima during the round-the-world flight. The article went on to discuss the impending initiation of 747 service by Air France later in the year.

"It is believed that the landing of the jumbo of the French Company, in the Mariscal Sucre Airport, will cause grave danger. The runway is not in condition to support the 580,000 pounds of weight of the giant airplane—besides—and this is only one detail—the landing and consequent braking will cause deterioration to the pavement, even putting the security of the passengers at risk."[2]

Alarmed, I made an appointment to visit Colonel Gudino, the new director of Civil Aviation, replacing Colonel Suarez.

"Colonel, I'm inquiring whether this article is an official opinion." I handed him a copy of the article.

He laughed.

"The newspapers say a lot of things," he said, "most of which are not true."

"I'm glad to hear that. As you know, with its sixteen main wheels, the unit loading is actually less than a 707."

"We understand. We have an old airfield out there. We need to strengthen it up anyway. Actually, we're already going ahead with a top coat. We'll be ready for the big Air France 747 in November, on schedule."

While in Quito, dozens of calls came in from consultant "wannabees." The word was getting around that the government was serious in their procurement plans for Ecuatoriana. Visions of big bucks danced in the heads of every retired military officer who had even the slightest association with the government. Lawyers, businessmen, and even a few *gringos* were also throwing their hats in the ring.

One of those candidates was particularly intriguing. He asked to come over to the hotel, and we met in my room.

"Mr. Bauer, I have just come from a meeting with General Leoro," he said.

My ears began to vibrate.

"Yes?"

"I'm a good friend of Leoro. I just called him to find out his position on buying an airplane, and he asked me how much there was in it."

I listened.

"I told him I didn't even represent Boeing, I just wanted to know if the government was serious."

I continued to listen.

"Leoro said, 'Yeah, we're going to buy an SP, but I have to convince Duran (Army) and Poveda (Navy). They might have some different ideas.'"

How could I possibly evaluate those remarks? They could be a fabrication out of thin air. On the other hand, I might be within arm's reach of the only person who could make it happen.

I acted casual. "What do you think the commission would have to be for this thing to go through?"

"What's the price of the airplane?"

"About $40 million."

The man stroked his chin. "I think about $2 million—5 or 6 percent will do it."

"I'm sorry," I said. "We've already committed to someone else."

While the evaluation was proceeding at Ecuatoriana, I returned to Seattle to spend the last two weeks of May and early June getting ready for another round of presentations at BWIA.

On June 7th, Ricardo came to Seattle to sign a one-year contract. For better or worse, Boeing had a sales consultant in Ecuador.

Ricardo had complained to Alfredo about the fee, claiming he could do nothing for 2 percent, but finally conceding to do the best he could. He was enthusiastic and knowledgeable, an engineer who ran a consulting business in Guayaquil. He also claimed to be a personal friend of General Leoro, knew most of the executive management at Ecuatoriana, and was in partnership with his cousin Francisco, in Quito. It appeared that we had made a sound choice.

1. *Annual Report*, The Boeing Company, 1976, 4.
2. *El Universo*, 3 May 1977.

# 29

While Ricardo was in Seattle for the contract signing, I filled him in on more details of our campaign.

"Ricardo, we're at a very critical point in the negotiations in Ecuador."

"I understand."

"I'm going to Trinidad for about ten days, and I want you to get your finger on the pulse of things in Quito right away."

"No problem, I'm heading straight back."

Allowing two days for Ricardo to get home, I gave him a wake-up call in Quito. His secretary told me he was in Los Angeles.

"Oh, yes, I guess he stopped there on his way to Quito."

"No, he'll be there for a week or so."

"Oh! Do you have a number where I can reach him?"

"No problem, he lives there."

I almost dropped the phone. *My God, what's going on!*

I was completely unprepared for that development. Calling Los Angeles, I was unable to talk to Ricardo directly; however, I found out a lot more about his activities. He was an Ecuadorean citizen, but actually lived in Los Angeles most of the time, commuting to Quito.

I was mortified! Many consultants, particularly those in Latin America, had no loyalties except to the almighty dollar. Sometimes they worked both ends, tilting to the winner at the last moment. Visualizing Ricardo in the same city with McDonnell Douglas and Lockheed gave me the creeps.

My schedule was cast in concrete. I was due in Port of Spain, where the timetable was speeding up. To make matters worse, Beth was in the hospital with colitis. I didn't know how serious it was and couldn't stay to find out. In airplane sales, the job managed the man. I decided to call when I arrived in Port of Spain.

At BWIA, a three-man Boeing team covered corrosion protection, systems operations, maintenance, and ground operations. A second three-man team covered aerodynamics, performance, and flight-handling characteristics, primarily addressing the pilots. Peter Morton, our marketing director, made a comprehensive review of the latest improvements in the airplane. Aerosystems began working with BWIA and a Trinidadian architect to finalize plans for a modern cargo-handling building.

The pilots clamored for a demo in Trinidad. Boeing rejected it as too costly. Three days later, still another team presented a thorough review of engine/airframe combinations. We were covering all the bases.

For the performance data alone, over 500 pounds of computer runs were airshipped to BWIA, covering thirty-two airframe and engine combinations. The sheer magnitude of the computer data overwhelmed the BWIA planning staff, and Peter Look Hong postponed the decision date.

Before leaving Trinidad for Quito, I sent a telex to General Revoredo in Lima congratulating him on the occasion of his eightieth birthday.

Arriving in Quito on Monday, June 20th, I hurriedly called Ricardo at the office of the partners. I was told he was still in Los Angeles.

Furious, I tried to contact him by phone, but after three days of bad connections and unanswered messages, I called Tom May and asked him to call from Seattle.

It was not until Friday that I was informed that Ricardo would be detained in Los Angeles, but that his partner, Francisco, was already up to speed in Quito and would handle all the details. They allegedly worked so closely together that each filled in for the other. I felt a little better.

Next, I called Francisco, expecting good news. He was in Miami! His secretary did not expect him to return to Quito before Monday. *Two more precious days lost!*

Meeting with Oswaldo on Monday morning, I was informed that the evaluation was proceeding very slowly, and a decision was not expected before the second week of July. Considering my consultant woes, postponement amounted to good news.

Returning to the hotel, I found a note from Francisco to call. *Progress at last!*

"This is Mr. Bauer from the Boeing Company. How are things going with the SP discussions?" I inquired.

"SP? What's SP? I don't know what you're talking about."

I started at the beginning. "You know—the contract we signed with Ricardo the first week of June to be our consultant in Ecuador for the 747SP sale. He was tied up in Los Angeles and said you would go ahead with the contacts. I understand you are partners."

There was a long silence.

"What did you say your name was?"

"Bauer. Gene Bauer from the Boeing Company."

"Look, Mr. Bauer, I haven't done a single thing. I don't know anything about a contract. Ricardo didn't tell me nothing."

Francisco seemed very agitated.

I was agitated, too. For over a week, I had been trying to reach one or the other of my alleged consultants, who stood to collect over three-quarters of a million dollars on a sale. The pit of my stomach felt moldy. *Something was very wrong! Very wrong indeed!*

"When can we get together to talk this over?" I inquired, somewhat irately. "How about lunch?"

"Lunch is out. I already have an appointment. Is four o'clock okay?"

"Fine, I'm at the Colon, room 410. Come right up when you arrive."

To say I was confused was a gross understatement. *What the hell had happened?* I cursed myself for not trying harder to contact Francisco back in March. It seemed that he was the senior partner. Besides, he lived in Quito.

At 3:50 p.m., I opened my hotel room door so Francisco could come straight in. I was expecting calls and might be on the line.

The Ecuadorean half-hour of "polite lateness" was religiously followed, so at 4:30 sharp, I was not surprised when a little, black-haired man with a sharp intense face, dark eyes, and an immaculately groomed waxen mustache appeared at the door. He was wearing a suit and tie and carrying a folded umbrella. Full of nervous energy, he loped into the room.

At exactly that instant, the phone rang, and I motioned to Francisco to be seated, greeting him out of the side of my mouth. The General Electric engine salesman was on the line from Miami, wondering if he should come to Quito. I advised him of the delay.

Turning to Francisco, I handed him my business card, apologizing for the phone interruption.

He leaped up from the chair, and began pacing the room at a furious pace.

"That bastard Ricardo—he doesn't have the authority to represent me."

He pounded his chest with a clenched fist.

"My name should be on that contract—just like the one with Aerosystems."

I went to my briefcase for a copy of the contract, and pointed to Ricardo's signature with the Quito address.

"That's the address of your business, isn't it?"

Francisco grabbed the contract, riffled it quickly, and stared at the signature and the address.

"Of course! Of course! But that son-of-a-bitch won't give me a cent! Don't you see, he's trying to bypass me entirely."

He waved his arms in a futile gesture.

"The only way I can help is if you can get my name on that contract."

"I'm afraid that's impossible. It's already signed, and you guys are supposed to be partners. Boeing doesn't know anything about you're personal arrangements."

"That son-of-a-bitch," Francisco repeated, his black eyes flashing.

He fairly leaped toward me, pointing a finger.

"He's not my partner at all, only an employee—and a damn poor one at that! I'll fire the bastard!"

Between bursts of outrage and sessions of pacing, Francisco listened while I explained what had happened, and that Boeing was trying to sell a 747SP airplane to Ecuatoriana. A committee was deciding, and a constant should be finalized in a few weeks, probably by the middle of July. Boeing needed all the help possible to neutralize the opposition, particularly to maintain Quito as the port of entry. The consultant could help convince the committee to make the choice for the SP.

"Time is too short to waste haggling about a contract that has been signed," I urged.

"Who're on the committee?" Francisco snapped.

"There's Colonel Pazmino—"

"Pazmino! Hell, I went to school with him. He's in my pocket—that bastard Ricardo—oh hell, this is terrible! Who else?"

"Colonel Lara, Colonel Camacho, Senor Guevara, and Senor Muller."

"I don't know Muller or Guevara, but Lara is my old friend—and Camacho, too—damn that son-of-a-bitch Ricardo!"

Francisco had momentarily sat down, staring at the floor. He leaped up again and danced around the room like an oversized puppet.

"Christ, Mr. Bauer, I have all those guys in my pocket. Don't you see? You have to get my name on that contract!"

I stared at him, incredulous. *How in hell did I ever get into this situation anyway? Was there no sanity left in the world?*

"Let's go over to your office and call Ricardo in Los Angeles," I suggested.

"Good idea—that son-of-a-bitch!"

Francisco could not stop cursing Ricardo.

We went down to the street and Francisco led the way to a sparkling new blue Mercedes. The air-conditioned interior was luxuriously carpeted, and immaculately maintained. He drove down *Avenida de Amazonas* to *Avenida de Octubre.* Stopping at a truck agency, Francisco explained that he owned the franchise for selling trucks in Ecuador for a large United States firm. It appeared to be lucrative. He escorted me into his inner office, an extravaganza of tropical woods and gold trappings.

The call to Ricardo was a dead-end. He was out.

"Look, Gene, I can't do a damn thing for you. I must have my name on that contract. The important guy in this decision is the minister of Finance. He's in my pocket. He always calls me for advice. Christ— goddam that Ricardo!"

I had an idea. "Maybe we can get Ricardo to send a telex to Boeing informing them that any commitments made on his behalf were to include you also."

"Okay, okay! That'll do it! Fine! Good idea. You'll call right away?"

"Certainly. And I expect to give Ricardo hell. If he won't send the telex, we'll cancel the contract!"

That was sufficient for Francisco.

"Fine, I can get started right away. The finance minister will settle for $300,000—this will be a piece of cake."

I held up my hand. "Hold it," I snapped. "You'd better read the contract. You're working with the Boeing Company according to strict rules, and you are explicitly forbidden to offer bribes or payoffs. I don't want to know anything about your personal dealings. Just convince those people that the 747SP is the best product. I have all the documents for you to study so you can understand the airplane and its performance."

Francisco took another look at the contract. I pointed out the paragraph about bribes.

"I understand, fine—we can go ahead."

When I returned to the hotel, I called Tom May, and told him exactly what Ricardo must say in the telex.

"If he doesn't agree to get the telex to Seattle within twenty-four hours, tell him the contract will be canceled."

"Gotcha!"

The speed of the subsequent events was amazing. At 9:05 a.m. the next morning, Boeing had a telex from Ricardo with the identical wording that I had demanded. I called Francisco, informing him of the telex, and wrote a letter to Colonel Banderas, advising him that Ricardo and Francisco had been retained as consultants, and were available to help Ecuatoriana.

On Friday, June 24th, McDonnell Douglas was scheduled to do a repeat performance of their DC-10 presentation. The first attempt, on May 20th, had been poorly attended, as both Colonel Lara and *Señor* Guevara had gone to Buenos Aires on the inaugural flight of the Ecuatoriana 707-320.

Now, it was my turn to spy on the competition. Stationing myself at a convenient place in the lobby, I took a nose count of those who came in from Ecuatoriana. Colonel Lara did not appear, and soon Alfonso came through the door. He reported that Lara had decided to fly the New York flight that morning and had designated Fiallos to attend in his place. Colonel Lara wanted the SP, and wasn't interested in the DC-10 story.

For the past several months, we had been planning the Cotopaxi climb, and had scheduled it for Saturday and Sunday. However, the three other Ecuadoreans in the party wanted to leave on Friday afternoon, instead of Saturday, so Fiallos had to get out of the meeting early. The meeting started late, but Alfonso promised he would stay only an hour and excuse himself for important business.

At one o'clock, he joined me in the lobby. "They didn't have anything new to say," he reported. "Their main pitch is the old theme that Ecuatoriana doesn't need nonstop flights out of Quito. They propose to stop at Guayaquil."

I knew that argument all too well. It pitted the Quito faction directly against the Guayaquil faction, and was probably the single issue that would decide the outcome.

"Okay, let's head for the mountain," I urged.

The others were waiting outside in a jeep, and I went to my room to bring my mountain gear. In addition to personal items, I had agreed to furnish body harness, prussic loops, ropes, carabiners, rescue pulleys, and a mountain stove. We originally planned two rope teams of three men each, but one guy dropped out so we decided on one with three in the front, and one with two in the back. The front team of three Ecuadoreans was headed by a young college student who had climbed the mountain twelve times. I led the second team, with Alfonso, who had the least experience, last.

Leaving Quito at 2:45 p.m., we reached the maximum limit for the jeep, at about 13,000 feet, at five o'clock, then put on our packs and headed for the *refugio*, a rustic cabin at the 15,800-foot level. Following an easy ridgeline, we reached there about an hour later, passing the snow level at 14,000 feet.

It was nearly dark, but there was still time to lay out the ropes and tie in the prussic loops to be ready for morning.

The afternoon we arrived, a party of twelve was on the way down. They had attempted the summit on Thursday, and were turned back at the 18,000-foot level by a blizzard with sixty-mile-an-hour winds.

Even though we got up at 2:00 a.m., it took too much time to get the inexperienced climbers ready, and we didn't get out of the *refugio* until 3:05 a.m. I vowed to make better preparations the next time.

Outside, in the pitch blackness, banshee winds were wailing, and visibility was less than a meter in the swirling snow.

By 5:00 a.m. we reached the glacier to the right of the main approach. We were suddenly caught in an endless series of crevasses, having drifted too far to the right. We began to traverse to the left, but it was slow going. Alfonso was not dressed right and was getting cold. The storm got worse.

We hunkered down at the 17,500-foot level to wait for daylight. There was a brief break in the storm, and we had a glimpse of the sunrise and Quito, so we started up again, feeling new confidence.

As we approached the final ridge, the winds increased, threatening to blow us off the mountain, and we turned back, reaching the *refugio* at 7:15 a.m.

We decided to try again in December, schedule permitting, when we could expect gentle winds.

Back at the hotel, a telex from Seattle was waiting.

"We regret to find it necessary to inform you that the Model 747 aircraft offered on an interim lease to Empresa Ecuatoriana de Aviacion by proposal . . . has been sold to another Boeing customer. Boeing's offer is hereby terminated in accordance with the provisions of. . . ."

There went the lease part of the deal. Down the tube. McDonnell Douglas gained the advantage for providing early lift.

I delivered the message to Colonel Banderas. It was anticlimactic. The airline had belatedly recognized it would be a far bigger job to introduce the jumbo than they had imagined, and decided to drop the lease idea, take more time for study, and postpone the decision date another thirty days.

# 30

With postponements all along the line, it was time to go home. My family life had been almost nonexistent with the simultaneous campaigns at BWIA and Ecuatoriana. There was scarcely time to schedule even the most important events. My daughter Cheryl, residing in Los Angeles, was getting married on Saturday, July 16th.

Ecuatoriana had begun weekly flights to Los Angeles, and I was on board. I presented my card to the flight attendant, requesting a visit to the cockpit.

"*Hola, mi amigo,*" I announced, opening the cockpit door and putting my hand on the pilot's shoulder.

He turned his head. It was Oswaldo, with his big, open-faced smile.

"*Bienvenida, Eugenio! Que sorpresa!* I didn't know you were on this flight."

"Well, I cheated," I said, as I sat down in the observer's seat and buckled up. "I asked Alfonso who was flying today, and got lucky."

"I still love to fly these 707s. But that SP is something else!"

"I know, it'll be great out of Quito."

"Gene, there's too much politics here. My brother works for the government, and it's very discouraging."

"How's our consultant doing?"

"I saw your letter to Banderas. Well, we haven't heard from him, but I suppose he's working with the government."

Oswaldo was silent for a moment. "Everything with the airline goes through Leoro."

"That's what I understand."

We talked for a while longer and I returned to my seat, promising to come back for the landing in Panama.

The night landing was my first from the cockpit. It was spectacular!

*"Okay, mi amigo, see you in Quito. Hasta luego!"*

*"Hasta luego!"*

My daughter and her fiancé met me in Los Angeles, and we had a short reunion between planes, for my Seattle flight.

"Happy Father's Day, Dad," Cheryl greeted with open arms.

"I'm only a week late, but considering my schedule, that's pretty good," I joked.

"I'm due back in Ecuador on the 17th, but I can stay a whole day here in Los Angeles for the wedding."

"Unbelievable!"

Back in Seattle, I had a few days to prepare for the next events in Quito and Port of Spain.

Beth and I took a morning flight to Los Angeles on Friday the 15th, went through the rehearsals that evening, and I gave the bride away on Saturday afternoon.

Right after the wedding, I took Beth to the airport for a plane back to Seattle. I said goodbye and took a flight two hours later to Miami to make connections to Quito via Ecuatoriana, scheduled to depart Miami at 2:30 a.m. on Sunday morning. The plane was two hours late out of Miami, and it was midmorning when I arrived in Quito.

After the emotional high of the wedding, followed by fifteen hours in airports and on airplanes, I was overcome by a feeling of sadness. After resting for an hour in my room, I went downstairs for a late breakfast.

I sat in the little stucco coffee shop with its quaint, round, frameless windows. Outside, the scintillating sunlight composed the distant, contoured hills in a crisp montage beyond the stark white buildings. A stately palm tossed its sharp fringes in the cool breeze, soft in the sunshine.

To the northeast, the white-capped peak of Cayambe towered above the ridgeline, encircled by a random necklace of gray and white clouds.

The quiet was broken only by the cadenced, persistent crow of a rooster somewhere in the distance, a seeming anomaly for late morning in the depths of the city.

As I watched, unaccountably melancholy in that pleasant setting, the morning was suddenly shattered by the foreign blast of a jet airplane cleaving the sky over Quito, the noise of its engines crackling and roaring as it appeared over the crest of the mountains.

*Was there no place left on this small speck of universe, however primitive, however remote, that was not influenced by man's intrusive machines?*

Ecuatoriana was still locked in the throes of indecision, the committee hopelessly split. Pazmino and Muller were holding fast to the DC-10, while Lara and Guevara would speak of nothing but the SP, and no one was championing Lockheed. Banderas, reluctant to break the deadlock with his vote, opted for continued postponement, requesting an extension of all the offers to the end of August. I departed for Trinidad.

In Port of Spain, the political pot, always volatile, boiled up in spurts all summer. The government was still smarting from press stories and charges in Parliament of bribes in the DC-9 acquisition. BWIA continued its money-losing ways, adding further embarrassment to the government.

Tobagonians were increasingly fretful at the poor performance of the DC-9s and worried by the greater attention that BWIA was paying to other routes, while letting the Piarco-Crown Point shuttle stagnate.

Peter Pena forecast 60,000 boardings for August, double the number for the same month only two years previously. He began to lobby anew for approval to purchase their own airplanes, again recommending the 737. BWIA responded by promising one of the new DC-9-50s that were about to be delivered, to be assigned exclusively to the shuttle.

In late August, Lockheed stunned competitors and recipients alike with a bargain-basement offer of a new L-1011-500 to Ecuatoriana, for delivery in March 1979, at a price of approximately $31 million. At the time, the DC-10-30 was being offered at approximately $41 million, and the SP, $43 million, depending on engine selection.

Surprising even his closest advisors, Colonel Banderas switched to favor the L-1011-500.

On September 9, 1977, the executive committee submitted its final wide body evaluation report to Banderas, who had been promoted to full General a few weeks previously. The report did not make a positive recommendation. It mentioned the superior performance of the 747SP, but went on to say that "all three airplanes" would perform satisfactorily on the planned Ecuatoriana route system. It also used a much more conservative traffic forecast than Boeing had proposed, which drastically impacted the revenue stream. The revised cash flow prediction favored the trijets, with their lower capacities, three engines, and lower airplane/ mile costs.

With my help in supplying data, Fernando Guevara, Director of Maintenance, wrote a strongly worded recommendation for the 747SP, leaking it to agencies outside the airline. He was promptly fired by General Banderas, who then formally recommended the L-1011 to the government.

Colonel Lara threatened to resign. General Leoro interceded, convincing Lara to stay—promoting him to executive vice president. Colonel Pazmino was replaced and assigned as general manager of TAME, replacing Colonel Mora.

When the shouting was over, General Leoro turned Banderas down on the L-1011. Concerned about getting spare parts and technical service, the Air Force did not want the Rolls Royce engines, the sole option on the Lockheed plane.

By September, the talk in Trinidad was swinging toward the 747SP; the 747-100 was too large. That put the SP head to head with the trijets, an unequal battle, since special performance was not required. In October, I brought the marketing team back to Trinidad to update the traffic analysis and show why a 747SP/747-100 mix looked better than ever.

BWIA paused yet again to restudy.

"We'd like to do some computer runs of our own," Castagne told me one day.

"Good idea. Why don't you come on up to Seattle and use our computers. You can adapt some of the programs we've already set up for your system."

"Fine, we'll do it!"

I almost fell off my chair. "When can you come?"

"How about January?"

"You name the date. We're always ready."

Reluctantly, I allowed myself to believe that Glenn was tilting toward Boeing.

In December, the head of the pilots association announced that the SP was the most popular airplane. There was a rumor that the decision had already been made to equip BWIA with two 747SPs in 1979! No ands, ifs, or buts! The Prime Minister was said to favor a "real jumbo with upstairs features."

My optimism increased—and my caution!

At AeroPeru, new currents of change were surfacing. The airline had purchased a second used 727-100 airplane, and although the airline was in an overall loss position, the 727s were both operating at a profit. By September, activity had heated up for a fresh look at new equipment.

As a result of the recommendations of the government commission, they brought in an interim general manager, Robert Booth, from Braniff Airlines. He convinced the government that one of the airline's main problems was the unrealistically low level of paid-in capital when the airline was formed. Based on Booth's recommendations, the government passed a decree increasing their paid-in capital from approximately $4 million to $25 million. The net effect was to wipe out all long-term debt, putting AeroPeru on a current profitable basis.

When I met with Mr. Booth in September, he was upbeat.

"Mr. Bauer, the government is letting us do some new things which I believe will help to pull us out of our slump."

"That's the best news we've heard for a long time."

"Your *Plan for Profitability* has many features that fit our system, and we're going to follow up on that."

In November, AeroPeru requested a firm proposal for delivery of three 727-200s and one 747SP in 1979. We included extensive concessions in training and field service support—totalling one million dollars. The deadline for acceptance was February 15, 1978.

Airbus Industries, who came on the scene late, upped their ante to bring in A300Bs, with no money up front for the first two years, and a ten-year repayment schedule at a fixed rate of 7.5 percent.

In Quito, I recommended that Boeing increase the concession package one more time by offering a cost-sharing proposal, consisting of an operating subsidy for the first year—not in cash—but in credit memos for Boeing goods and services, primarily training. The result would be to equalize the operating cost of the 747SP to the trijets, allowing an additional year for traffic buildup. Then the extra twenty-nine passengers in the SP would surpass the trijets in earning power. Management in Seattle accepted the recommendations and the offer was telexed to Quito.

Banderas expressed interest, requesting an extension of the deadline for acceptance, but insisting on no slide in the delivery date. I called Seattle.

"Tom, I need another miracle here in Quito."

"And what's the latest?"

"Ecuatoriana wants more time to consider—but we have to hold the delivery date firm."

"I think the firing line is filling up, but I'll check it out with the big brass."

Tom called right back.

"Sorry, Gene, the July 1979 position is sold. The best we can do is September."

"I'm afraid we're in big trouble. McDonnell Douglas is holding to a promise for a June delivery."

"That's the way the cookie crumbles."

There was nothing more to do but wait.

Meanwhile, balance of payments problems were mounting for Ecuador. The finance minister was finding it difficult to justify a $40 million subsidy for an airplane purchase, particularly when rats were gnawing the children's toes while they slept in their beds in Guayaquil.

I spent all the time I could in Quito, sandwiching in quick trips to Port of Spain and Lima.

Time dragged. In November, Air France initiated twice-weekly 747 service to Quito via its Lima-Paris run. I was on the field when the plane came in, taking photographs and reporting for *Boeing News*.


"Quito turned out a hero's welcome on November 2, 1977, in the brittle-bright sunshine of this ancient, nearly two-mile-high city, the second capital of the Inca Empire. Thousands of Quitenos had come to Mariscal Sucre International Airport to watch the Air France 747 arrive.

Vehicles scurried about nervously to service the big plane, and clusters of people tried to break past police barriers to touch it. The Quito press was enthusiastic in its coverage, making special note of the ample interior, and low noise level of its engines.

"Considering that the airport was originally designed for DC-6s, the operation was very smooth. The field had recently been improved with a four-inch overlay of asphalt on the main runway, with blast proof lights and a jet fence on the ramp.

"If *Atahualpa*, the last Inca ruler of Quito, could have taken a peek at this, he surely would have thought that his God had come to take him home in this magnificent carriage."[1]

With continuing postponements, I returned to Seattle in the middle of November. On the way, I stopped in Los Angeles to discuss the latest developments with Ricardo, who was expecting to hear from the government very soon. He expressed optimism.

In early December, Ricardo called.

"Hey, Gene, we have good news!" he exclaimed.

"Great, what's the latest?"

"I'll be going to Quito tomorrow to finish up the whole deal."

"Good show!" I could hardly believe my ears, but I held excitement in check. History had dealt many disappointments. I had learned to take consultants' claims with a bushel of salt.

Ecuatoriana requested still another extension of the sales proposal, but insisted on holding the July delivery date firm.

I went directly to the top.

"Clancy, we can do it. Here's a new customer, just about in the bag."

Clancy listened calmly, puffing on his pipe.

"Our consultant says he is finishing up the details."

"Okay, Gene, you got the airplane."

Lockheed came back with a dramatic "final offer" of $29 million for the L-1011-500. Boeing was out of concessions—already at breakeven.

General Leoro turned the Lockheed proposal down for the second time. I felt the last hurdle had been cleared when I returned to Quito in December. General Banderas had switched back to the 747SP. Colonel Lara, new executive vice president, was making most of the decisions. It was rumored that he would be the new president when Banderas moved out the following spring. *The ducks were lined up!*

Glenn Castagne and two associates came to Seattle for a full week in January to work with the Boeing computers. With an agreement on the market projections and the expected BWIA share, a new economic forecast was completed.

I decided it was time for a showdown in Port of Spain, scheduling the team into Trinidad for the last week of January 1978, right after Castagne returned from Seattle, hoping for a decision before the end of the month so our competitors would not have time to restructure their proposals.

1. *Boeing News*, 1 December 1977, 2

# 31

After two years of investigations and charges by the SEC, indictments by the Justice Department, and marathon committee hearings, the U.S. Congress formulated a bill which specifically addressed itself to the problem of bribes. On December 19, 1977, President Carter signed into law the Foreign Corrupt Practices Act.

The Act was intended to put an end to bribery overseas, imposing heavy fines and/or prison sentences of up to five years on the officers of offending companies.

Although U.S. airplane manufacturers were still left in the uneven position of competing with government-subsidized foreign firms—as in the case of Airbus—at least the act provided an even field for U.S. companies to compete against one another.

Feeling a little more relaxed, I decided to implement my plans for a week of vacation in Trinidad during Carnival.

BWIA was flying 707s to Toronto, via New York, and I routed myself to meet their southbound flight on Sunday, January 22nd, with Beth coming later. Quite often, wives were able to improve the chemistry of relationships with airline management.

Having achieved a good rapport with Eric's wife, Liz, during the Seattle visit, I did not hesitate to call her at home soon after I arrived.

"Liz, I believe that Beth needs a little break, and I'm bringing her down for the Carnival."

"Oh, Gene, I'm so happy to hear that—nobody should miss the Carnival. What day is she coming?"

"Well, she arrives on the 4th, and we've planned on that week, but I expect there'll be lots of interruptions for me. She goes back on the 11th."

"You must reserve one day to come out to the house for dinner—and I want to show her the island—so if you get too busy, just count on me."

"Fine. She'll be pleased. We want to be sure to take in the *Diamanche Gras* on Sunday night and the main parade at the Savannah on Tuesday."

"Oh, I'm so excited she's coming."

"Good, we'll be in touch. I'll be seeing Eric on and off during the week."

*Good show*, I thought, when we finished our conversation. Liz had found a new friend in Beth, sharing common interests, and my linkage with BWIA was on a firmer footing.

The Boeing team arrived on Monday evening, and the main presentation was scheduled for Wednesday morning. The Blue Emperor room was in immaculate condition, having been completely refurbished following the flood.

Glenn Castagne and the planning committee arrived promptly. However, there was no sign of Peter Look Hong.

I glanced at my watch. The scheduled meeting time of 9:30 a.m. came and went. I decided to postpone a little—this was the final shot—and I needed the biggest fish. The room was full, with anxiety mounting. I leaned on Glenn.

"What do you think? Shall we start?" I asked.

Glenn appeared embarrassed. "Peter was ready to come, when he got a call from the pilots association demanding an immediate audience," he replied lamely. "Eric is there, too. The pilots' contract is up and they're talking strike."

"Strike! That's all we need!"

I had been hearing rumors, but didn't realize how deadly serious the situation had become.

"Then I suppose there's no use in waiting?" I said.

"Let me call headquarters one more time."

Glenn called the office.

"They've barely started their meeting," he announced, looking forlorn.

It was 10:15 when we got underway. I instructed the team to go through everything as planned—no short cuts. I was unwilling to trade polish for pace. Lunch could wait.

The delay proved to be fortuitous. Around 11:30, both Captain Mowser and Peter Look Hong arrived—in time to hear the economic and financial forecasts.

The bottom line was impressive.

The next several days were devoted to more detailed discussions with middle management, but attention was beginning to flag as Carnival approached. Friday was the first of a series of *fetes*—stand-and-shout dance festivals—also called "jump-ups," which went on all during the following week. They danced to the music of the popular steel bands, a world-renowned trademark of Trinidad and Tobago, dating back to the *Tamboo Bamboo* men of the early 1900s.

Glenn Castagne had suddenly become downright friendly, inviting me and the others of the Boeing team to visit the most popular of the *fetes*, put on by the yacht club. He even invited me to dinner at his home.

*Panorama*, the next big event of Carnival, was the competition among the steel bands. A total of forty-six competed, and six were chosen as finalists for the grand parade the next week.

Beth arrived on the BWIA flight on Saturday evening. Three flights came in over a span of thirty minutes, and 450 people were jammed in a mass in the customs area. Some passengers were asked to sit in the parked airplanes for an hour or more in the oppressive heat, while others cleared customs.

On Sunday evening, we attended *Diamanche Gras*, the parade of the kings and queens of the bands, who were competing for the most spectacular costumes.

Theoretically, I was on vacation for the entire week, but I never felt free to take any full day off. However, I did take time for us to join Eric and Liz in a grand tour of the island on Monday, followed by dinner in their home overlooking the harbor.

The next day, Shrove Tuesday, Beth and I had reserved seats in the grandstand on the Queen's Savannah for the grand parade.

The dizzying Carnival atmosphere had mesmerized the islands; it was a marathon of music, madness, parades, and dancing.

In the darkness of early morning, the bands and dancers began to form in the central area of Port of Spain. Around 8:30 a.m., they started the three mile march to the grandstand of the Queen's Savannah, where the festivities officially opened at nine o'clock.

In a seemingly endless procession of riotous color and pounding pans, an estimated 35,000 multihued, costumed dancers, carrying banners depicting the themes of the bands, passed over the boardwalk on center stage between the opening ceremonies and the last gasp at midnight. The endurance of the participants was extraordinary in the 90-degree heat.

Individual bands ranged from 150 dancers to a high of 3,200, their colorful names carried before them on huge banners: All that Jazz, Pacific Festival, Adventure on the High Seas, Under the Jolly Roger, Somewhere in Africa, The Lost City of Angkor, Sails, Zodiac, Love Is . . . . , on and on, sixty-two bands in all. Directly behind each banner came the King with his court, followed closely by the Queen with her court.

At the stroke of midnight, it was all over. Ash Wednesday, the beginning of Lent, marked the end of the revelry.

On Wednesday evening, we invited the Mowsers and Peter and his wife to the world-famous international buffet at the Hilton, an indescribably delicious culinary extravaganza.

Peter appeared pale and haggard, worn down by his problems with the pilots, and concerned about his own job. Bruce had advised me that he was on his way out.

One of their captains had been suspended for alleged erratic personal behavior, and the association refused to continue bargaining until he was reinstated. The deadline for a strike was now only about twenty-four hours away.

Neither side in the controversy had acted responsibly, each working from narrow, selfish interests, creating an intensely adversarial climate. There was also a shadow of revenge on Peter's part, because of the "pilots' revolt" two years before. The relationship had steadily deteriorated, each side issuing ultimatums, with no fallback strategy.

When the strike date and hour had been announced, Peter promptly threatened to fire all the pilots if they observed it—only adding to their determination.

The pilots hoped for a face-saving gesture from management—which never came. On Thursday, at midnight, they went on strike, and the entire fleet of seven 707 and two DC-9 airplanes came home to roost.

Look Hong ordered letters of dismissal delivered to the pilots' homes.

Now, the air transport situation looked so bad that it was doubtful if people would be able to leave Trinidad. BWIA attempted to arrange charters to take the people out.

Beth and I had reservations to fly to Tobago on Thursday to swim in the world-famous lagoon where the Robinson Crusoe movie had been filmed. Regretfully, we canceled out and abruptly ended our vacation.

I was due in Ecuador the following Monday, then on to Nicaragua and El Salvador, accounts which I had acquired only a few months earlier.

Putting Beth on a charter plane to Seattle, I attempted to obtain a reservation to Quito via Caracas. All flights had been canceled. I was forced to go back to Miami to connect with Ecuatoriana from there. Arriving in the early evening, and catching a few winks, I was on the 1:00 a.m. plane to Quito.

The pilots' strike in Trinidad settled down for a long siege. The year of 1978 had been expected to be the year of breakeven for BWIA, and instead, they were losing $200,000 a day. Hopes, so bright a month earlier, had turned to dust and ashes.

The decision to purchase wide-body airplanes was hopelessly derailed. Indeed, the very survival of the airline was in doubt.

In Quito, the government's feet had begun to drag. With national elections due in March, people in power had become less inclined to stand up and be counted. The $40 to $50 million investment suddenly seemed overwhelming.

On February 23, 1978, I wrote in my report under *Sales Outlook*:

"Cloudy. The obvious stalling by the government is evidence that the investment has become a political issue and subject to more than the usual pressures."

While the government was locked in indecision, Ecuatoriana purchased another used 707-320, bringing their exclusive Boeing fleet to five airplanes.

The "buy cheap and plan short" philosophy had ratcheted Ecuatoriana down a notch in world air competitiveness, and the rats in Guayaquil were back in the headlines.

Urgent business awaited in El Salvador. The previous December, on the same day I departed for Port of Spain, Senor Francisco Balzaretti, newly elected president of TACA International Airlines of El Salvador, came to Seattle to inquire about the availability of a 737-200 airplane.

TACA had been added to my territory in September, but the intense campaigns in Trinidad and Ecuador had forced me to postpone a personal contact. After developing an agenda for Balzaretti's visit, I had turned the task over to Tom May as I departed for the airport. After the meeting, Tom had reported to me in one sentence.

"Gene, I think this is a live one."

# 32

We were flying at 8,000 feet, skimming over the countryside of rolling hills, scrub forest, and neatly arranged fields of Central America.

I was headed for San Salvador, scheduled to make a quick stop in Managua, Nicaragua, to visit LANICA, the national airline—also a recent addition to my sales territory.

After arriving in Panama, events had rapidly overtaken my well-laid plans. All flights north were booked solid! Fridays were particularly bad, and as I cooled my heels all day in Panama City, I called George McHugh, vice president of Traffic and Sales at TACA headquarters in San Salvador. He was quick to arrange a ride in the cockpit of their Saturday morning flight.

Now, I was resting comfortably in the observer's seat, rewarded with the unexpected opportunity of meeting Captain Jules Caroma and First Officer Mario Montalvo, the crew of the TACA BAC-111 airplane.

One of the first things they told me was that their vice president of Operations, stationed at the New Orleans maintenance base, was pro-

McDonnell Douglas. I also learned that the British were lobbying hard to sell the BAC-111-500, their latest derivative—guaranteeing brisk competition.

My goal was to replace the three-airplane fleet of BAC-111s with 737-200s.

TACA had a high-density, profitable route structure, flying daily from Panama City to San José, Managua, San Salvador, and Miami, and back to Panama City for overnighting. The airline also provided service to New Orleans and Mexico City.

I deplaned in Managua, with permission from George McHugh to fly in the cockpit again on the last leg to San Salvador.

Phoning the president of LANICA from the International Hotel early Saturday morning, I was in luck—the office was open until noon, and I was invited for an 11:00 a.m. meeting.

A review of their traffic history and financial position left me unimpressed, and concluding that new equipment was a long way into the future, I added them to my yearly visit list.

The Saturday meeting with LANICA put me back on schedule to go to San Salvador the next morning.

At the airport in San Salvador, I was surprised when a smiling George McHugh greeted me, helped clear customs, and drove me to the hotel in his own car. Then he invited me to his home for lunch in the afternoon and a swim in the pool. Unprecedented in four years on the road!

"I suppose you realize you have a gold mine here in the airline," I ventured. "I believe you have a 12 to 15 percent spill factor."

George responded with a hearty laugh.

"Would'ja believe 18 to 20 pucent?" he said in his southern drawl.

"Which means you're turning away a few thousand passengers over a year's time. You really do need bigger airplanes—fast!"

"Yer damn betcha we do! We bin needin'um for the last three years. Owa load factors ah ova 75 pucent."

The southern accent and wonderful hospitality branded George as someone from Main Street, U.S.A. I asked if he was from the deep south.

"Hell yes, a'hm down hea' from New Orl'ns. We love the place. "Bin hea' goin' on eighteen yeahs."

The next morning, George introduced me to Dr. Jaime Quesada, vice president and general manager. Middle-aged, growing heavy, he still had coal-black hair. His round, pleasant face was wreathed in a perpetual smile. I took an immediate liking to him—cool, calm, and professional. He was a lawyer, and in San Salvador, lawyers are afforded the title of "Dr."

Quesada came out from behind his cluttered desk. "My friends call me Jaime," he said, extending his hand.

He appeared anxious to get on with the business. "Let's go to *Pancho's* office," he suggested. "We need to talk together about getting a 737." He winked at George, who was wagging his head in affirmation.

Balzaretti was busy with a single stack of papers in the center of his desk, and everything was neatly arranged. As Jaime led us in, he was lingering over a last letter. Quickly rising, he came to the center of the room to greet me.

He was tall, and thin as a rail. His steel-gray eyes were set in a sharp face, and his sparse greying hair flowed around his ears and came over his shirt collar. He moved rapidly, catlike, a man with a mission—restless for results.

I was aware that Balzaretti had been thrust into the presidency less than three months earlier—following the sudden death of Mr. Kriete— long-time chief executive and major stockholder. An architect by profession, Balzaretti knew nothing about running an airline, but he was no outsider, married to Kriete's sister.

"It's a pleasure to meet you, *Señor* Balzaretti," I said shaking his hand. "I'm sorry I missed the opportunity in December."

Balzaretti scowled.

"*Pancho!*" he shouted. "Gene, you call me *Pancho!* None of that *Señor* Balzaretti crap!"

"Okay, *Pancho.* Good!"

"Gene, you absolutely have to find an airplane right away. I understand if we ordered a new one today it would take two years to deliver. We can't wait."

"That's right, almost two years—January 1980. Boeing has the biggest order backlog in the history of the 737."

"And what's the price of a 1980 airplane?"

"Around $10.5 million."

"That's about $2 million more than today's price?"

"No. About $1.5 million."

I explained that sales prices were always quoted for the delivery year, and we included an inflation factor.

"We can't afford a straight purchase. That's why we want to lease—but a lease/buy arrangement would be even better."

Balzaretti's gray eyes pierced right through me. "You must find an airplane for us to lease!"

"Will you be keeping the BAC-111s?"

"Hell no! We want to replace 'em as soon as possible. As a matter of fact, the British Aircraft Company is our biggest problem. They hold a note on our fleet, and TACA is not allowed to buy—or even lease—without their written permission."

The only new 737-200 available for lease was a Southwest Airlines nonadvanced machine, being offered through ITEL, a San Francisco leasing company. They were asking $120,000 a month, viewed as outrageously high by TACA. ITEL also insisted on a five-year lease, terms which TACA could not accept—and the lack of the advanced features for takeoff and landing would limit their passenger load on their prime leg, San Salvador to Miami.

The alternatives were to buy a used 727-100 or a 720B, and Jaime was already working to win approval from the governmental financing agency, INSAFI *(Instituto Salvadoreno Fomento Industrial)* for the guarantee of a $3 million loan to purchase a used 727-100.

After two days of reviewing balance sheets, annual reports, and traffic histories, I returned to Seattle on February 22nd with nothing but superlatives for TACA and the country of El Salvador.

Smallest country in Central America, approximately the size of Massachusetts, it is a dazzling continuum of lush, tropical vegetation. The many varieties of flowering trees during the early spring envelope the countryside.

With a high sky and billowing white clouds nestling over the green hills, where the coffee trees creep up the slopes to the very tops, the country must rank as a queen.

I was impressed, too, with the people of El Salvador—as friendly as any I had encountered south of the border.

The tiny country secured its independence from Spain in 1821, gradually moving toward constitutional government while retaining many dictatorial features.

The government took a generally positive and welcoming attitude towards foreign investment, with a good record in its dealings with foreign firms. Two U.S. banks, Citibank and Bank of America, had branches in San Salvador, while Manufacturers Hanover Trust had a regional office there.

The economy had grown by an estimated 5 percent in real terms in 1977, with an inflation rate of 16 percent annually, low by Latin American economic standards. Coffee, a highly prized mountain strain, accounted for about half of the country's exports.

I noted that TACA was privately owned, well organized, and apparently well run. The company was forty-four years old, and retained a solid core of knowledgeable personnel. I could find no evidence of middlemen, and no one discussed consultants. Whether this was a post-Corrupt Practices Act environment or not, it was a fresh new atmosphere.

McDonnell Douglas had also become active, with a multiman team having visited in January, offering the DC-9-30. Capacity to Miami was 115 passengers, compared to 130 for the 737-200, with equivalent seat pitch.

Fate seemed to smile a little in my direction when I discovered that VASP, one of Rischbeiter's airline accounts in Brazil, was unable to finance two previous orders, and the airplanes had become white tails. The planes would come off the assembly line in June—barely three months away.

Demand for the white tails ballooned—and with good reason. In the equipment-hungry market of 1978, they were immediate delivery airplanes, being sold for $8.8 million—the price established when they were ordered almost two years earlier. For Boeing, they were as much a curse as a boon. Every customer seeking more lift clamored for them, justifiably feeling they deserved some kind of priority over new buyers. But how could priorities be established? At the time, Boeing had seventy-four 737 customers.

Clancy's policy was to handle white tails on a personal basis, edicting which salesman would be given the opportunity to offer them. TACA qualified for his prime criterion—a new customer.

The second criterion was financial. The airline must be able to pay for the airplane or readily arrange financing. To eliminate pretenders, Clancy required potential buyers to make a $100,000 nonrefundable deposit within ten days, considering one buyer at a time. Meanwhile, the airplane remained on Boeing's books, incurring mounting inventory costs.

The third and final criterion was the status of the competition. If the candidate buyer was leaning toward a competitor, Boeing would make extra efforts in its behalf.

On the initial analysis, TACA was not taken seriously, and did not appear on Clancy's list, so I hesitated to mention the white tails.

First, VASP was given until the end of February to change the Brazilian government's mind. They failed.

Second, one airplane was offered to a current customer, and Frontier Airlines was given the nod over Aloha, both with urgent needs and money in hand. Holding Aloha off with one hand, Clancy reserved the other airplane exclusively for a new customer. That decision put TACA on the list.

Topping the list was Peter Stross, regional director for southern South America, offering the plane to Austral, an Argentinian domestic carrier. While I held my breath, waiting out the crucial five-day decision period, I called *Pancho* in San Salvador.

"I might have good news. Boeing has a white tail which is currently being offered to Austral. They have five days, and counting, to accept. If they decline, TACA is up to bat."

"Hey, Gene, that's great!"

"Now I have two $64 questions. First, can you make a decision within five days if Boeing offers the plane?"

"Damn right!"

"Second, can you plunk down a $100,000 cash, nonrefundable deposit within ten days after you accept?"

"Damn right. I can authorize it myself. I'm sure I can get a bank loan, and INSAFI will guarantee it."

Austral held the suspense all week. Then their management came back with a negative decision, and on March 8th, Clancy moved TACA up to the front burner, and we offered the airplane.

Now, just as my parade was ready to get under way, Alfredo called me in to his office.

"Gene, we're putting a new face into your territory."

Well aware of the fluidity of salesmen, and our avowed understanding of sudden moves, I was nevertheless stunned.

"What in hell is going on? It looks as if we have a live customer, and you're asking for a change?"

"It won't make any difference to the airline. They buy Boeing airplanes, not salesmen's personalities."

"And when do you want this to happen?"

"Right away."

I sat frozen for a long minute.

"Look, Alfredo, we've argued and fought over a lot of issues, but this is insane. I'm going to the boss and ask for a reprieve."

"That's your prerogative."

I went to O.M. "Rusty" Roetman's office, director of international Sales, one notch under Clancy.

Rusty was cordial, as always.

I came straight to the point. "Alfredo just told me about the new sales plans for my territory. You need to know he and I haven't hit it off well, as we have different ethical standards, but this is a bad time to make a switch at TACA."

Roetman listened, nodding.

"Rusty, I'll make you a straightforward proposition. Give me the green light and I'll do a balls-out effort on the TACA account. I expect to make the sale, and when I do I'll walk away. No ands, ifs, or buts."

With two degrees in engineering, and an MBA in international business, I was unworried about my post-TACA career. I had changed course many times before in my thirty-seven years with Boeing.

"Gene, that sounds fair. You have my blessing to go ahead. Good luck."

There was no time to do traffic, fleet, or economic studies. It was Wednesday, and TACA had until the next Monday to accept. With no time to lose, I asked Phil Lindsay, our airline analyst assigned to TACA, to begin immediately on an Ex-Im Bank financial feasibility study.

"Be ready to leave for San Salvador on Friday!" I told Phil. "We're setting up shop in Balzaretti's boardroom!"

All flights were booked until Monday, the same day we had asked for acceptance. Clancy, always understanding—to the point of being wise— extended the deadline to the following Friday at midnight. If the offer was not accepted by TACA by that time, the plane would go to Aloha.

As I entered the terminal on Tuesday afternoon, my name was being announced over the loudspeaker. A TACA hostess met us and escorted us through customs. Tourists filled the city and, officially, there were no hotel rooms available. George McHugh performed a miracle, arranging for rooms in the Sheraton Hotel, within a mile of TACA headquarters.

Early Wednesday morning we hurried to the TACA offices, our hopes high.

George had assembled the top management people in Jaime Quesada's office. In addition to Jaime and George, we had Bill Daly, vice president of Finance; Bobby Padgett, treasurer; and Bill Handal, director of Planning.

*Pancho,* the ramrod, had flown to Minnesota, where he had taken his suddenly critically ill wife to the Mayo Clinic.

Jaime slapped his knees and turned to me. "We're ready for that 737 white tail right now!" he announced, smiling.

"Financing is the big task," I replied. "An application to the EX/Im Bank will be the best bet. Then commercial banks will jump in, and we can get the lowest interest rate."

I paused. "But time is short. There's only one airplane, and everybody and his cousin is clamoring for it. They're standing in line with checkbooks in hand."

I motioned toward Phil. "Phil Lindsay is prepared to work with TACA to quickly finish the financial feasibility study."

"How much time do we have?" Jaime inquired anxiously.

Our proposal expires Friday night, but if TACA accepts by that time, you have until the end of March to put up the $100,000 deposit."

"I understand that's nonrefundable."

"It comes off the sales price—yes, those are the terms."

Bill Daly put on a glum face, blowing clouds of smoke from his ever present cigarette. "There's no way we can do a financial plan in time," he exploded. "We have a stockholders meeting in May, and the annual reports and proxies have to be in the mail by the end of March."

He directed an appealing look to Quesada, who quietly listened.

"Besides, you can forget the nonrefundable deposit," Daly continued. "British Aircraft would have to approve, and that'll take three months. I say we forget the whole deal."

# 33

Shaken by Bill Daly's negativism, I glanced toward Jaime. *Momentum! I must not lose momentum!*

"Gentlemen," I said, "we know there are obstacles to overcome—but we have to start someplace. I propose we go ahead with the financial exhibit. Boeing may be willing to extend the deadline if results look promising."

"Hell, we can buy the used 727," snapped Daly. "We already have INSAFI concurrence on a loan guarantee."

"Only a verbal promise," Dr. Quesada corrected.

"It's easy to show that a new 737-200 is a better economic decision," I interposed, turning to Jaime. "We don't expect an opportunity like this to come up again soon. It was an amazing coincidence that it occurred at this time."

"We'll be in a helluva shape if'n we don't get that airplane," George McHugh broke in.

Quesada decided to give it a try. "Bill, let's do the financial analysis. We need the numbers. We can talk terms later. Why don't you and Bobby get started with Phil here."

Daly, Handal, and Lindsay left the office to go down the hall to the boardroom to get to work. George McHugh stayed and the three of us discussed the British Aircraft approval problem.

Quesada reported that it boiled down to the terms of the original purchase contract for the three BAC-111s. A separate clause required prior advance written approval from British Aircraft before any commitment of company funds could be made by TACA, either for a purchase or a lease. Failure to observe the terms would be cause to call the note, resulting in default. In that event, British Aircraft could repossess the entire fleet.

"It looks as if you have the same problem, whether you lease or buy— even if you buy a used 727," I observed.

"Precisely," Jaime replied. "Besides, we have a second mortgage with the Mercantile Bank of New Orleans. That obligation is a promissory note of slightly over $1.4 million. Mr. Ken Lott, vice president of the bank, agrees with the British."

*Another problem had crawled out of the woodwork!*

"That's why ah believe we might's well bite the bullet, and go full boh for the new ai'plane," George put in. "They'is no sense in goin' for an in'trum fix."

"Why don't we make a conference call to Ken Lott?" I suggested. "Maybe we can get him on our side."

Dr. Quesada, anxious to keep the action going, agreed, placing the call.

"I have Mr. Bauer on the line from Boeing, Ken," Dr. Quesada began. "He wants to discuss the sale of the new 737-200 that I talked to you about."

"Good morning, Mr. Bauer. I don't know what you're trying to do, but you might as well forget it. There's no way we could get all the arrangements made in less than thirty days. Why don't you just go home!"

I flinched, not expecting an attack, but this was no time to be timid. I pressed on.

"We don't see it that way at Boeing, Mr. Lott. We're trying to take the first step. We can't predict all the details right now, but we want to approach the British and seek approval to go ahead with the deposit, while providing them assurances to protect their interest."

"What makes you think they'll agree to anything? I've dealt with those people."

"Mr. Lott, there's no harm in trying. We have two weeks before the money has to be put at risk. By that time we'll have a detailed financial feasibility study completed. We expect it to show that TACA can pay for the airplane out of earnings."

"Whatever your study shows won't make any difference. Making a deposit is against the agreement. It indicates an intent to buy. BAC can foreclose. I'm opposed to it."

"This is TACA's best opportunity. If they don't take advantage of it, they'll begin to lose market share. Eventually, everyone involved will lose, including your bank."

"Mr. Bauer, I'm not the least bit worried about that—I don't think we have anything to talk about," Lott replied tersely.

The conversation was getting nowhere. Mr. Lott had his mind made up—regardless of the facts—just like Bill Daly.

"Thank you for discussing it, Mr. Lott. Please think it over. Maybe we can talk about it again." We hung up.

Dr. Quesada shook his head. "Ken is a very stubborn man."

"Wow! Did he ever come on strong! I can see we're in for a big job. But it's only Wednesday. We can accomplish a great deal in three days. Phil will be well along in the financial analysis by the weekend. You'll see!"

I proposed an acceptance telex to reduce the anxiety back at the plant—hoping Dr. Quesada would sign it, agreeing to put the $100,000 in escrow by March 31st. He declined. Ken had convinced him that a nonrefundable deposit could get TACA into trouble—even the promise of making such a deposit.

With Friday midnight staring me in the face, I made another call to Boeing, proposing to make the deposit fully refundable, and recommended an April 21st cutoff date. That would give TACA the month that Ken Lott wanted to get the BAC clause taken care of. I was promised a decision before the deadline.

In the meantime, Phil Lindsay was working nearly around the clock to complete the Ex-Im loan exhibit. Bill Daly was determined to derail the study—increasing the contingency fund, reducing revenue expectations, and adding to the cost estimates.

Nevertheless, at our meeting on Friday morning, I had reason to hope. In spite of Daly's added conservatism, the cash flow looked better than he predicted. Thus, I expected TACA to step up to the responsibility for starting negotiations with the British.

"Good morning, Jaime, I think we're making progress," I announced confidently.

"Oh, that's good, that's good."

"The preliminary figures are encouraging."

Jaime smiled weakly. It was obvious something else was worrying him. "Yes, okay, but we still have the problem of the default clause in the contract."

"Jaime, I'm trying to get more time."

"We can't afford to risk the airline."

"Why don't we call *Pancho* and discuss it?"

Jaime placed a call to the Mayo Clinic in Minneapolis. *Pancho's* wife was scheduled to undergo surgery that very day. The clinic telephone operator could not locate him, and vain attempts took up the rest of the morning. With *almuerzo* and *siesta* time, nothing more could be done until three in the afternoon. *Some things are cast in concrete and cannot be changed.*

During lunch, Tom May called me at the hotel.

"Gene, Clancy will stall Aloha a little longer," he said.

"Good! How about my request to extend the clause to the 21st of April, and make it refundable?"

"Good news! The refundable has been approved, but only until the 14th."

"That's progress. Maybe I can get TACA off dead center."

In the afternoon, I was back in Jaime's office. "I had another call from the head shed," I told him.

Jaime perked up. "What did they say?"

"Boeing is willing to make the deposit refundable—and to extend it to the 14th of April."

Jaime broke in. "Good, good."

"There's a catch. The present proposal expires at midnight tonight, as you know. In order to get the clause extended, Boeing needs a conditional acceptance."

Dr. Quesada frowned. He looked out the window and tapped on his desk. "Let's try *Pancho* again."

The operator finally located him. *Pancho* was firm. "Do nothing until I return on Saturday afternoon," he ordered. "Remember, you don't have the authority to sign an acceptance telex."

Jaime put the receiver down, throwing up his hands in frustration.

I decided to take a still bolder approach. *There was nothing to lose.*

"Jaime, you haven't even checked with the legal people. You keep refusing to do anything to find out. Boeing has made all the concessions. A brand new airplane is waiting in Seattle. TACA needs it. The next airplane is almost two years in the future. It's time for drastic action."

Jaime stared at me. "You're right, Gene, but we have to be careful— excuse me."

He got up and went to *Pancho's* office to call the lawyer.

I waited. I was alone, and it was suddenly very quiet. I glanced around the expansive office. A curl of gray smoke rose slowly, lazily, from the ashtray on the desk—contorted, diverging and diffusing as the currents from the air conditioner disturbed its upward motion. I reflected on events.

Papers, half written telexes, annual reports, copies of contracts, route maps, traffic figures, all scattered over the room, contained the elements of confrontation. Otherwise, there was no evidence of conflict. The comfortable, high-backed chairs of the boardroom were all empty, proxies to the real actors who would soon return to the stage. The ornately encased electric clock on the wall announced 4:00 p.m. We had been discussing the same thing all day.

Outside, quiet heat gripped the city. March and April were the hottest months of the year. Through the half-drawn venetian blinds, I could see the unhurried workers moving along the sidewalk. In the square, the beautiful flowering trees exuded their fragrant elegance. My mind sifted the possibilities of making the TACA deal.

Abruptly, the door opened, breaking into my thoughts. Dr. Quesada moved quickly into the room, with Bill Daly at his heels.

"The lawyer says there's no problem with the language," Quesada announced, beaming.

"Oh, I figured that all along!" Bill Daly broke in. "I read the fine print, and it didn't say anything definitive."

Jaime studied Bill Daly, a curious expression on his face.

I perked up, surprised. From previous conversations, I assumed the contract had been studied meticulously—but now it appeared as if Jaime had not bothered to read it—and he was a lawyer himself! Another thing bothered me—even more. If Bill Daly had read the contract, why had he not spoken up? His suspicious behavior made me wonder if he was another Glenn Castagne—possibly pulling for McDonnell Douglas. But why the sudden turnaround?

Boeing didn't have a consultant in Salvador. Things had happened very fast, and no one had discussed the subject. I was beginning to have second thoughts.

"I figured we could even get by with a nonrefundable deposit under the BAC-111 terms," Daly continued.

"That certainly puts a different light on it," concluded Dr. Quesada.

The lawyer's opinion pumped new energy into Jaime. It was nearly six o'clock. "I have to get *Pancho*. Maybe we can get a telex out after all."

It was of no avail. Balzaretti had checked out, already on his way to the airport.

Quesada's face fell, and he lapsed into silence.

"I think everybody needs a break," I cut in. "How about being my guests at *Siete Mares* for dinner?"

"Only if everybody comes to my house for cocktails first," retorted Dr. Quesada.

In the TACA office all day Saturday, Phil and I worked on the Ex/Im loan study, to be ready for the meeting with Balzaretti, who was due to arrive at the airport at six.

At seven, *Pancho* burst in. "Gene, I'm ready to talk."

*Pancho* led the way to his office. He seemed tired and drawn.

"I've written an acceptance telex for the proposal, which expired—"

"I know all about it!" *Pancho* interrupted. "Dr. Quesada filled me in. There's absolutely no way we can do it!"

*Pancho* could not have been more definite. *The last grain of sand was running out of the hour glass.*

"The $100,000 deposit is no problem. I can authorize it without board approval. The government guarantee is no problem—the president of the country is a good friend of mine. He owes me a favor. It's only the EGCD."

The EGCD was the British financial agency similar to the Ex-Im bank in the United States. They were the final approval step for the British.

"I talked to Ken," *Pancho* continued. "They need forty-five days to even consider it."

"I'm sorry to hear you make the decision so final—no wiggle holes."

"I know! I know! There's nothing we can do. Let's go to my house and have a drink to drown our sorrows."

I briefly returned to the hotel, to pick up the telex that Tom May had promised with a new proposal from Boeing. I said nothing to anyone about it.

*Pancho* took us on a tour of his home; an extravaganza of glass, stone, and fine woods, covering a half acre. He designed it himself.

After a few drinks, *Pancho* talked grandly of his excellent personal relationship with Senor Romero, president of El Salvador.

"I'm sure we could do this thing if Boeing would give us a little more time."

I was getting exasperated. TACA kept asking for more time but did nothing positive. I held my tongue.

*Pancho* looked at his watch and joked bitterly. "The proposal expired last night. Whose time? Seattle time would have given us another three hours!"

He glared at me.

"Big deal! Why can't Boeing be realistic and give us enough time to work out the details?"

I decided it was the opportune moment, and reached in my briefcase for the copy of the latest telex.

"I've been working on that. Here's a new proposal. It provides for the deposit to be fully refundable until the 14th of April, assuming TACA makes progress on the financial arrangements. If not, Boeing reserves the right to sell the airplane to another customer."

*Pancho* was startled.

"It's a step-by-step approach. This extension gives TACA twenty-seven more days. If progress continues, I guarantee you Boeing will extend the time again."

I reached over and slapped *Pancho's* knee, laughing.

"*Pancho*, we're going to sell you that airplane whether you like it or not! All we ask is that you keep working."

*Pancho* extended his hand. "Okay, I'll accept that. Keep working."

We agreed to begin early in the morning.

Just as I was ready to leave the hotel, *Pancho* called.

"Gene, we have to forget it. I just talked to the lawyer, and he says if there is any chance of losing the deposit, there's a chance of default!"

"But I understood on Friday that he said it was perfectly legal."

"This is a different lawyer—he's in Mobile—the man who wrote the original contract on the BAC-111s."

I was out of rebuttals. It would be TACA's loss to fail to get the airplane. George McHugh, Bill Handal, and Bobby Padgett had put their hearts into the work.

"I'm sorry, I'm out of ideas," I replied.

*Pancho* called his people and told them to stay home. I gave Phil Lindsay the bad news. "You might as well get in some tennis. It looks as if we're dead!"

Still recovering from the shock, I was surprised when the phone rang again. It was Seattle. *Who would be calling so early on Palm Sunday?*

It was Dick Allyn, the Boeing contracts man. He had been trying hard to help me with the deal.

"Hey, Gene, I thought it might help if I told you confidentially that the reason Clancy put the progress clause in was to hold TACA's feet to the fire."

"I figured that."

"But here's the good news. He's decided to hold the airplane all the way to the 14th, regardless of what happens."

I grabbed for the straw. There was still a glimmer of hope, and I called *Pancho* at home. His daughter said he had gone to the office to talk to that "Boeing fellow."

*What the hell was going on?*

I called Phil. "Drop the tennis, we're alive again! You better get over to the office as soon as you can. I'll fill you in later."

Since I couldn't reach *Pancho*, I called Dr. Quesada, relating my latest information. He started reviewing the difficulties again.

"Jaime, please listen," I urged. "We'll go stepwise. If the cash flows are poor, we'll drop it. If they're good, we'll go back to INSAFI—step by step."

A half hour later, Jaime called back. "I called to tell you that I asked Bobby Padgett, Bill Handal, and Bill Daly to go on over."

I gulped. "Please, Jaime, do me a favor. Don't send Bill Daly. Tell him to take the day off. He's been working pretty hard. Just send Bobby and Bill."

Jaime agreed. I knew Bill Daly would keep everybody else from getting anything done. He was a bookkeeper, with no vision, not a financial man.

Before I could leave for the office, the phone rang again. It was *Pancho*, in the lobby. I invited him up for a drink.

"I have some important news," I announced, as he came through the door.

"You don't give up, do you?"

"Not while there's a chance. After we talked this morning, I heard from Contracts at Boeing. The vice president of Sales will hold the airplane unconditionally for TACA until the 14th of April."

"But we need more time than that."

"*Pancho*, listen. It's our only chance. TACA hasn't signed a thing. Don't give up yet, you have nothing to lose."

"It may be a waste of effort, but I'll go along. If you do this, it'll be a miracle. I'll see the president of the country tomorrow. By the way, is there any way we can get the price reduced?"

"Absolutely not! It's already a million and a half below market—but I'll see that the overwater equipment is included."

After *Pancho* departed, I felt the momentum was building up again, and I hurried over to the TACA offices.

George McHugh called, inviting everyone to lunch. I regretfully declined, deciding to work straight through. We couldn't afford to lose three hours. The bottom line was close.

Phil had a big bag of popcorn. We made it do for lunch, and worked into the evening.

The next morning, Jack Kinder, the vice president for Operations, arrived from New Orleans, bringing updated information on labor and maintenance costs.

By the end of the day Phil had completed the cash flow for five years, through 1983. It was thin for 1978 and 1979, but there were no minus numbers.

We took the results to *Pancho*. The glum expression did not leave his face. I was surprised, expecting enthusiasm.

But it was not the numbers that bothered *Pancho.* He had just met with President Romero.

"Gene, we can't do it. Even though the cash flow looks good enough for the Ex-Im loan, we need a government guarantee because TACA is a private company. They're afraid of public criticism if they take the risk."

I nodded. We had reached a chasm.

"I think we'll have to postpone a new airplane until January 1980, *Pancho* said. "I've written a telex to Boeing just now. Here's a copy for you to look over before we send it out. Does it look okay?"

Numbly, I reached for it. I read it reluctantly, my mind racing. *Where else to turn? I was out of aces.*

". . . we therefore regretfully conclude that we are unable to accept the Boeing offer to purchase the 737-200 white tail."

I handed it back to *Pancho.*

"Yes," I said, swallowing a tear, "it looks okay."

# 34

The equinox brought a change of weather to El Salvador. In the mornings, fog hung on the hills where the coffee trees nestled under the protective branches of their larger native cousins, safe from the unbroken heat of the dry months of winter. The spectacularly beautiful *maquilidats*, with their cascades of pink flowers, began to change their dress. The petals fell and a fresh set of leaves formed as the rain heralded a new season.

The sound of cicadas was shrill and overpowering, filling the air with a crescendo of sound, not unlike the incessant whine of a giant turbine.

Winds swept in from the sea, with gusty capers of forty to fifty knots. Thunder rolled across the ridges, and lightning snapped at the volcanos' peaks.

It was a happy and a not-so-happy time. Gone were the clear, lazy days with their blanket of quiet heat on the land, but gone, too, was the dust of the dry season. Downpours followed the gentle rains, the countryside gasping for breath in the deluge. Reservoirs filled to brimming, and it was the time for the *malo de mayo* to begin to disappear from the children's stomachs.

I was not so fortunate. The *malo de mayo* caught up with me on that disappointing Monday when *Pancho* threw in the towel.

It was 6:30 p.m. when we returned to the hotel after that ill-fated meeting. I felt only half alive, and the telex to Seattle, giving up the white tail, burdened me. But I put aside the pain in my stomach, searching my mind for new approaches.

The phone was ringing when I entered the room. It was Tom May. He was anxious to hear the latest news.

*How could I tell him?*

"The news isn't good," I complained, my right hand pressing against my severely cramping stomach. "Balzaretti just sent a telex calling off the whole deal."

Tom was thrown off balance. "Gene, that's all we need! Clancy will probably let it go to Aloha. What's the problem?"

"The big hurdle is approval by the British. Balzaretti finally gave up and decided to start planning for a January 1980 airplane. We better crank up the long-range fleet plan. I'll set it up here for the 24th of April."

"Okay, but our finance guys have a new idea to bypass the British. ITEL is still interested, and they're proposing to buy the airplane and then lease it to TACA."

"Does that mean Boeing is keeping the airplane off the market?"

"Hang on. I'll call Clancy on the other line."

Sitting on the edge of my bed in the semidarkness of my poorly lighted room, I waited. I glanced toward the window at the spectacular evening sky. A long, lazy contrail lingered in the fading sunlight. For one grand, beautiful moment, I was unchained from the earth—free—up there soaring in the crimson clouds.

"Yeah, Gene, you're still alive."

The words jarred me back. "Fine, I'll keep working."

The next morning, I reserved meeting rooms for the Boeing team presentation and luncheon on Monday, April 24th—just in case. My personal plans were down the tube. I would have to remain in Salvador over Easter—the third Easter on the road. Phil and I went back to the TACA offices to discuss the ITEL lease proposal.

While Phil mulled over the numbers with Bill Handal, searching for loopholes and opportunities, I went to see Dr. Quesada.

"Gene, why couldn't TACA buy the airplane on a conditional basis, just like we're doing with the BAC 111s?"

"Jaime, we're working on something like that. ITEL has offered to buy the airplane and lease it to TACA."

"That's exactly what we need!"

Maunday Thursday was the beginning of the long Easter holiday. TACA closed at noon. No matter the urgency, no business could be conducted until the following Monday.

John Woods, Boeing regional director of finance, called from Seattle in the afternoon with news that a U.S. bank was interested in making the loan. More important still, they would not require government approval, only the INSAFI guarantee.

On Easter Sunday, Phil and I attended services at the Episcopal Church. When we came out for coffee, there was Bill Daly, nonchalantly puffing away on a cigarette. "I thought you guys had gone home by now!" he exclaimed in surprise.

"Of course not! We don't give up that easily," I replied.

"We thought you might reduce the contingency reserve," Phil joked. "Then maybe *Pancho* would change his mind."

Daly was immediately defensive. "But there are a lot of unknowns."

"For example?" I snapped.

"Well, look at accommodations. We'll need extra serving trays—er, ah—there are a number of items like that."

"But Bill, they're included in the spares package."

Daly threw his half-smoked cigarette down and ground it out on the multicolored tile floor, quickly lighting up a fresh one. He had a stubborn look—like a Missouri mule. "I'm not so sure. We had plenty of problems with the 111s."

"I guarantee you this'll be different."

"We'll see."

It was a long walk back to the hotel. The expansive homes with ample lawns and large patios were partially hidden behind vine-covered stone walls and iron fences, adorned with fragrant hibiscus and colorful bougainvillea. It was the wealthy district, belying the poverty of the rest of the city. We walked along silently, each with our own thoughts.

I broke the silence. "Phil, I think we're going to get a second chance."

"How's that?"

"Some U.S. bank is getting interested. They may make a loan without a government guarantee."

"So what's the next move?"

"We need the most optimistic forecast we can get, but one we can still defend." I let that sink in. "Can you do a refinement of the study by tomorrow morning?" I challenged.

Phil looked shocked. "But the damn rules!"

"Use your own rules. Forget Bill Daly's."

"I'll see what I can do."

Phil worked all night, reaching the bottom line at five o'clock Monday morning. I arranged a meeting with Jaime and *Pancho* for 8:15.

"We have new numbers, using more realistic cost and revenue estimates," I announced.

"I don't think it'll make a bit of difference," *Pancho* replied. "You don't know how tough those British are."

I continued, unfazed. "Another thing, we have a U.S. bank interested. If the cash flows look favorable, they'll make a 100 percent commercial loan without the Salvadorean government approval. The only thing the bank would ask for is the INSAFI guarantee."

"So?"

"So we have two new $64 questions."

"Shoot!"

"First, if the cash flows look good, will TACA go back to INSAFI again?"

"Of course!"

"Next question. If INSAFI is favorable, will TACA contact the British for a preliminary expression of approval?"

*Pancho* stared hard at me.

"The numbers better look damn good! I'm assigning Bill Daly for the final review. If he says okay, then we go."

*Daly again. That man was damn near impossible. But there was no other way.*

"Let's get started," I suggested. "But I'll tell you a fact. Bill has made the rules to guarantee failure!"

*Pancho* raised his eyebrows.

I continued. "Yeah, he wants to escalate the costs by 9 percent a year, and the revenue only 4 percent. If that's the real world, you're programmed to go out of business. No bank will accept that kind of analysis."

"Let's get Daly in here," *Pancho* broke in.

Jaime went down the hall and quickly returned with Daly close behind. *Pancho* explained the problem.

"Phil Lindsay claims the historical data justifies a closer spread between the revenue and cost escalations for the forecast," he said firmly, his grey eyes piercing Daly's composure.

"Er ah, I suppose we could use 6 percent for revenue escalation. The traffic growth looks pretty healthy for the last few years."

"Okay, six it is," I interjected, before Daly could throw in a second thought.

*Pancho* was satisfied. "Let's get going."

Jaime set up a meeting with INSAFI that very afternoon. I went to McHugh's office to call Seattle, and Phil and Daly headed for the boardroom.

The work session was difficult. Daly kept trying to back away from his earlier agreement. With no sleep the night before, it was a long day for Phil.

Tuesday morning, I arrived at the TACA office early. Jamie reported dejectedly that the INSAFI meeting was a draw. They said maybe. *Pancho* was more pessimistic than ever, and refused to call the British.

Lilian, *Pancho's* secretary, confided to me that a McDonnell Douglas team had arrived and a presentation was scheduled at the Sheraton Hotel at 11:00 a.m.  Pancho had kept the meeting a secret from his own managers until late the previous afternoon.  I decided to do a little private snooping.

I went to the hotel.  The McDonnell Douglas team was making a 35mm slide pitch.  All the important TACA people were there.

In the afternoon, I asked Bill Handal about the McDonnell Douglas presentation.  He scoffed.

"Junk!  Pure junk!  It was a waste of time.  We don't want the DC-9. We want the 737. You can take a look at the documents if you wish."

He motioned to a stack on the side table.  "Unofficially, of course!"

"Naturally!"

I glanced over the main points.  They offered a complete fleet plan of three DC-9-30 airplanes: one in January 1980, one in June 1980, and a third in 1981.  A second document showed growth capability into the larger DC-9-50, and eventually the "dash 80," a paper airplane with a very long body stretch.

Later, I met with *Pancho*.  "I understand you're looking at Brand X," I mentioned casually.

He was candid.  "We haven't ruled anything out. You were right about availability though.  McDonnell Douglas doesn't have any planes before 1980 either."

I relaxed.

"But they have a better financing plan than Boeing," he continued. "They can do direct financing through a subsidiary."

"I'm aware of their program."

"They promised TACA a conditional sale and didn't ask for a guarantee from anybody.  We have no secrets.  I plan to send them a letter telling them TACA is interested."

I changed the subject.  "Don Garni from ITEL will be here tomorrow to talk over their lease/buy proposal."

"Yes, I know.  We have a meeting at five."

On Wednesday, Phil and I stayed in the hotel, fine tuning the financial exhibit.  In the evening, Alfredo arrived to "push the ITEL deal over the top," and invited the TACA officials to a banquet.

*Pancho* had seen the ITEL proposal the night before and was not impressed. It was a package—three airplanes in a complex deal.

"This proposal is unrealistic for TACA. We can't afford the luxury of planning for three airplanes. We need to concentrate on the first one. Let's forget it."

Meanwhile, back at Seattle, John Woods was working day and night on a different deal—lining up commercial banks. By Friday, he had convinced Citibank of New York to request their local San Salvador office to contact INSAFI, indicating their conviction that TACA's finances were sound and encouraging them to guarantee the loan.

By afternoon, the president of INSAFI called Jaime saying he was in favor and had the votes. All he needed was an "expression of favor" from President Romero.

The ITEL negotiations ground to a halt. Alfredo returned to Seattle, and Don Garni to San Francisco. I decided to stay indefinitely— until Christmas if necessary—to keep the process moving. It was the fourth time I had postponed my return home.

On Saturday, I sent Phil back to Seattle to help John Woods with the new financial plan.

By Tuesday, ITEL had sharpened their pencils, improving their offer by splitting the white tail out as a single transaction.

The favorable combination of Bill Daly's softening, INSAFI still talking, and ITEL improving their terms gave renewed hope. Balzaretti flew back from Guatemala in his private plane, bringing Garni with him. It was already seven o'clock Thursday evening, but the meeting continued into the night. Garni hopped around—all nerves. For one last time he called his superiors in San Francisco, winning a final concession. That left only the problem of paying for the spare parts.

"Gene, what do we do about the spares? Will Boeing finance them?" Balzaretti inquired.

I stalled. "We should be able to do something. Let me call the head shed again."

It was past quitting time at Boeing. I called Alfredo at home. He was out. Later, I reached him but he could only promise an answer the next morning, and I needed an immediate solution. The ITEL offer to lease the airplane to TACA was tied to its purchase from Boeing. *Both proposals expired at midnight!*

At this point, I felt that maybe Alfredo wanted me to lose, so I wrote some "weasel words" of my own.

It was 9:00 p.m. ITEL had backed off from their initial demand for a full INSAFI guarantee, but still insisted on the last two years of payments.

*Pancho* kept glancing at his watch. "I have to leave," he abruptly announced. "I have some Mexican visitors at my house. Dr. Quesada is the INSAFI expert. If he can work out a clause by midnight, I'll sign the agreement."

Don Garni and I hurriedly finalized the conditional clause for separate financing of the spares package, and Jaime added a paragraph conditioning the agreement to an INSAFI guarantee for the last two years of lease payments.

At 10:00 p.m., we were still working on the language when *Pancho* called.

"We're up at the *Él Mar*. Why don't you come and join us? We can finish the discussion here."

Don looked at me and I looked at Jaime.

"We won't be able to write anything at the restaurant," I lamented. "Let's steal a little more time and get it written before we go."

Garni and Quesada agreed.

We worked another half hour, hand lettering two copies of the agreement, and departed for the *Él Mar*.

The dinner party was in a dimly lighted, smoke-filled room, at the rear of the restaurant. We could scarcely see. While I held a flickering cigarette lighter, *Pancho* read the agreement. Then he and Garni argued the fine points for an hour. At last, more from weariness than satisfaction, *Pancho* acceded.  He held up his pen.

"Gene, shall I sign this thing?" he asked, laughing.

I looked at my watch.  "If you don't sign in the next twenty-five minutes, the 737 will turn into a pumpkin!"

Everybody laughed, and *Pancho* signed.

# 35

G arni departed for San Francisco the next morning. I had booked a nine o'clock flight to Seattle, but still needed Jaime's signature on the financial feasibility study. I took a taxi to TACA headquarters and waited. He was late, and at 8:30 when he drove in, I was biting my nails.

"My flight leaves in a half hour!" I announced. "It's twenty-five miles to the airport, so I don't think I'll make it!"

"Don't worry," Jaime said, "I'll take you." He exceeded all the speed limits as he raced through the city. We arrived just as the flight was being called.

Relaxing in the airplane on the trip home, I reflected on events. There was still a long road ahead. The agreement in my briefcase was a bare first step. However, since I would be leaving sales soon, I had only to complete the TACA deal.


Colonel Lara called from Miami and requested an extension of the 747SP proposal to the end of May. The pilot's strike dragged

on in Trinidad. Those accounts would soon be someone else's
responsibility.

John Woods was still afraid that the ITEL/TACA/INSAFI financial
arrangements would unravel, and he continued to work on the commercial banks.

I called Dr. Quesada early the following week. "How are things holding up?" I inquired.

"Not good. INSAFI has backed out again. They won't even guarantee the final two years of lease payments. They insist on full collateral."

"So where are we now?"

"The total value of the loan will have to be increased to include the
$2.8 million still owed on the BAC-111s, so the British can be paid off.
Then we can offer the planes as collateral to INSAFI."

"That means the $11 million loan we were talking about is suddenly
up to almost $14 million."

I could hear Jaime's groans all the way from Salvador.

Clancy continued to be patient, extending the deadline to April 28th,
and I notified *Pancho*.

"We need more time than that to twist INSAFI's arms," he
replied dejectedly.

"Well, I have to tell you one thing, *Pancho*. Clancy Wilde is at the end
of the rope. On April 28th, it's sudden death."

John Wood's negotiations were approaching the bottom line. There
was only one sticky point. Citibank insisted that Boeing itself assume
part of the risk—a rare concession—requiring approval by the corporate vice president of finance.

At this stage, I would have gone to the president of the United States,
if necessary, and I requested a letter of credit, recommending that Boeing
provide a loan guarantee for the spares package.

It was approved!

On April 28th—showdown date—TACA begged for another week, and I asked Clancy for an extension to the 5th of May.

"Gene, there has to be an end somewhere."

"Look, Clancy, here's my proposal. I'll take a team to San Salvador this weekend with the authority to close the deal or get out."

After almost three months of frustration, one more week didn't seem to bother him.

"Okay, let's do it!"

On Sunday, Roy Peterson, regional director of Contracts, joined John Woods and me, and the three of us flew to San Salvador.

Monday, May 1st—Labor Day—was a holiday there—as it is in most of the world. TACA had taken the day off. That extra week of grace gave them ample excuse to postpone until *mañana*.

The following morning, John Woods presented the finance options to Jaime and *Pancho*. He had negotiated with more than thirty banks in the United States, sifting out two possible deals. The best option for TACA was a 100 percent Citibank loan for eight years, at 11 percent interest.

Balzaretti requested that John review the financial details with Bill Daly. As they left the boardroom, I caught John's eye and held up my right thumb. I felt sorry for anybody who had to work with Bill Daly.

Roy and I stayed to discuss contractual terms with *Pancho* and Jaime. Roy presented the formal proposal, making it clear that it must be signed by May 5th or the airplane would be lost to TACA. *We were down to four days!*

*Pancho* sent a copy of the proposal to the Mercantile Bank in Mobile, Alabama, via the morning TACA flight to New Orleans, for their approval. The bank promised a reply the next day.

In the meantime, John Woods was still struggling with Bill Daly.

At four o'clock, the official letter offer was delivered to TACA from Citibank. Boeing agreed to a partial guarantee. In return, the company requested a remarketing clause. Under the clause, Boeing would be reimbursed for the cost of flying the plane home in case of default, as well as storage and remarketing costs.

At this point, a new chemistry began to develop behind the scenes. Citibank was a prestigious name in Salvador. Merely having them involved created a domino effect on the local Salvadorean banks, who immediately clamored for a piece of the action. First, *Banco Agricola*, largest commercial bank in the country, offered a $2 million loan to help pay off the outstanding debt on the BAC-111 fleet. The other major bank, *Salvadoreno*, lobbied for TACA to consider them instead.

*Pancho* began to view the impending transaction as a major personal triumph. Negotiations with INSAFI were no longer necessary. He could now go to the government, claiming that he had arranged financing single-handedly, establishing a good position to secure their support when TACA was ready to finance the second and third 737 airplanes.

The critical piece of the puzzle was the negotiation between Boeing and Citibank for the Boeing guarantee on part of the primary loan— that and the remarketing clause. Those negotiations were taking place at the corporate levels of both firms.

Late Wednesday afternoon, our team got together with all the TACA managers in the boardroom, with the goal of reaching final agreement on the cash flow to be presented to Citibank.

Bill Daly continued to vacillate. He would agree on a set of rules, and then turn around and add a new condition to increase the conservatism.

When the final figures showed a net of $500,000 positive cash flow for 1978—the worst year—Daly arbitrarily reduced the expected proceeds from the sale of the first BAC-111 from $1.5 million to $900,000, creating a $100,000 negative cash flow.

John Woods was heating up. It was clear that Daly was still intent on creating a forecast that would show a negative cash flow for both 1978 and 1979, hoping to panic Balzaretti into dropping the deal.

John finally agreed to a figure of $1 million, only $58,000 above book, a conservative figure since the used airplane market was strong and the BAC-111 was in demand as an executive airplane.

With the financial exhibit structured in the usual convention of thousands of dollars, that put the cash flow entry at exactly "$000" for 1978.

*Pancho* interceded. "Bill, tell me if I'm right. You're saying that we're so close, we might come out at $000?"

Daly's face lighted up, certain he had won the argument. *Pancho* would definitely not want to go ahead.

"Yes, *Pancho*, that's precisely right!" he eagerly replied. "It could be $000!"

*Pancho* pounded his fist on the table. "The worst case is $000!" Laughing loudly, he looked at John and me. "Great! We'll buy the airplane!"

The breakthrough had arrived.

On Thursday, when John and I met for breakfast, we were quietly confident. At 9:30, John received an urgent call from Seattle. Boeing wanted a better break with Citibank. We hurried over to TACA headquarters. Citibank wanted Boeing to guarantee 15 percent of the loan, in addition to accepting the cost of default and remarketing. Harold Haynes, Boeing corporate vice president, said it was too steep. Further, he wanted additional collateral from TACA in the form of a second mortgage on the remaining two BAC-111 airplanes. We gave Balzaretti the bad news.

"If TACA would agree to pay the costs arising from a possible default," John explained, "I think Boeing would go along with the Citibank proposal. Of course, you would also have to agree to the second mortgage."

"You guys keep making it tougher," *Pancho* lamented.

In spite of what he said, it was clear that *Pancho* had crossed that crucial psychological barrier. He had *decided* to buy the airplane.

"How much would it cost?"

John thought it over a few seconds, and responded on the spur of the moment. "Let's say $50,000 a year for the eight years of the loan," he stated firmly.

At that instant, *Pancho* could see a very bright light at the end of the tunnel. "Okay," he said. "We can do it."

He tried to phone Mercantile Bank in Mobile to see if they had received the copy of the agreement, but was unsuccessful.

TACA's lawyer came over. Bill Daly began a long harangue on the problems with the deal.

*Pancho* told Daly to back off.

We recessed while *Pancho* went to another meeting downtown. At 5:30 p.m., everyone was back in the boardroom.

After studying the papers, the lawyer said they were in order.

*Pancho* finally reached Ken Lott at Mercantile Bank. There had been a tornado in New Orleans. With eight feet of water in the streets, traffic to Mobile had been halted all day Wednesday, but they had finally received the proposal, and agreed that it was satisfactory.

I inquired about the $100,000 dollar deposit. Jaime said the check would be delivered at 9:00 a.m. on Friday morning. *I had visions of another Friday night cliffhanger.*

Jaime announced he would need two days to get the check converted from *colones* to dollars.

I invited everyone to *Siete Mares* for dinner. At dinner, *Pancho* announced he would sign the agreement in the morning.

On Friday morning, May 5th, I called Tom May.

"We have good news," I reported. "*Pancho* agreed to sign."

"You don't sound very excited," Tom shot back.

"It's been a long time—a long hard road—and the reality hasn't hit me yet."

"But it's finished. You should be celebrating."

"We still have to find out if Boeing and Citibank have agreed to terms."

"I think it will go through."

I went back to TACA to ride herd over the final details. Bill Daly looked glum. Everyone else was in a holiday mood. George McHugh and I were postulating the probable delivery date when the phone rang.

It was John Woods, calling from the hotel. "You better sit down!" he exclaimed. I was certain that Harold Haynes had rejected the Citibank terms.

"Let me be the first to congratulate you!" John shouted over the phone. "Boeing and Citibank have agreed." He paused. "Wait a minute. I'll come right over."

I waited, and we went in together to give Dr. Quesada the good news. Jaime's face was a solid smile from ear to ear.

At 11:45 a.m., the *Agricola* messenger brought the check for 250,000 *colones* ($100,000). In the afternoon, the letter came with the $2 million loan commitment.

We went in to see *Pancho*. He could scarcely contain his pleasure. With a flourish of his pen, he signed the agreement to purchase the white tail, bringing TACA into the Boeing family as the seventy-fifth customer for the Model 737 airplane.

A superior product, backed by the expertise and perseverance of a dedicated organization, had prevailed in the face of strong competition and a maze of indigenous problems. Moreover, no consultants were involved, renewing my faith in honest dealings.

On August 1, 1978, the airplane made its maiden flight to San Salvador. Beth and I were on board, invited by *Pancho* Balzaretti to participate in the delivery ceremonies.

# THE BOEING FAMILY OF AIRPLANES
## DECEMBER 31, 1979

| MODEL | SEATS (mixed class) | RANGE (nautical miles) |
|---|---|---|
| **747** (study) | 550-650 | 4,600-5,700 |
| **747*** (service) | 452 | 5,700 |
| **747**SP (service) | 331 | 6,400 |
| **767** (study) | 260 | 2,900 |
| **767** (ordered) | 211 | 2,900 |
| **757** (ordered) | 178 | 2,200 |
| **707** (service) | 160 | 4,800 |
| **727** (service) | 143 | 1,900 |
| **737** (study) | 112 | 1,900 |
| **737** (service) | 100 | 1,900 |

*Available in six versions.

(Source: Boeing Annual Report - 1979)

# EPILOGUE

The tiny, struggling TACA airline, beginning with its feet in the sand, but its head in the clouds, proved to be the jewel of my sales career. After selling the BAC-111s, they continued to add 737s, and purchased a "new technology" 767 in the '80s.

Still privately owned by the Kriete family, TACA embarked on an aggressive program of expansion. Forming the TACA Group, they assimilated all of the airlines of the small countries of Central America, including COPA of Panama. Acquisition of equipment continued apace, and in 1996, the fleet consisted of thirty-seven airplanes; twenty-nine Boeing 737s, two 767s, and six A320 Airbuses.

What happened in my other accounts?

AeroPeru continued to expand its 727-100 fleet to six airplanes, while also purchasing two Boeing 757s, bringing the fleet to eight in 1996.

Faucett scaled up their capacity, replacing the 727-100s with two 727-200s, and acquiring six 737s.

BWIA sold their 707s and DC-9s, replacing them with seven McDonnell Douglas MD-80s and five Lockheed L-1011s.

Guyana was flying a Boeing 757 in 1996.

Ecuatoriana went out of business in 1995.

TAME of Ecuador purchased a new 737, and subsequently added seven 727s and a Fokker F-28.

Transbrasil continued as an exclusive Boeing customer, now flying one 707, fifteen 737s, and eight 767s.

In the area of payoffs and bribes, Boeing did not escape unscathed. In spite of corporate diligence and explicit rules in acquiring and managing consultants, a few instances of questionable payments occurred.

As with Lockheed and McDonnell Douglas, the U.S. Justice Department pursued Boeing, finding that certain facts had been withheld from previous reports. The investigation was concluded in July 1982, when Boeing pleaded guilty to the charge of concealing from the U.S. Ex-Im Bank $7.38 million in irregular commissions, paid to agents in Spain, Honduras, the Dominican Republic, and Lebanon. Payments in Spain and Lebanon accounted for 95 percent of the total.[1]

Later in the decade, responding to questions about occasional ethical lapses on the part of an individual employee, Mal Stamper, vice chairman of the board, summed the company's approach to its business:

"We have an obligation . . . a moral imperative . . . to be above reproach. We can neither hide behind statistics nor make excuses about only a few untrustworthy people out of tens of thousands of good employees . . . or isolated breaches of trust out of countless legitimate actions. Our goal is to be without fault. If that takes forever, then we will work at it forever."[2]

*For Boeing, the '70s proved to be the defining decade for international market dominance.* In 1972, when McDonnell Douglas closed its DC-8 production line, the aging 707 showed new life. Over the next several years, Boeing sold an additional eighty-one airplanes overseas. Of even greater significance, was the acquisition of new customers. Noteworthy among those were Tarom of Rumania, the first customer in an Eastern Bloc nation; Iraq in Asia; Egypt and the Sudan in Africa; and most significant of all, the People's Republic of China, with CAAC—its sole airline—ordering ten airplanes in 1972.

The 727-200 continued to be the cash cow during the '70s, but the 737 was rapidly moving to center stage. At the beginning of the decade, 737s had been sold to twenty-six customers, and by the end of 1979, the total had grown to ninety.

In the long-range category, the 747—queen of the skies—continued its steady sales, as a result of a long series of derivatives offered to meet the continuing differentiation and specialization of the market.

In sum, new orders for all models by foreign airlines in the '70s more than doubled those for all previous years (1955–1969), and by the end of 1979, the Boeing family of airplanes encompassed a complete spectrum of sizes and ranges. (See illustration.) Indeed, the intense foreign campaigns of that period, searching even the smallest airlines over six continents, spawned a new sales explosion in the '80s.

By 1991 the backlog for commercial airplanes reached the alltime high of $92.8 billion, with foreign orders accounting for nearly 80 percent of the total.

With the last 727 delivered in 1984, representing 1,831 total units sold, the 737 and 747 models stepped up to assume the role of cash cows, providing Boeing with the resources to invest in the huge Model 777 twinjet, with a capacity in the 375-400 passenger range.

The People's Republic of China exhibited the most spectacular growth of all foreign buyers. By the end of 1995, mainland China was operating eighteen airlines, flying 243 Boeing airplanes—representing every model of the Boeing family—including the new 777.[3]

For the United States, Boeing's export contribution to the balance of payments was of profound significance. In the world market for commercial transport, Boeing consistently maintained about a 60% share.

According to Fortune magazine, cumulative exports of Boeing commercial airplanes during the five-year period of 1990–1994 exceeded $65 billion—leading all U. S. corporations.[4] Further, a recent Boeing marketing group study estimates that for the period of 1995–2014, two-thirds of all commercial airplane sales will be made to overseas airlines.[5]

Finally, what happened to Alfredo Dodds and me? In September 1985, after twenty-seven years of service, Alfredo took early retirement—bowing reluctantly to a company request.

In 1979, I went back to engineering, joining the Customer Support organization. Beth and I moved to New York for that year, where I was attached to Pan American at the JFK International Airport. However, my eye was on the People's Republic of China, a colossus that appeared to be on the verge of emerging from the shadow of the late Chairman Mao.

The previous December, President Carter had met with Deng Xiaoping, paramount leader of the PRC, to begin the normalization process between the two countries. At the time, I had indicated my desire for the assignment to manage a possible future Boeing office in Beijing.

When the Chinese purchased three 747SP airplanes, the position became a reality, and in January 1980, thirty days prior to the landing of the first 747SP, we were sent to China, where I opened the Boeing office. I remained there as manager for five years, aiding the Chinese airlines and witnessing their spectacular growth. Following a similar assignment in Brazil, I retired in 1988, after nearly forty-six years of service.

1. *Wall Street Journal,* 1 July, 1982, 40.
2. M.T. Stamper, "If We Are Smart," (speech before the National Contract Management Assn.), Los Angeles, 22 July 1988.
3. *Boeing News,* 1 December 1995, 2.
4. *Boeing News,* 22 March 1996, 1.
5. *Boeing News,* 19 January 1996, 1.

# BIBLIOGRAPHY

## BOOKS

Bauer, E. E. *China Takes Off.* Seattle: University of Washington Press, 1986.

Boulton, David. *The Grease Machine.* New York: Harper and Row, 1978.

Daley, Robert. *An American Saga.* New York: Random House, 1980.

Godson, John. *The Rise and Fall of the DC-10.* New York: David McKay, 1975.

Jacoby, N. H., P. Nehemkis, and R. Eells. *Bribery and Extortion in World Business.* New York: MacMillan, 1977.

Noonan, John T., Jr. *Bribes.* New York: MacMillan, 1984.

Schon, Donald A. *Technology and Change.* New York: Delacorte Press, 1967.

## PERIODICALS

*Aerospace Historian,* December 1979, Page 208.

*Aviation Week & Space Technology,*
December 8, 1975, Page 15.
August 4, 1980, Page 21.

*Boeing News,* The Boeing Company
December 1, 1977, Page 2.
December 1, 1995, Page 2.
January 19, 1996, Page 1.
March 22, 1996, Page 1.

*El Universo,* Guayaquil, Ecuador, May 3, 1977.

*La Prensa*, Lima, Peru, March 27, 1976.

*The Evening News*, Port of Spain, Trinidad. May 20, 1976.

*The Express*, Port of Spain, Trinidad, May 20, 1976.

*The Guardian*, Port of Spain, Trinidad, May 20, 1976.

*Time Magazine*, "The Big Payoff, Lockheed Scandal, Graft Around the Globe," Cover Story, February 23, 1976.

*Wall Street Journal*
    December 4, 1975
    May 7, 1976
    February 20, 1979
    July 1, 1982

**SPECIAL REPORTS**

Annual Report, The Boeing Company, 1975, Cover.

Annual Report, The Boeing Company, 1975, 5. ,

Annual Report, The Boeing Company, 1976, 4.

Annual Report, The Boeing Company, 1979, 33.

T. Wilson. *U.S. House of Representatives Testimony on Foreign Trade*, 14 May 1973.

M.T. Stamper. "If We Are Smart." Speech before the National Contract Management Assn., Los Angeles, California, 22 July 1988.

## INTERVIEWS AND PRIVATE COMMUNICATIONS

Countless conversations and meetings by the author with other Boeing employees and executives, as well as their counterparts in nine countries in Latin America.

## PERSONAL JOURNALS

Daily appointment records and travel notes over the period of September 1973 to August 1978.

# INDEX

# Eugene E. Bauer

E. E. "Gene" Bauer, joined Boeing's engineering department in 1941, went away to war in 1943, and returned to Boeing in 1946. He was appointed to a management position in 1956, upon completing his masters degree in metallurgical engineering under the G.I. Bill at the University of Washington.

During the 1960s, he earned an MBA in international business from the University of Washington—stretching his day to work fulltime at Boeing while attending school parttime. Graduating in 1971, he left engineering to take over the international desk in the Office of Corporate Business Development.

Becoming enamored with the potential of selling commercial airplanes overseas, he joined the Boeing sales force in 1973 as a regional director of sales in Latin America. Learning both Portuguese and Spanish, he sold airplanes in nine countries over a period of five years.

Bauer's next assignment was to open and manage a customer support office in Beijing, in the People's Republic of China, where he remained for five years. Following a similar assignment in Brazil, he retired in 1988.

OTHER BOOKS BY EUGENE E. BAUER

*China Takes Off*
University of Washington Press, 1986

*Boeing in Peace & War*
TABA Publishing, Inc., 1991